/I\ Defrag your soul...

To Deb,

Love is the path upon which
when you walk, you become
the path.

Love & best wishes
Shine on...!

Paul

By Paul C Burr PhD
http://paulcburr.com

3rd April 2013

/I\ Defrag your Soul /I\

Transform your consciousness:
a practical guide for the beginner
and seasoned traveller within

By Paul C Burr PhD
http://paulcburr.com

If you deem that excerpts from this book are worthy of people's attention, please use them with specific direction to the original content, namely: *Defrag your Soul* by *Paul C Burr PhD.*

Thank you.

/|\

Paul C Burr PhD

Email: doctapaul@paulcburr.com[1]
Facebook page: http://www.facebook.com/PaulCBurr
Twitter: paulburr

---

[1] I'm from Newcastle, a Geordie from the North East of England. I was given the colloquial nickname Docta-paul by my late pals Geoff and Ernie (who was a proper GP). When referring to my doctorate, a PhD, Ernie would joke, "Doctapaul here's got a Paper-Hanger and Decorator diploma in Statistics". God bless you Geoff and Ernie. Howay the Lads.

I dedicate this to fellow apprentices and spiritual masters in this world - occultists, healers, teachers, bards, orators, alchemists, seers, leaders, psychics, shamans, peace warriors, light beings, clerics and angels - who seek to serve the greater good; humankind's return to oneness.

Contents

Self Help Exercises

Foreword by Professor John Ditch

Paul Burr is an incredibly interesting man. I met him in 2005 when he agreed to be my 'career coach'. At the time I held a senior position at a UK university and it was rather fashionable to undertake 'management training'; every member of our senior team was expected to devote time to 'continuing professional development'. I approached Paul because he offered something different, something a little more challenging. We met regularly over the course of a number of months. Paul was a good listener and quickly identified a number of issues that we could work on together. That was part of his style: he didn't teach, he didn't preach, he had no axe to grind. What he had was insight, humour and a remarkable capacity to facilitate self-questioning and reflection: he had a 'tool-kit' but he didn't carry spare parts. Our 'sessions' were always well organized and when I'd done my 'home-work' thoroughly they were both demanding and rewarding. Paul is a seriously bright 'numbers-person' (he has a PhD in statistics) and can do all the technical stuff that management consultants come out with. But he is more than that: he is also in touch with the right (creative/emotional) side of his brain. Thinking back there were three things that Paul facilitated or encouraged in me: first, he supported me to think about (or imagine) ways of 'doing things differently'; second, he emphasized the importance of 'authenticity'; third, he helped me develop additional capacity for 'resilience'. Time with Paul was all time well spent.

A few years later Paul and I re-established contact via Facebook and LinkedIn. Paul had moved on and so had I. I saw from his postings that he was now writing and I offered to read his work in progress. I don't always agree with what he has written, indeed I don't always really understand. I find that I can't share some of the rather mystical and deeply personal experiences that Paul sometimes writes about. But, and this is important, there is an honesty about his writing and a modestly expressed insight embodied in his work that I find to be engaging and helpful. Paul makes me think about life in a positive

I

way: about success and setback, sadness and fear, joy and happiness; he helps me to be contented and fulfilled.

This is not a book that must be read in one sitting; indeed it is designed so that its sections can be read out of sequence. There is autobiography, there are fictive case-notes, there are homilies and there are exercises: I recommend this book; just go with the flow and it will work for you.

Professor John Ditch
Wheldake, York.
October 2012

How 'Defrag your Soul' Came About and Evolved.......

I've done a lot of 'grasping'.
I've read quite a few books on how life works. In many instances, I found myself **'grasping'** to get my head around the concepts laid down. The books fall mainly into three categories:

1. **Quantum Science (the study of the sub-atomic world)** – I often find myself reading paragraphs over and over again. I am enthusiastic to understand the concepts extolled but I often struggle to **'grasp'** either their meaning or how to apply them to my life.

2. **Abstract Ancient Wisdom** – in which words and phrases have been carefully constructed and combined with several layers of meaning. Parts of sentences have a deep meaning. When you combine the parts they have a deeper meaning. It can take my conscious mind several minutes to take in the whole meaning of a single sentence. I can get lost because I get into a state of mind bordering on the unconscious to **'grasp'** what's being said.

3. **Spiritual Revelations/Epiphanies** – I sometimes find these types of books difficult to **'grasp'** because the revelation isn't mine. I'm not saying I doubt the words of the revelators' experiences - but even the most profound revelations or epiphanies, in my experience, aren't always accurate.

   I owe it to you to watch what I say here. I reference a few 'out-of-this-world' events in *Defrag your Soul*. I use them to explain what happens when you have an epiphany as opposed to relating to you superior wisdom from on high. If I do have a mind-blowing experience, I write it up as a dream or a thought guidance process - for example, in the two chapters *The Castle* and *The Cathedral* respectively.

In 2011, I was reflecting on all the grasping I'd done on what is the most important subject to me in my life. I asked myself, "What if you were to write such a book about life, Paul? What would you do differently?"

Such a book would need to include some fairly abstract concepts using language I use every day. After quite a bit of 'umming' and 'arring', I decided to write a book and gave it the working title: *How Life Works and What to Do about It*.

I began by writing about how to take practical, *spiritual steps* to:

1. Release all the things that we allow to hold ourselves back, namely: *shame, anger, sadness and fear* (the *four seeds of negative karma*).[2]
2. Find, open, become and express our *true selves*.

As I wrote, I started to 'live the book'. I invoked the experiences I was writing about. The book changed.

Taking *spiritual steps* required me to develop a much broader range of inner resources: especially temperance, courage, compassion and gratitude. These didn't come easily.

I found out that courage, for example, is a choice and <u>not</u> a trait that only some of us possess. We all possess courage but we don't always choose it. I haven't, certainly.

The book changed again. I began to realise that my *life's journey* is about restoring the divided self within me, from *separateness* to *oneness*. I reflected that in every personal relationship I'd ever had, I'd send out love (which is nice) combined with a boat-load of subliminal fear and occasionally anger (not nice). These negative emotions would often manifest themselves in the form of over-protectiveness and jealousy. I needed to switch these negative emotions, many of which I

---

[2] I came across these four categories of emotions when I took my master practitioner qualifications in *Time-Line Therapy* by Tad James. I use the word, "shame" instead of "guilt". I find the word "shame" more powerful because it feels deeper than "guilt". Furthermore, it embraces anything bad you feel about yourself (e.g. I'm overweight, I'm no good in company) as well as anything you may have done that you feel guilty about. These *four seeds of negative karma* seem to be adequate enough to cover all the negative emotions I've come across. For example, *self-doubt* could come under *shame* but ultimately comes under *fear*.

If you take this one step further, you could aggregate all four (*seeds of negative karma*) categories under one heading - *Not-love*.

was unconscious of, into positive powers such as poise, compassion and grace.

In the attempt to unearth my unconscious negative emotions, the book changed again - I became aware that the path I was on led to a beautiful form of magic - the ability to manifest my heart's desires. Here's the awakening I had....

Manifestation is not about making stuff (e.g. money, lovely people, and success) appear in our lives to satisfy our egotistical desires. Not that there's anything wrong with money, lovely people and success – they are usually great fun! I wanted something else as well. I began to realise that manifesting was a process of cleansing my mind - so that spirit could manifest what I truly desired in my heart of hearts. And...

When you manifest through love, truth and oneness, you practice compassion.

So this book is ultimately about the *path of magic* which is synonymous with oneness; the bringing together of the divided self, the upper (heart) and lower (head) desires; the upper and lower stretches of the Nile, as symbolised by the ancient Egyptians.

When the pure waters from the upper source of the Nile feed the lands in its lower reaches steadily, the harvest will be abundant.

THE *PATH TO MAGIC* SPIRALS, AS DOES THIS BOOK. IT IS NOT WRITTEN IN A CONVENTIONAL FORMAT THAT BUILDS UP AND DESCRIBES EACH SUBJECT IN A LOGICAL SEQUENCE.

INSTEAD, THE BOOK RETURNS TO LOOK AT THINGS IN DIFFERENT WAYS - AND SOMETIMES TO DIG MORE DEEPLY OR 'PEEL ANOTHER LAYER' FROM THE SURFACE.

I'VE TRIED TO WRITE *DEFRAG YOUR SOUL* SO THAT YOU CAN READ ANY PART IN ANY SEQUENCE. IT ALL FITS TOGETHER, HOPEFULLY, LIKE A JIGSAW PUZZLE. THE SEQUENCE IN WHICH YOU COMPLETE THE PUZZLE IS UP TO YOU. YOU CAN READ IT FRONT TO BACK OR... START BY READING PART I, THE BOOK'S SPIRAL CORE. AFTER, GO TO THE TABLE OF CONTENTS AND SELECT THOSE PIECES OF ITS

PUZZLE THAT APPEAL TO YOUR INTUITION THE MOST. THEREAFTER YOU CAN FILL IN ANY MISSING PIECES AS THEY BECOME APPROPRIATE TO YOUR JOURNEY.

YOU WILL FIND THAT THE PUZZLE THE BOOK DESCRIBES HAS NO STRAIGHT EDGES. ACTUALLY, IT HAS NO EDGES AT ALL, ONLY MORE PIECES - FOR WHICH I CONTINUE TO SEARCH.

Acknowledgements: I Thank...

Jeanne Ayling, Spiritual Mechanic and Tai Chi Master, who knows more about working with spirit than anyone else I know. Without her guidance and editing I would have floundered to write this book.

David Loxley, Chief Druid, and **Brenda Sanderson** of the Druid Order, London, have patiently guided me to understand and apply the wisdom of the ancients to my life. I've had many spiritual ups and downs over the last four years and feel blessed to have the friendship and support of my companions in the Druid Order, London, who devote much energy to helping one another on the road to the Light.

Andrea Kurucz

Andrea applied her very talented imagination and hands to craft the illustrations within. I thank Andrea for her patience whilst I attempted to explain my ideas for designs to illustrate the concepts laid down. I wouldn't say that Andrea ignored my design ideas but rather she had the confidence and nous to create illustrations far more imaginative and insightful than my vain attempts. Andrea has achieved 'more than a thousand words' can explain in her drawings.

Lucille White: I have been evolving the *Etheric Cleansing* technique described within for three years. It was inspired by a mind-body-soul diagnostic process called *The Truth Model*™ designed by Lucille. *The Truth Model*™ is the most significant single piece of therapy I've ever taken myself through. It influenced me to change my life. Subsequently it helped me to help other people change their lives – much for the better, I am told!

A number of kind and very patient friends volunteered to proof read, review and improve this book. They are **Romilla Ready** (lead author of NLP for Dummies™), **Jeanne Ayling, Kelly Scales, John Ditch, Heather Harte, Cat Lee, Tara Leaver, Penelope Walsh and Amanda Giles**.

To the divine spirit within me:
I am sorry.
Please forgive me.
I love you.
Thank you.

Glossary

Phrases and names that perhaps require explanation are normally found at the end of a book. I've placed the glossary at the beginning to help you get into this book more quickly from the outset.

- **Act 'as if...'** – Whether you're viewing real life situations or dreaming about them, the brain executes the same neural pathways in the same way. The mind cannot tell the difference between the real world and an imaginary world. By acting as if you already have what you want in your imagination – you fool the mind into thinking the same. The mind then signals your DNA to send out a vibe to attract what you want in your imagination.

- **Atma** – the spirit at the core or centre of the body where you feel oneness; where you experience the present moment or present tense; there you experience your *true self.*

- **Body cell** - Each and every cell within your body tissue contains your whole life history, your memories, feelings, actions and reactions. Untainted and uncensored by thought, everything you've given and received in your life, knowingly and unknowingly, is stored in your cellular memory.

- **DNA** - is your transmitter to the universe. It transmits your signal of how you are feeling in the moment – your vibe. Its signal is governed by your unconscious mind.

- **Entities** - are etheric. They are usually invisible in my experience but not always. Entities can be higher or lower vibrational spirits. They can appear in the form of a human, an angel, an animal or perhaps just the feeling of a presence. I've not met any entities personally that I would call evil. What 'looked' or 'felt' like evil spirits turned out to be tortured souls.

  Whenever talking to spirit I recite the following incantation: *"I wish to speak only with the highest vibration available to me from the divine source. Everything else will leave. Show me only truth".*

- **Etheric Region** – the Physical World is split into two vibrational regions, the lower and higher:

1. The lower is the **Chemical Region** – consists of the solids, liquid and gas all around us.
2. The higher is the **Etheric Region** – is all around us but at a vibration beyond the reach of our five senses. For example a human's *Etheric Body* exists in the *Etheric Region*.

- **Etheric Body** - stores away information that pertains to every sinew, every nut and bolt of every thought, every intention, every action and every response you've either made or been on the receiving end of in your life. It's collected every impulse your mind and physical body has ever given and received. It has collected information from the very start of your embryonic journey into life, your very first body cell.
- **Etheric Cleansing** – is a process I've developed over time to remove the effect of the negative emotions stored in the *Etheric Body* and enable a client to take their next *spiritual step* toward their *true self*. I help the client to pinpoint the nature of their next spiritual step, usually in the form of an affirmation (e.g. "I am discerning") and create a pathway of vibrations (or feelings) forward to complete their next *spiritual step* in life.
- **False-ego** - is the keeper of shame, anger, sadness and fear. It has a dual-edged sword type of existence. It holds on to these negative emotions and attempts to control your mind with them. Also, it knows that its purpose is to reveal the source of these negative emotions to you when the time is right – so that you can release them.
  In a paradoxical way, your *false ego* beckons your light. It knows when to submit to your light which shines within in its dark shadows. Each time you shine more light into your *false ego's* shadows, you take a *spiritual step* on your chosen *life's journey* – toward your *true self*.
- **Four Seeds of Negative Karma** - only four things hold you back in life: shame, anger, sadness and fear. All four emotions lurk within the shadows of your psyche. When you invoke thoughts and actions based on these emotions you invoke an equal and opposite response.

- ***Imagination*** – takes place in your mind. It means place an image-in-ions (atoms). Your conscious mind passes the information (your emotional state) pertaining to that image to your unconscious mind. The unconscious mind then signals your DNA to send out the corresponding vibration to the universe.
- ***Inner World*** – has four main constituents: your spirit, soul, mind and body.
- ***Karma*** - you invoke a karmic response, an equal and opposite reaction, to everything you think and do. When you veer from the path of your chosen *life's journey*, negative *karma* (e.g. in the form of an upset) tells you that you are allowing shame, anger, sadness and fear to cloud your decisions; that you have gone astray. Positive *karma* (e.g. the synchronicity of receiving unexpected help) informs you that you are on the 'right path'.
  I use the words 'positive' and 'negative' to illustrate *karma's* didactic purpose. *Karma* is neither good nor bad. It is not retribution, it just is!
- ***Kinesiology*** - also known as *Human Kinetics*, is the scientific study of human movement, which addresses physiological, mechanical, and psychological mechanisms. Applications of kinesiology to human health include: biomechanics and orthopaedics, rehabilitation, such as physical and occupational therapy, as well as sport and exercise.
- ***Kundalini Yoga*** - is a physical, mental and spiritual discipline for developing strength, awareness, character and consciousness. Practitioners call it the yoga of awareness. Kundalini Yoga focuses primarily on practices that expand sensory awareness and intuition in order to raise individual consciousness and merge it with the Infinite Consciousness.
  Considered an advanced form of yoga and meditation, Kundalini Yoga's purpose is to cultivate the creative spiritual potential of a human to uphold values, speak truth, and focus on the compassion and consciousness needed to serve and heal others.
- ***Law of Attraction*** - where or how you focus your feelings is the vibration you send out to the world. For most of us, it is a complex combination or signature made up of positive vibrations (e.g. love,

oneness, joy, and self-worth) and negative vibrations (e.g. shame, anger, sadness and fear). You attract like for like.

If you focus your feelings on abundance and gratitude they are what you'll attract. If you focus on their opposite, scarcity and yearning, guess what you'll attract?

You get what you focus on

- *Law of Duality* - To know love, for example, you need to know what not-love is. So learning not-love serves a purpose. You are indirectly learning about love and you won't experience love wholly until you complete your learning. Here lies the rub of duality. This is how life works.

  All the things that you experience - even those that you don't want - serve a purpose.

- *Law of Reversibility* - adds depth to the *Law of Attraction*. If situations (events and people) can affect your emotional state, then inducing that same emotional state will manifest the same events and people into your life. To do this effectively you need to find out what your unconscious mind is attracting or repelling that helps or hinders your power to imagine what you truly want - to make it happen instantly.

- *Life's Contract* - like any commercial contract this has precise details of what you agreed to achieve in this lifetime. It specifies the outcomes by which you will know for yourself that you achieved your life's purpose – or soul's quest.

- *Life's Path (or Journey)* - put simply, this is the shortest journey available to you from wherever you are right now to achieve your *life's purpose*. It may not be evidently clear but the path is always there. You sometimes can't see the path when your mind is clouded in negative emotions: shame, anger, sadness and fear. When you release all these four negative emotions, you surrender to the path. You become the path – for the greater good of all humankind, with whom you are now one.

- *Life's Purpose* - is what you are here to achieve in this incarnation. The specifics of your *life's purpose* are found in your *life's contract*.

Before you were born you chose this life to achieve that purpose. Generically, your *life's purpose* is to find, open, become and express your *true self*.

- **Occult/Occultism** - The word *occult* means 'that which is hidden'. There is nothing innately sinister about the word - in the same way that there is nothing innately sinister about a kitchen knife. It's what people do with it that counts. I practise it to raise consciousness – which is in effect 'white magic'.
  There are millions of people around the world who practise the *Law of Attraction*. They are occultists.

- **Pranayamic Breathing** - *Prana* is the vital life-sustaining force of living beings comparable to the Chinese *Qi* or *Chi*. *Prana* is a central concept of yoga. It flows through a network of fine subtle channels called *nadis*. Its most subtle material form is the breath, but it is also to be found in the blood, and its most concentrated form is semen in men and vaginal fluid in women.

- **Soul** - knows the quest for your life, to seek and complete your *life contract* to meet your life's purpose. Your body cells store all the information needed to inform your soul where you are now and the direction you seek to take. Soul cross references your current intentions and behaviours with its (your) real quest. Soul then signals spirit via the mind - to inform spirit of new experiences needed or corrections to be made - to keep you on or return you to your life's path.

- **Spirit** - is the force which manifests form: people, things and events, to take you down your chosen life's path, to your *true self*, your soul's quest. But spirit can only manifest via the mind. The decision as to what to manifest is taken by the mind. The mind contains four things (shame, anger, sadness and fear – the four seeds of negative *karma*) that sully spirit's power, often unconsciously, to attract what your soul wants.

- **Spiritual Mirror** - what happens in your outer world reflects what's happening in your inner world and vice versa. Success mirrors success. Issues mirror issues, as without so within, as within so without.

- **Spiritual Steps** - are what you take when you release all the shame, anger, sadness and fear in your life that stops you from taking that step. Each step takes you closer to your *true self.*

Illustration 1: L'Étoile (The Star)
Major Arcana card from the Tarot of Jean Dodal, 1712.

- **The Star** - number 17 of the major Arcana (cards) in a Tarot deck. The picture denotes a female figure, creative energy, pouring water onto the land and into a lake. The land signifies humankind's material needs. The lake signifies emotional needs. The figure thus nourishes humankind materially and emotionally.

I often encourage clients to use seventeen-second visualisation techniques for seventeen days. Some occultists recommend forty days (and nights) as symbolised in the bible story. If you haven't got what you're seeking after seventeen days, go the whole forty.

- **True Self** - the purpose of your life is to find, open, become and express your *true self*. If you don't know it already, you find the purpose of your life by following your heart's passions. Once you find out what your purpose is, open it up to understand the implications it holds for you. Becoming your *true self* takes time. You have to find and open each *spiritual step* on the way. As you take each step, you become closer to your *true self*. You gain wisdom. You complete that step when you apply that wisdom to serve humankind. You shine. You express more of your *true self* - an 'everlasting solar star'.

- **Unconscious Mind** - passes on the decisions made by the conscious mind to each and every cell in your body along with information that you are unconscious of - e.g. deep rooted early childhood memories. The unconscious mind protects you from information that it feels you cannot cope with. All the information, joyful and sad, is stored away in your holographic *Etheric Body*. Each and every body cell is a fractal (the whole is contained in each fractal) of your *Etheric Body's* hologram.

- **Vibe** - is the aggregate vibration that your DNA sends out to the universe. You increase the positive power of this vibe by acting as if you already have what you seek to attract.

- **Yoga** - is the union of the True Individual Self (Jiv Atma) with the Universal Self (Param Atma). At the very core of the body, we move closer to experiencing this union or oneness.

Paul C Burr

Wee Notes About:

.... The Phrase 'You'

When using the phrase 'you', I mean me, you, we and us. I refer to all seekers of truth and fellow apprentices in the Light. I refer to all humankind.

.... Gender Specificity

When using phrases like mankind, warrior, hero, magician, alchemist, occultist, salesman, chairman, spirit, soul, you, we, us and God, I refer to the andro-centric generic sense, unless the female or male form is specified.

.... 'Hu-man' Means 'Light Being'

I use the phrase 'hu-man' often and deliberately.

The letter H (ה) in Hebraic is pronounced 'hay'. ה - represents the symbol of elementary existence, spirit.

The letter U (ו) spelt vav (sometimes pronounced "vov"), represents a connection from the timeless centre of existence to the here and now.

Added to together, ה ו (HU - the Hebrew symbols are written in reverse order), renders that which makes elementary existence manifest and obvious, i.e. *light*.[3]

.... The Spiral Structure of Defrag your Soul

I stopped writing this book for a two month period as I wrestled with how to build the contents into a logical sequence. I couldn't figure out how to do it. I was talking through the problem with my mentor, Jeanne Ayling. I described to Jeanne the trouble I had, writing about the spiral nature of life in a linear sequence; how I kept wanting to

---

[3] Ref: *The Hebraic Tongue Restored* by Fabrice D'Olivet, 1815 - documents the 'true meaning' of Hebrew words, specifically the first ten chapters of the Sepher containing *The Cosmogony of Moses* - a subset of which was later translated as *Genesis*, but lost its full meaning in the translation.

write next about things I'd already written. I kept reshuffling the chapters (like a deck of cards) but didn't feel comfortable with any sequence I came up with.

Jeanne's reply was simple, "Why don't you write you book in a spiral format?"

Durrrr???? Why didn't I think of that?

Later a friend, Professor John Ditch, came up with the metaphor of a spiralling double helix like that of DNA. John's words inspired me to contemplate the image of the light and dark serpents that entwine around one another - and both around the central staff of the caduceus carried by *Hermes*[4]. The central staff or metaphorical ray of light forges the connection between the sun within you and the body. When you light the staff, your spinal column, you shine.

So I have created the book's structure to begin at its very core, the heart of the matter. As it travels its spiral journey, you will revisit the light and dark of many concepts laid down early on, only with (hopefully!) deeper and richer meaning on each subsequent visit. The purpose of each revisit is to reinforce and expand the learning laid out earlier.

As you journey the spiral, my wish is to pass on to you what wisdom I have learned along with tools and exercises to light up the core staff, the path to your truth.

.... Fictitious Names

The case stories use fictitious names to preserve anonymity. They bear no connection to anyone with the same name as any of those used.

.... The Symbol 'Ω'

I use the symbol 'Ω' to denote the end of a case story, sub-story or learning exercise to inform you that you are about to return to the main thread of the book. Ω

---

[4] Ref: The 'myth' of *Hermes* and its allegorical connection to human wellbeing is described in Chapter *Physical Body* in *Part VIII: Mind, Body, Soul and Spirit.*

Preface:

You know when someone can't remember your name. Maybe it's something in the tone of the voice or slightly shortened sentences or maybe it's just that the other person doesn't address you by name.

"I notice that you highlight a lot of sentences with a green ink marker. Why's that?" enquired my fellow traveller. He sat across the table we shared. I had spoken to this man several times before. I felt he could not remember my name. I could not recall his name either. We had travelled this 280 miles each way train journey together for thirty years, along with forty to fifty fellow Newcastle United Football Club supporters. We caught the 9.30am train from London Kings Cross and had three hours to while away on the way there and three more hours on the way back. (Hopefully with a victory to celebrate.)

"I'm researching for a book I'm writing", I answered. "When I feel that particular sentences or points are noteworthy, I highlight them. So when I review the book later, it makes scanning and searching a lot easier."

"What're you reading about?" he continued.

"About life after death and reincarnation", came my reply.

"Do you believe in that?" He pried with one eye half closed and chin tilted slightly to one side. A friendly voice interjected from the side, "Oh, don't get Doctapaul (my Geordie nickname) going, you should read some of the stuff he writes in the supporters' mag."

Behind my smile I felt defensive because from past experience the "Do you believe...?" question puts me on the spot. If I answered in the affirmative, I would have to justify my belief and prove myself. I knew that I couldn't and this discussion sounded as if it was heading down the rationalist road. I would be asked for irrefutable evidence which I could not provide. Even if I could, was the inquirer genuinely curious or simply filling time on our train journey?

By the time I said "Mmmm, how do I answer you?" out loud to myself, about eight or nine heads had turned, all looking my way. Some of those heads had voices waiting to pounce. One did not bother and jumped straight in just as I was taking a long in-breath to reply.

"Here we go." One voice blurted out mirthfully, "Doctapaul speaks", as I was about answer. We all laughed and nodded.

"I find the verb 'believe' is often misconstrued - especially when it is substituted for the phrase 'know for certain' ", I replied. "So my answer is 'yes, I have a very strong belief..... 'faith', you might say, in life after death - but I do not know it to be true for certain. Perhaps what's more important is... Am I instinctively curious about life after death? Yes! So rather than profess 'I believe', I ask myself 'What if? What if what I read is true? Does it feel right? Sound right?' And if so, 'What are the consequences for me? How might I want to live my life differently?'"

A long discussion ensued. It still went down the 'there's not a shred of evidence' route. I had attracted a conversation about my spiritual path and my experience of that path. But it is my path, not my fellow traveller's or anyone else's for that matter. I cannot prove that my experiences are valid for others. I have experienced enough personally to write this book and can only talk about what I've experienced. What I have experienced increases my curiosity to experience more and ultimately, I feel more fulfilled for my experiences.

For example, two days ago, I read a description of the *Desire World,*[5] an ethereal world where all your desires or wishes come true. It is uncannily similar to a vivid dream called *The Castle*[6] that I blogged about on my website a few weeks earlier. I had the dream originally some two years ago. One can shoot down such a claim of first-hand experience of something like the *Desire World*. That is not the point.

The experience was real enough and proved instrumental in my decision to find out more; to journey within to find my *true self*.

Along the way, I keep experiencing more 'coincidences', 'synchronicities' and the occasional epiphany, by my humble standards at least. I've been helped to make discoveries and made a few of my own. For that is all they can be, self-discoveries. My intent for this book is to help you make similar if not more insightful discoveries for yourself.

---

[5] Ref: *The Rosicrucian Cosmo Conception Mystic Christianity* by Max Heindel, 1922, published by the Rosicrucian Fellowship Press.
[6] Ref: I write of my experience in *The Castle* in *Part III*. You can read the original blog at https://paulcburr.com/2011/08/15/the-castle/.

I've created tools that I used initially on myself and then with clients, to create their own inner experiences. Sometimes these tools make clients curious to find out more, to evolve their lives to the good, in their inner worlds and subsequently the world around them. Such is the path of the mystic or occultist. All occultists are fallible, especially apprentices like me. I will relate a few 'corkers' I've made, later.

Psychic senses are not infallible.....as it took years after birth to educate the sense of sight....it may take that long to develop...a comparative degree of accuracy.
CC Zain[7]

I've also been blessed with both help and wisdom which I now do my best to relate to you.

There exists an inner life experience. An inner world far richer and more profound than anything I've come across in the physical world. Don't get me wrong, I love the beauties and wonders of the physical world. I love to travel and experience new places - as without so within.

I've been what you might call 'spiritually proactive' for about 6-7 years. Prior, I'd done a bit of reading on spiritual matters, including novels such as *The Celestine Prophecy*[8] and its sequels. It's fair to say that I hadn't pursued a great deal of spiritual study for 30 years – when I was in my early 20s.

Whilst at university, in the 1970s, I read up on Hinduism, Taoism, Sikhism and various hidden scriptures. I joined the *Divine Light Mission*[9]. I became a *premie*,[10] a follower of the teachings of Guru

---

[7] Ref: Chapter 1, *Occult Data, Laws of Occultism, Inner Plane Theory and the Fundamentals of Psychic Phenomena* by CC Zain, published by the Church of Light.

[8] Ref: *The Celestine Prophecy* by James Redfield, an insightful novel for newbies and seasoned spiritual travellers within.

[9] *The Divine Light Mission* (Divya Sandesh Parishad) was an organization founded in 1960 by Guru Shri Hans Ji Maharaj for his following in northern India. During the 1970s, the *Divine Light Mission* gained prominence in the

Maharaji. The teachings and religious studies stayed with me in spirit (just) throughout my subsequent corporate career. But I spent most of my time <u>not</u> putting them into practice.

I worked hard at university and in my corporate career. I dedicated myself to success during working hours and also gained a reputation as a bit of a 'pioneering free spirit' or 'maverick'. One senior manager called me "the unmanageable talent", another - less complimentary - told me to avoid becoming known as a "space cadet". Most customers seemed to like my approach though - my sales results proved consistently good. I thus avoided the forfeiture of <u>not</u> being allowed to manage myself.

Outside of work, I loved to party. In my bachelor days I collected the nickname "Bonker Burr, Bon Viveur" after a Viz cartoon comic character. This flattered the *false-ego* - were it only true in reality. I partied hard and had my fair share of relationship flings.

I never set out to deliberately hurt anyone. I made wise and not-so-wise decisions. Like most of us, I've hurt and been hurt many times often through repeating the same old habits in relationships; habits that once served a purpose but no longer helped; habits that ended relationships in anger, hurt or blame.[11]

It's fair to say, that between the ages of 25 and 54 I wasn't fast-tracking my spiritual development. (I'm not saying I am now but I do work at it much more. The input is there if not the output.)

In 2003-4, aged 52-3, I became fairly depressed about the world at large. I'd spent two years or so researching what was really going on behind the scenes of wars in the Middle East. I'd lost faith in Western governments.

I recall listening to an old recording of Aldous Huxley speaking at the University of California, Berkeley[12]. Huxley spoke of "scientific dictatorships" whose ultimate aim was to "to get people to consent to

---

West under the leadership of his fourth and youngest son, Guru Maharaj Ji (Prem Rawat).

[10] *Premie* - from the Hindi *prem, meaning* "love"

[11] You can read more about repeating habits that hold relationships back, in my first book, *Learn to Love and Be Loved in Return.*

[12] Search www.youtube.com for *'Aldous Huxley speech at uc berk'*

(if not love) servitude" through fear, "refined terroristic .... and more modern techniques". His words rang, sadly, so true in my ears. I often exacted my misery on friends and family. I wasn't much fun to be around in those days.

I started to study religion again. However, I couldn't connect with the notion that God would choose one of the mainstream faiths in the world and bar all others from entering the Kingdom of Heaven. I could connect with godliness or, better still, goodness. I could connect with a human being rewarded for his actions and deeds but not his creed of faith; unless that faith was in himself and all humankind, regardless of race, colour and heritage.

I came across Druidism in 2005. I attended a series of public workshops. I listened to and meditated upon words sourced from ancient wisdom that made sense – far more sense than anything else I'd read about, witnessed or heard prior. Following my request to join, I was welcomed formally as a Companion into *The Druid Order*, London,[13] in August 2006.

There's quite a bit of misinformation about Druidism. For example, it's often confused with Paganism. It's recognised by the UK government as a religion, although in my experience, it isn't.

To me, Druidism is more of a school of science in the natural laws of the universe. It's often associated with nature and natural cycles which is true. But it isn't all about oak trees, seasons of the year and the like. Outside of London, some of the Druids I've met study and practice ancient Celtic wisdom. Some model themselves on Arthur and the Knights of the Round Table, others practice Wiccan Magic. All have a common symbolic and ethereal bond – to find and practice truth in harmony with the natural laws of the universe.

In London, I joined the 'Townies' (my affectionate nickname for The Druid Order) where the focus is around consciousness development.

In workshops and classes I've studied: the spiritual nature of man, consciousness development, homeopathy, how man connects with the stars, practical advice on making decisions, working in and with a group, dealing with crises, practicing patience, Rosicrucian teachings,

---

[13] The poet and artist, William Blake, was once a chief of (as it was then known) the *Ancient Order of Druids*.

Gnostic Christianity, Mathematics, deciphering Stonehenge, the energy of Hebrew glyphs, the significance of the four seasons and natural cycles of the year, and Egyptology. The list goes on and on. I have at least another five years of study material to get through - as far as I can work out - and then maybe start again?

Outside of Druidism, over the last three years I've studied astrology, Tarot reading, casting runes, dowsing with a pendulum and working with spirit.

You now know some of the (my) contextual bedrock for *Defrag your Soul.*

About the name, *Defrag your Soul*

'Defrag' your hard disk, in PC[14]-speak, means 'clean up, tidy up and optimise for use'. You arrange all your frequently used and helpful data files close together. You delete all the data files that no longer serve a useful purpose. You create a void in which to place new and helpful data for new programmes as they come on stream. *Defrag your Soul* means something analogous.

Replace the phrase 'PC' with 'life purpose' and 'data files' with 'habits and thought patterns'. Release those habits and thought patterns that no longer serve a useful purpose. They slow you down if not hold you back from your soul's quest, your life purpose. **Defrag your soul to cleanup and optimise the resources available to achieve your life purpose.**

I seek to fire your imagination; to help you explore new possibilities and experience an increased level of fulfilment. Not *'to boldly-go where no man has gone before[15]'* – but to boldly-go, directed by...

- What ancient wisdom has been telling us throughout the ages
- What non-prejudiced, modern day science measures, models and discovers about human consciousness.

---

[14] PC – the abbreviation for 'personal computer' predates 'political correctness'. Otherwise I'm in deep trouble. ☺
[15] I admit it. I am a Trekky for the 60's and 70's series of Star Trek with Captain Kirk, Mr Spock, Doc, Scottie, Lieutenant Uhura and the rest of the crew of Starship Enterprise. "Live long and prosper!" and "Make it so!"

Imagination is key. You cannot create abundance, fulfilment and prosperity, until you imagine it, have faith in yourself, choose courage to go for it, and work with the science of **spirit** to manifest it. I ask you to focus on two words: **spirit and imagination**.

More about Spirit:

Spirit moves one step at a time.

Spirit is the force that manifests form or put simply, the things you see, hear, feel, smell and taste in the world. You possess a three-fold spirit.
1. **Divine Spirit** – the highest level of vibration within us that, as it implies, connects with the divine. The highest state of our real ego as opposed to our vain *false ego*.
2. **Human Spirit** – that level of vibration within us that connects, cares and possesses compassion for our fellow species. That part that harkens sadness when we see a child cry and rejoices when they laugh and smile.
3. **Life Spirit** – the force within us that drives our heart's will to find, become and express our true selves, unfettered by our *false ego*.
When I use the phrase 'spirit', such as 'raise up to spirit', I refer to your threefold spirit that manifests the things you attract in your life.

About Imagination:

Imagination is more important than knowledge. Knowledge is limited. Imagination encircles the world.
Albert Einstein

Your mind has access to the *World of Thought*. It can think thoughts that do not limit themselves to the day-to-day, time-space continuum you live through. Your mind imagines. It dreams. It senses. It fantasises. It ponders. It speculates. It evaluates. It filters what spirit tells you. It distinguishes you from the animal kingdom.

Your understanding of life, the universe and how it works, is limited solely by your willingness and courage to explore your imagination and apply the creative wisdom you find. You possess limitless imagination. Your ability to conceptualise, understand and create has no boundaries, unless you choose to confine your thoughts. When you limit thinking, you limit possibilities.

Text Messages about Imagination

My friend BJ sent me a blog about cold fission. My imagination started to wander. I dreamt of a new world, as I texted with my pal. I imagined.

[12:03:55] Paul Burr: *Soon science and mysticism will join in one accord - this alone will transform man's conscious consciousness*

[12:03:57] BJ: *I'm into the unknown. So don't hesitate to forward information. Unknown is what I seek. Got to go, as I'm in the library ;)*

[12:04:36] BJ: *only if the elite will adjust*

[12:04:57] BJ: *had to answer that b4 I go..........*

[12:05:04] Paul Burr: *and - almost free energy MIGHT be the catalyst. It will put an end to oil wars and facilitate the feeding, clothing and provision of clean water to everyone on the planet. Once you have everything you need, as a separate individual, there is only one thing left to focus on ...... oneness.*

Imagine!

Many of us define a straight line, like the edge of a jigsaw puzzle, around our thoughts. Even when our intentions are good, we set limits as to the scope and size of possibilities in our *Jigsaw of Life*. Why?

Often because someone, whose influence we allow in our lives, tells us not to step outside accepted limits. That influencer may be a partner, a parent, a teacher, a cleric, a boss, a peer who pressures us to conform, a scientist, a politician or a little voice in our head.[16]

These restraining voices, with good intention or not, attempt to:

---

[16] I do certainly NOT advocate that you ignore the little voice inside that says "look both ways" before you cross the road. Instead I ask you to question the so called 'truths' you are spun.

- Apply pressure on us to conform. They present facts, data and logic to persuade us to limit our thinking. Sometimes these voices lie deliberately.

And/or

- Dictate and instil fear. They create laws. When persuasion does not work they tell us to 'not venture' across a line. They threaten us with severe consequences from violation of their rule of law. They attempt to make us feel not-good about ourselves. They attempt to increase our sense of insecurity - so that we do not trust ourselves and place our trust in their decisions instead.

I'm going to cover some heavy stuff now (but not for long). I want to talk about the darker side of humankind today.

I speak of global issues that invoke <u>not</u> human wellbeing, <u>not</u> world peace, <u>not</u> prosperity, <u>not</u> health, <u>not</u> wisdom, nor equal honour between people and nations. I speak of <u>not</u> the adequate provision of food, water, clothing or shelter for every living soul to thrive. I speak of the 99% exploited by the 1%. I speak of <u>not</u> oneness, separateness. (*Defrag your Soul*, I stress, is all about a return to oneness, 100%)

Humankind has gone far enough with separateness. Neither apartheid nor, in extreme cases, ethnic cleansing brings peace or cleanliness. The separateness these policies forge never cuts clean.

Furthermore, separateness does not put an end to things nor bring about peace. Separateness increases separateness.

War = separateness,
Love = oneness

Look at the no-end-in-sight wars that drag on and on around the globe. Can you imagine that the wars between tribes and races will bring peace to the Middle East? Will China's unlawful annexation of Tibet bring peace, freedom to practice religion, and prosperity to Tibetans?

Consider humankind's attempts to control - and its abuse of - nature. The war between humankind and Mother Nature reminds me of when I found myself inadvertently between a wild mother elephant and her baby. There was only going to be one winner so I retreated as far and as fast as I could. But humankind's governments and corporate powers do not cooperate universally with nature. Some act knowingly for profit borne of separateness from one another and, equally importantly, from Mother Nature and Her laws.

If humankind does not turn around, it will destroy itself or be culled severely - such is the karmic *Law of Consequences*. All the suffering and injustices carried out in the physical world stem from separateness: nation against nation, religion against religion, sectarianism, capitalism against socialism, authoritarianism against anarchism, liberalism against conservatism, highlanders against lowlanders, one colour against another colour; the duality is endless.

Instead, humankind can ready itself to evolve to a more informed level of consciousness between everyone and everything - oneness. Consciousness will not rise from manmade structures or dogma. It will evolve through personal volition, one person at a time.

About six or so years ago I decided to start with me! I've discovered that *life's journey* to fulfilment is more than about heartfelt joy and happiness, much more. It requires me to learn wisdom and transform from separateness to oneness.

Only this year I discovered that I made a secret pact with myself, as a very young child, to bring harmony (oneness) to my immediate family. I say "discovered" because the pact was wrapped up in my unconscious memory as soon as I had made it. I 'unearthed' this hidden pact in therapy only four months ago.

I was too young, at the time of making the pact, to appreciate that I could only bring harmony to my surroundings by harmonising the divided parts within myself. I was too young to appreciate that to change what was going on around me, I had to stop trying to control anyone but myself. But, I was and still am fully empowered to change myself (i.e. heal the divided self within me) at anytime I choose.

In doing so, I seek to do my bit to share what 'wisdom' I find and hopefully raise the consciousness of humankind; to help you find, open up, become and express your own *true self*; to create a world in which children everywhere can thrive.

Paul C Burr, 21 July 2012.

Paul C Burr

xxx

Part I: You Are All Magicians

Start at the Heart-centre

This book spirals. The heart of the spiral is found in *Part 1.* The heart of *Part 1* is found in a single paragraph.

Love is divine[17]. All that is <u>not</u> divine is <u>not</u> love. Shame, anger, sadness and fear are not love, not divine, nor are they borne of love. They dwell in the past or future, not the now. They reside in the head not the heart. They exist to be released, not conquered or embraced. And when you release them, nothing holds you back from your journey beyond <u>their</u> illusory boundaries, to love, truth and oneness.

The heart of the above paragraph is found in its first sentence.

Love is divine.

The heart of the above sentence is found in a single word.

Love!

Defrag your Soul equips you to journey the spiral path to love, oneness and truth; your *true self*, an everlasting solar star, the divine destiny your soul seeks to reach. What better place to start than love? Start with love. When you reach your destiny you return to love, only infinitely wiser (I 'ain't' there yet!). When you walk with spirit, the

---

[17] Instead of the word *divine*, you can replace it, if you wish, with the phrase *the highest spiritual influence of humankind.*

1

path is love. You become the path you walk on. Love is 'the Word', the vibration and (*"love, love, love, love..."* ☺) is all you need, for...

Love created the universe. The love within you can create the universe your heart truly desires - as if by magic. Tis' called 'Alchemy'.
Paul C Burr

I've never wanted to be a witch, but an alchemist, now that's a different matter. To invent this wizard world, I've learned a ridiculous amount about alchemy. Perhaps much of it I'll never use in the books, but I have to know in detail what magic can and cannot do in order to set the parameters and establish the stories' internal logic.
JK Rowling, Author of the *Harry Potter* books.

When you filter out, ignore or deny feelings of low self worth, you filter out self worth as well. Remember, the 'wet and dry' of life. You can't know one without the other. So life is about knowing self worth and its shadow, low-self worth. When you understand both, and how to transmute the shadow into light, then you understand the alchemy of life.
Paul C Burr

The glory is in the shadows, the seeds of love, plenty and gladness are scattered upon the waste places of the earth.
Druidic Wisdom

Unconscious Attracts

Nothing is random. You attract everything that happens to you. Most of us do it unconsciously, i.e. our unconscious mind directs our DNA to send out a signal that corresponds to the feelings we experience.

When something you want very much happens, you feel joy and elation; you feel good about yourself. When you feel good, you tend to attract more good things - until.... you start to contemplate or fear that these good things won't last forever. Then you project fear - and fear attracts that which you fear.

When that something unwanted happens, more negative feelings such as anger and hurt can well up in your conscious mind as well. They move from your conscious straight to your unconscious and you project these additional negative feelings outwards subliminally too. Unless you check yourself, you can create a vicious spiral from which there seems no escape. If you over-embrace your fear you can become frozen, like a rabbit in headlights. If you put up a 'mental shield' to protect yourself, you go into denial of your taboo fear.

People see your 'armoured shield' not the true you within. People are less attracted to and more wary of an armoured tank than love and truth. As a 'tank' your influence and ability to communicate effectively is thus limited if not futile. You may attract other like for like 'tanks'. You might shoot at one another - or join forces and shoot shells collectively at anything that threatens to penetrate your 'ring of steel'. You join a gang of like minded people, each with their own suit of like for like 'mental armour'.

What is this armour? It manifests itself in the form of shame, anger, sadness but most of all fear (the *four seeds of negative karma*). You cannot hide inside the armour but you can get lost.

For example, if you insulate yourself from hurt through drink, drugs, TV or a similar escapist distraction, you are in conscious denial of your hurt. The trouble is, you cannot be selective when you are in denial.

3

When you deny the existence of hurt,
you deny true joy and happiness at the same time.
Paraphrased from Brene Brown PhD,
Research Professor, University of Houston[18]

On the other hand, if you over-embrace your negative feelings, you restrict yourself from releasing them.

As another example, you may commit to work long hours so that you avoid failure or portray loyalty to compensate for perceived incompetence. No matter how successful you are; no matter how much fear you successfully avoid, you never release the fear

Notice, I say '<u>release</u> the fear', not 'defeat it'. It takes courage to defeat fear, but it takes more courage to release it. Warriors defeat fear, alchemists release it. And in doing so they achieve fearlessness – which is not about bravery; it's about wisdom.

On the far side of fear and hurt, lies wisdom.

Release the *four seeds of negative karma* (shame, anger, sadness and fear) and you ready your unconscious self to shine.

More about *Karma*....

Karma means action and reaction, cause and effect. It invokes the *Law of Consequences*. Every thought, every action you commit, goes out to the universe. Its energy is amplified and eventually returns to you. Put simply, if you complain a lot, even in your thoughts, you will attract a lot more things to complain about. If you get angry, you attract anger. If you are compassionate with yourself, you will attract compassion from others.

Notice the feelings in the preceding sentence are directed towards your-self. Project the feelings which you want onto yourself. (Imagine your inner child. Give it compassion, care and love; cherish yourself.)

---

[18] Ref: http://www.brenebrown.com/

And that is what you give out to the universe. What you give out, the universe gives back.

Many texts refer to *karma* as retribution. Instead, think of *karma* as the universe giving back what you put into it, abundantly. When you give out love, compassion and kindness, you will eventually receive these wonderful gifts in return. The 'trick' is to release the negative feelings that sully the vibrations of love, compassion and kindness that you are trying to put out. The negative feelings that take you away from the path your soul wants you to follow.

The *path* to your *true self* is always there, no matter how far you veer from it. When you walk that *path*, you do so <u>without</u> shame, anger, sadness or fear. You free yourself from creating any further unpleasant consequences, over and above those you have already created.

Police your thoughts. Curb negative actions borne out of separateness in which you seek to gain without sharing. Trust the divine completely. Let its current lift and set you free. Choose courage. Be patient. Spirit moves one step at a time.

The Spir(itu)al Path to Magic

Spirit, the highest form of vibration, resides in the heart. Spirit manifests form filtered by the mind. Unfettered, spirit governs all lower vibrations but only through the mind.

For truth by biased minds is ne'er divined;
Therefore seek wisdom, but first cleanse the mind.
From *Message to the Hierarchy of Selene,* the opening of
the Crown (7th) Chakra, the Moon Goddess[19]

Spirit radiates unconditional love. Spirit speaks truth. The mind fetters and distorts spirit's ability to manifest until you free it from the

---

[19] Ref: *The Restored New Testament, The Hellenic Fragments,* by James Morgan Pryse, published by The Theosophical Press.

clutches of the *false ego*. That dark shadow within lurks in the shadows between your persona[20] (what others see of you) and your *true self.*

Illustration 2: *The False Ego*

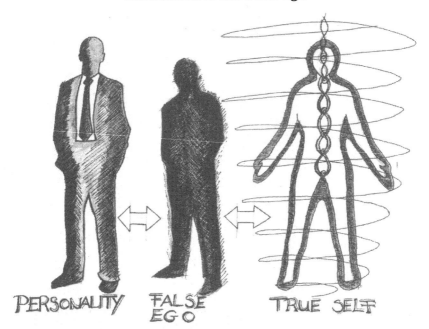

PERSONALITY   FALSE EGO   TRUE SELF

Spirit shines light into the shadows which beckon its beam of love. But Spirit's light is often clouded by the smoke and mirrors of the *false ego.* Be wary of what you find when you travel within, for you venture the path between truth and illusion. Choose inner truth and you will experience truth in the outside world. Choose illusion and.....

You will need to finely hone your skills to <u>discern</u> between the two. This insight smacked me right between the eyes a few years ago. I felt I could only be happy if I was in a relationship with someone else. I attracted a series of non-relationships, illusory relationships. Each individual I attempted to partner up with had a magnetic appeal but the relationship with them would falter quickly. I needed to learn to love/be compassionate with myself, independent of anyone else. I kept ignoring self-love and compassion until the penny finally dropped.

---

[20] Persona – derived from the Ancient Greek word for a theatrical mask.

I continue to improve my sign reading skills to recognise illusion when I come across it and hopefully select truth instead.

Truth, as the prose says, is *'ne'er divined by biased minds'*. Until your mind frees itself from bias, you encounter not-truth, i.e. illusion. I know of no short cut to truth.

To find, open, become and express your *true self*, you need to release the negative emotions within; the troubles that fog or deflect your light from the truth. As stated earlier, four emotions hold you back from finding your *true self*:[21]

1. **Shame** – impacts your feelings of self esteem and self worth.
2. **Anger** - at yourself (a form of extreme shame pointed inwards), sometimes unconsciously, for things you have or have not done, knowingly or unknowingly, that contributed to the harm of others. It can isolate you from self love, self care and self compassion; entombed in a smoky bubble of despair.

    Anger, towards others whom you feel have wronged you badly, can create clouds of emotion. You can't see through the cloud. You can't see what needs to be done. You can't help anyone. And no one can see in. They can't help you.
3. **Sadness** – when extreme, can easily switch in and out of anger. Either way, sadness encases you in the past tense. It holds you back from daring to dream of new possibilities.
4. **Fear** – stops you more than any of the above three emotions. Fear lurks behind shame, anger and sadness. Fear stops you in your tracks. It locks you into an undesirable situation in the future. I describe later how you'll need to choose courage to allow your fear into your consciousness so that you can release it. As you do, you see through its illusory powers - eventually.

Each *spiritual step* requires that you release all the negative emotions you have that stop you from making that step. The spiral does not always adhere strictly to any specific sequence though. For example, when you release shame you may also find yourself clearing out some anger and sadness at the same time. Upon completion you are tested.

---

[21] Swami Sri Yukteswar in his book, *The Holy Science*, describes *'8 meannesses of the heart'* – hatred, shame, fear, grief, condemnation, race prejudice, pride of pedigree, and a narrow sense of respectability – as obstacles to *'salvation'*.

The path spirals; you return to the starting place. You find out if you have released each negative emotion. You attract a similar situation to that which would have upset you in the past. You discover if you really have put your feelings of shame, anger, sadness and fear behind you. You are tested to see if you're okay with yourself; that you no longer get upset.

When you're okay with yourself that means you have <u>learned and applied</u> what you needed to learn from within you. You have readied yourself to climb the next spiral of your *spi(ritu)al path*.

Illustration 3: Spir(itu)al Step - Release Shame, Anger, Sadness and Fear

You start your next *spiritual step* conceptually from above (higher in vibration) where you started your last one - only now you are wiser and lighter, literally and emotionally. You ready yourself to take the next step towards your *true self*, where you find magic, *the Philosopher's Stone*[22] to life. Such is the true nature of alchemy.

> *I therefore counsel you to buy from me*
> *Gold, pure as Wisdom, tested in the fire.*
> *That you may thus enduring wealth acquire,*

> *And garments white as Truth, that you may clothe*
> *Yourself in beauty, not in rags you loathe,*
> *And magic salve wherewith your eyes to smear,*
> *That you may share the vision of the Seer.*

> *All whom I love I teach, but first confute,*
> *Thus from their minds all errors to uproot.*
> *For truth by biased minds is ne'er divined;*
> *Therefore seek wisdom, but first cleanse the mind.*

From *Message to the Hierarchy of Selene*, the opening of the Crown (7th) Chakra, the Moon Goddess[23]

The alchemists of the middle ages spread the popular belief that they sought to transmute base metals into gold. They deliberately hid their true work in this symbolic way, to lull the suspicions of religious zealots who policed the injunction *'not to seek to know the mysteries of God'*. Instead of fusing metals whose collective elemental weight

---

[22] *The Philosopher's Stone:* a legendary alchemical substance said to be capable of turning base metals (lead, for example) into gold. It was also sometimes believed to be an elixir of life, useful for rejuvenation and possibly for achieving immortality. Both these explanations were symbolic myths that alchemists created to protect themselves from interrogation and prosecution.
[23] Ref: *The Restored New Testament, The Hellenic Fragments,* by James Morgan Pryse, published by The Theosophical Press.

matched that of gold, they sought to change their lower nature into spirit.

The essence of spiritual alchemy is thus 'the development of character (which) is more important than physical gratification'.[24] Spiritual Gold, truth, is acquired by spiralling upwards through levels of consciousness, each with their corresponding life experiences. And the *Elixir of Life* is to find, open, become and express yourself with 'deathless truth'.

> *The Conqueror I shall reward with food*
> *Ambrosial, that his mind may be imbued*
> *With deathless truth; and unto him, mine own,*
> *I shall present a precious pearly stone.*
> *And on the stone a sacred new name writ.*
> *Known only unto him receiving it.*
> From *Message to the Hierarchy of Ares,* the opening of
> the Solar Plexus (3rd) Chakra, Mars[25]

In the end, when you have released all the seeds of negative *karma* (shame, anger, sadness and fear) what remains is love. You reverberate with unconditional love, unfettered spirit, free to manifest truth, free from negative karmic responses.

> *The Truth Shall Set You Free.*
> John 8:32

Free to manifest in the service of humankind. At this level of consciousness, what else would you desire?   The *Law of Attraction* thus serves you best in the pursuit of truth, your truth. You may attract all the material things in the world which will bring you joy and

---

[24] Ref: *Spiritual Alchemy, The Hermetic Art of Spiritual Transformation* by CC Zain, published by Church of Light, Los Angeles
[25] Ref: *As 23.*

happiness whilst they are relevant. When they no longer become conducive to your journey within, by definition, they no longer serve you and could even hold you back – especially should you fear losing them.

Make sure that which you ask for, attract and conjure, serves your *life's journey*, in a timely fashion.

You Conjure

There is a commonly used phrase amongst those who study the *Law of Attraction*, *'Thoughts become things'*. It is slightly incorrect in that it misses a small step.

> *Thoughts that become feelings, become things.*

Your mind plucks a thought from *The World of Thought* and clothes it with the emotion of wanting it. You create a desire. You <u>feel</u> desire - and spirit responds to feelings, not thoughts. Your feelings of desire form an ethereal image know by the ancients as your *Desire World*.

The 'secret' is to feel as if your desire is already fulfilled. Then spirit has clarity about that which you desire. I speak not of the *Law of Attraction*; I speak of the *Law of Reversibility*.

> *Your task is to develop a transparent mind,*
> *to let spirit manifest your heartfelt desires.*

There are more laws as to how manifestation works, such as the *Law of Consequence*. If manifesting was simply the process of clothing that which we desire in our minds, I would not have any readers of this book.

Illustration 4: *Law of Reversibility* **- Sequence of Manifestation**

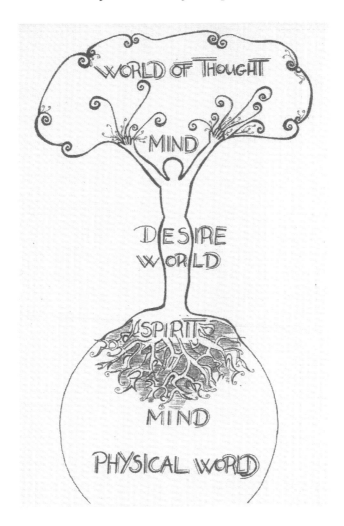

The mind is the gateway through which spirit manifests your heart's desires. The mind chooses ultimately but its choice may be a subconscious choice. I return to this aspect of manifestation in more detail later. [26]

Sometimes we seek to attract what we want. At other times we seek something not to happen; we seek to repel that which we don't want. It

---

[26] Ref: *Part IX: A Collection of Blogs and Essays*, chapter, *Fear Bypasses your Conscious Mind.*

is important to be clear about what you want. Wanting 'not-something' to happen creates a void; it doesn't necessarily create what you want instead. Furthermore, spirit moves one step at a time.

For example, let's say we seek 'not-war' and we succeed. We create a cease fire (a void.) This is far better than war but it is not peace, not yet. We would still need to invoke a lasting peace as step two. If we do not and turn our attention elsewhere, war can return. We serve ourselves better by informing spirit that our outcome is 'lasting peace', as opposed to 'not war'. There are further (laws of) consequences to focusing on 'want-nots' as well.

Consider the word 'antiseptic', it presupposes septicity. We label anti-ill health drugs to immunise us from maladies that could befall us. Likewise we see commonly used phrases such as 'anti-war', 'anti-terrorist', 'anti-bullying' and 'no-more-poverty'. With good intention we fight against that which we do not want, but in so doing, we invoke a problem, associated with duality.

Here's the issue. In order to achieve *not* poverty, for example, we attract poverty first in order to remove it. Why? For two reasons:

1. Those who have studied Neuro-Linguistic Programming know that our unconscious mind cannot process the word 'not'. For example, if you were to shout at a child "Don't drop that!" The child will invariably drop what they are holding because your command bypasses their conscious mind, they leave out the 'not' and obey your command. (Better to speak calmly and firmly, "Hold it carefully!")

Fun Exercise:

1. Think of a human-size pink bunny rabbit standing next to you.
2. Now, think of <u>not</u> that pink bunny rabbit.
3. Do you find yourself thinking of the pink bunny rabbit still?

---

2. Point 1 links to the *Law of Reversibility*, '*We attract what we focus with feeling on*'. The energy in the thoughts and language we use,

as we shall see later[27], influences the vibration of our DNA. So when we focus on 'not' something, the lack or scarcity - or more precisely, the gap between what we don't have and what we want - that's what we attract, a gap.

For example, when I have dwelt on not love or loneliness[28] (which I have been wont to do without thinking in the past) that's what I've attracted – not love. And, as you will see in the next section, the situation can worsen.

For every single thing we desire, there exists a corresponding not-thing. For example: we can attract wealth and not-wealth (poverty); joy and not joy (sadness); health and not health (disease), love and not love (fear[29]).

So a fundamental, although not the only, secret of successful attraction lies in your willingness to focus your language and thoughts on the positive (for example: 'peace' instead of 'anti-war') and allow spirit to take its course, to manifest that which you desire.

Neither Fight nor Feed Fear

Spirit doesn't work through intellect. Spirit attempts to pass good feelings to the conscious mind to be interpreted and experienced. If the conscious mind is receptive to these feelings, you feel good and become high spirited. Your conscious mind passes the feeling of goodness to your unconscious mind - which despatches signals to your DNA to expand and increase their vibration. Your DNA rejoices. You send out a good vibe to the universe.

If you have good thoughts they will shine out of your face and look like sunbeams.

Roald Dahl

---

[27] Ref: See chapter *DNA: the Biological Internet of the Universe*
[28] Alone or all one: when you embrace oneness you are never alone, you are all one.
[29] Notice I use "fear" not "hate" to describe 'not-love'. I discuss this further in chapter *Love, Not-Fear, and Karma.*

Imagine you are going to ask someone out on a date. Spirit attempts to pass on the feeling of self confidence to you. It whispers, "go for it, you can do this!" When the good feelings despatched by spirit touch a 'nerve', a fear, your mind becomes unreceptive. This fear passes straight down into your unconscious mind and on to your DNA which in turn sends out a negative vibe to the universe. It wasn't spirit that sent you a negative feeling; it was your mind that transmuted spirit's message into fear.

Spirit can't force you to choose courage instead of fear; it invites you to. Spirit is the voice of your intuition. You intuit what spirit says between thoughts. Your intuition might prompt you to choose courage - but your conscious mind has power of veto. It took me over fifty years to catch on to what phrases like, 'listen to your heart' or 'follow your instinct' really mean.

If you only acknowledge one thing from this whole book, let it be....
When spirit whispers in your ear, respond accordingly!

Using the overt phrase 'choose courage' however was a relatively new concept to me. What does it mean? Does it mean face or fight your fear? No! It means choose the courage to allow your fear into your conscious mind and <u>let it be consciously</u>. Neither feed nor fight that fear, acknowledge it and let it be. Your unconscious mind then has no corresponding negative signals to send to your DNA.

Allow fear 'in' and let it be. Fear that is neither fed nor fought gets 'bored' eventually – and leaves.

The learning process, to allow fear into your conscious mind, is subtle. Its subsequent release is even more subtle. It is not an intellectual process. But once you have experienced it, you'll know what I'm talking about.

Sometimes you might have an unconscious fear. You know it's there by the repeating unwanted patterns you keep attracting in the outside world. If you're in this situation, you might want to seek professional help to unearth your fear. Find out what it is, where it came from, how you got it, who gave it you – and the impact it's had on the decisions you make in life. And when you unearth your unconscious fear....

Let your fear be. It's part of you at this point in time. This is what the duality of human existence is about, to know fear so that you know not-fear.

Fear is invoked by the potential of not getting that which you desire. For example, 'I desire success but I'm not going to go for it in case I fail' or 'I desire not to be alone. I fear loneliness'. When you let your fear of loneliness be, you let your desire not to be lonely be at the same time. You free yourself from the 'not-love' aspects of your desire. What remains is love. And love creates magic.

When you let your desires and fears be, you create nothingness, a void in your consciousness. This means you practise 'being nothing'.

This doesn't necessarily mean 'do nothing'. Instead, attend to what the relationship or situation needs borne out of love and compassion, for yourself first of all. When you fill the void with love and compassion, for yourself, you walk with spirit.

Tread one step at a time with spirit. There's a temptation to rush ahead; to fill in the blanks of missing wisdom with fantasy; to join dots that aren't meant to be connected. Tread thoughtfully, truthfully, patiently and unassumingly - spirit will provide what's best for you.

When you present your truth to a situation, you have nothing to hide behind. You are defenceless. Your defencelessness is your strength.

The above phrase took me a while to work out and required a lot of faith. When you present your truth (including your desires and fears) to a situation, the falsity of others has no strength in that space and therefore leaves.

Exercise: Practise Being Nothing[30]

1. Think of a relationship or a project where you are not getting what you want.

2. Write down the outcomes that your heart truly desires from this situation.

3. Write down all your fears as well.

4. The summation of your desires and fears represent 'your truth right now'. You are human. Let it be ok to allow these fears into your awareness, without fighting or feeding them.

5. Avoid attaching yourself to (but do not deny) your desires and fears, as best you can. Let them be. If you find this difficult, pretend - 'Act as if!'

6. Practise 'being nothing' which means...

7. Watch and listen to, non-judgementally, what goes on around you.

8. Develop an awareness of things which you may have projected on to the situation or the others involved.

9. As you raise your awareness, attend to what's needed compassionately. Keep your fears and desires 'parked'. Bring truth to bear.

10. You might encounter some form of kick-back as others wrestle with their not-truth, i.e. falsity. Stay non-attached.

11. Notice any feelings of shame, guilt, anger or sadness that others might try to instil in you. Trap and park these negative feelings. Use them as feedback to inform your conscious mind that you are aware of these negative emotions but not controllable by them. Keep trapping and parking them. They will lose their power eventually.

12. As you trap and park each negative feeling, give a patient, compassionate and truthful response to things that happen.

13. The outcome now has only one destiny - truth. Regardless of what happens physically, you invoke truth into a situation when you stop trying to control it.

---

[30] Inspired by an exercise given by David Loxley, Chief Druid, The Druid Order.

Tip: **Being Nothing**[31]

We act upon our thoughts and feelings. So as you think about a situation or relationship, imagine putting all your associated thoughts into a circle. No thoughts are allowed in the centre of the circle. That is the place where you practise 'being nothing'.

Put all thoughts about the future in front of you. Put all thoughts about the past behind you. Put all thoughts about other people and their actions to your left. Put all thoughts about yourself and your feelings to your right.

If you find yourself thinking about what someone else is doing, take a mental step to the right. Likewise, if you find yourself thinking about yourself, step to the left. Step forward or back as the case may be if your mind wanders into the past or future. Keep to the centre of the circle.

> *'Being nothing' means being in the present tense - that present moment-by-moment of truth.*

Ω

You cannot change a situation by trying to control it. But you can change it into one of truth by being in your truth.

You Conjure Not Through Fear

In extreme cases we clothe a 'not-something-we-want' in fear.

In my childhood, I accepted a fear of poverty from my single-parent father. My father's intentions were indeed honourable. He wanted to provide enough income so that he and I could live comfortably and I could have a decent education. (I am mightily grateful.) But fear pays no heed to intention and when fear becomes an obsession, it drives intention. For example...

You can obsess about a relationship. Instead of love, the fear of losing someone dear to you drives your behaviour. You attempt to control the responses the other person gives you. You sometimes blame or

---

[31] Inspired by some advice from Jeanne Ayling, Spiritual Mechanic, Hove, UK.

find fault. At other times you may keep silent and hope to maintain some semblance of artificial peace. You avoid risk. You cease to trust either your partner or, worse still, yourself. In extreme cases you obsess yourself with fear.

If you find yourself behaving this way, a red flag is waving. Anything borne out of obsession is bound for a fall sooner or later. And even if you keep that which you obsess over (in this instance, losing the relationship) at bay, the obsession never goes away until you awaken yourself to new possibilities - your views on the relationship don't have to stay the way they have been - or being single is cool - or you can find a better relationship with someone else.

My own example: I would never go as far as to call my fear of poverty an 'obsession'. Luckily, I succeeded enough in my career, to keep fear at bay. However, no matter how much money I had in the bank the fear never went away. I only started coming to terms with my fear during the last year or so. I am slowly learning to displace the fear. Instead, I do my best to focus on prosperity in the fuller sense of mind, body and soul.

When you live in fear, you mirror the future with something that happened in the past.

My father, for example, was brought up through childhood periods of extreme poverty and debt. He took his childhood memories and placed them in a 'picture' of the future. He did everything he could to avoid that 'picture' becoming a reality. Easy to say in hindsight, for my dad and myself, 'there was another way, another picture, of something my father wanted, in the affirmative - wealth and happiness'.

The same holds true for the three other categories of negative emotions that we attach to our childhood memories - anger, sadness and shame. All such memories can hold tremendous sway over our adult lives; we replay those childhood memories often unconsciously.

If we give memories power, even unknowingly, they create emotions - sometimes good, sometimes not good. We recall memories in our mind but where do we get them from? Where do we store the past tense?

The Physical and the Etheric

Quantum science (for further information, watch DVD's like *The Living Matrix*[32]) is now on the fringe of assimilating that memories 'live' in every cell of your body. In each body cell resides a holographic model (or fractal) of something known by the ancients as your *Etheric* (or *Vital*) *Body*[33], which resides around your physical body. <u>You</u> have a *Dense Body* and an *Etheric Body*.

Your *Etheric Body* stores away information that pertains to every sinew, nut and bolt of every thought, intention, action and response you've either made or been on the receiving end of in your life. It's collected every impulse your mind and physical body has ever given and received. It collected this information from the very start of your embryonic gestation into life.

Your first DNA strand transduced information from your mother into your first human cell. The information stored was replicated in every subsequent cell in your body. Every cell in your body contains the whole history of your life from the moment a seed atom in your father's sperm connected with the seed atom of your mother's egg.

As the number of cells in your body grew, they formed a field of energy around them. Scientists at institutes like *HeartMath*[34] refer to it as *The Living Matrix*. Rosicrucians call it the *Vital Body*.[35] Druidic, Yogic and Hindi texts refer to it as the *Etheric Body*. Think of it as a highly advanced computer storage device, different to man-made devices in that it is:

1. Holographic – if you detach any living cell from your body it contains the exact same information as every other cell. Even if the living cell is relocated several miles from your body, the DNA of your in-host cells transmit information to the remote cell instantly. Scientists call this phenomena 'non-locality'.

---

[32] Ref: www.thelivingmatrixmovie.com
[33] You can find out about the function of the *Etheric Body* in connection with physical health in *Part V: Health = Mind and Body at Ease. Not-Health = Dis-ease.*
[34] Ref: http://www.heartmath.org/
[35] Ref: *The Rosicrucian Cosmo Conception Mystic Christianity* by Max Heindel, 1922, published by the Rosicrucian Fellowship Press.

Illustration 5: The *Etheric Body*

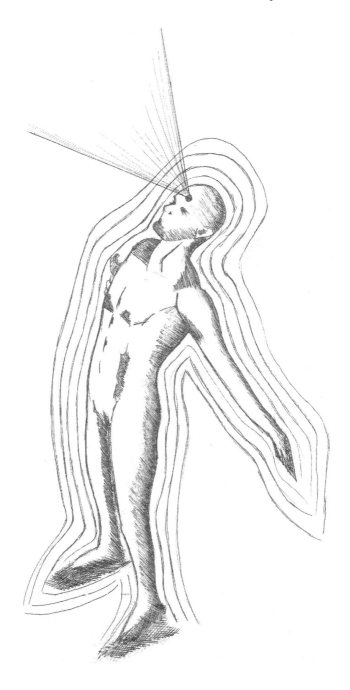

2. Solitonic – the data or information is stored in wave patterns of bio-photons emitted by your DNA.

The data (memories) impressed in the *Etheric Body* feeds the mind, your decision making machine. The mind decides what to do with the information (memories) presented. Does it make some animalistic 'fight or flight' response to some external stimulus without an intervening thought? Or does it pause, reflect and give a measured response? Better still, does the mind pass the thought up to spirit and be guided by a higher vibration?

Let's return our attention to the *Dense Body*. The mind signals the flow of energy/impulses to neurons in your body that activate your nervous and hormonal systems. These systems influence your well being.

Summary:

The information your mind downloads, from your *Etheric Body,* influences your wellbeing emotionally and, as we shall see later, physically. The closer you get to your *true self,* the 'cleaner' the data the *Etheric Body* dispatches to your mind - e.g. instead of sending a memory that you are fearful of being alone, it sends the memory that you've gotten over that fear now and that you are okay with yourself about the idea of being single. You raise your vibration. You radiate more light. You attract people, things and events that are tuned into that same higher vibration[36] - others who are okay with themselves about the same things as you are. You share and receive more wisdom - of truth, love and oneness. Your soul rejoices.

---

[36] You might also attract people, things and events of the opposite vibration. Such is the nature of duality. Although it may not be apparent, at some level, they seek you to share your wisdom. When the student is ready, the teacher appears.

A Précis: Successful Sorcery

Create the image of oneness.
Use your imagination.
Place the image in ions.[37]
I, magi, in ions.[38]
Imagine.

Alchemy, magic, sorcery – call it what you will – means at some level to craft an 'image in ions' (use the imagination); be it, for example, wealth, fame, health or love. You achieve that which you desire in the world outside by removal of that which within you stops you fulfilling that desire. You decide to remove the inner blocks to and leaks from spirit's force.

We make decisions in our mind and the decisions we take (consciously and unconsciously) cause and affect what we manifest. Sometimes we choose between what our heart tells us and that which our head says. We decide what we think is best. But we don't always choose wisely. By that I mean we invoke unhelpful repeating patterns in our life. We recognise them time after time again – and still do nothing about them until something inside screams, "Enough!"

For example, I decide to attach myself to someone whom I feel I love dearly, but they don't return my love in the same way. The thought of not having them in my life drives my thoughts and actions. I fear rejection and isolation. I do all I can to comply with their wishes and that which I think will make them happy. I hopefully keep some semblance of balance and continuity. I give them the power to determine my happiness. I give them my power. At some deep, deep

---

[37] *Ions:* an old word for atoms, later used by physicist, Michael Faraday to describe an atom in which the total number of electrons is not equal to the total number of protons, giving it a net positive or negative charge.

[38] *Magi:* an old word for a practitioner of magic, to include astrology, alchemy and other forms of esotericism.

23

level, my soul tells me that I no longer express my *true self*. I no longer place esteem in my *true self*.

My self esteem gets lower and lower. So low, I no longer trust my own judgement or ability to make the right decision. This other person, in effect, makes all my decisions for me. Those decisions are theirs, not mine. Eventually something inside of me cracks and I choose courage. I break free.

Courage is a decision, a choice, not a trait. We all have courage. But we don't all choose to use it. Neither does anyone I know personally, including me, choose it consistently.

When we choose not-courage, we invoke negative holding patterns in life. The negative patterns hold us back from finding, opening up, becoming and expressing our true selves. In order to find our true selves we need to take steps, *spiritual steps*, within ourselves. We take these steps to free ourselves from the endemic negativity of our *false-ego* (i.e. not our *true self*).

Each step, I have found, takes courage. You strive to do something differently and when you take that step, you cannot predict the outcome because, by definition, you haven't taken it before. You have no memory of the consequences so you attract a new outcome. Success or setback, you gain new wisdom about what works or what does not.

These days, you will find a ton of books about the *Law of Attraction*. Some claim to help you find happiness through the right job, the right partner, money or good health. I seek all these things for myself and why not? I have enjoyed much abundance in my life (for which I am hugely grateful).

By abundance, I mean everything that I felt I loved, needed, enjoyed or made good use of – money, a job, a loving partner, a lovely home, a nice car and good health. I have had all these things at times and each time it wasn't enough. So I looked for something else, something more.

When I have had everything I thought I might need, I tended to do one of three things (I can't recall ever doing nothing):

1. Go for more and horde what I didn't use or need.
2. Keep and maintain what I had. Bring in what goes out. Everything remains the same.

3. Get rid of what I had. Create the space to replace it with something different and better.

Each action has its own consequences. Action that avoids balance (temperance) invokes the karmic law that nature restores everything to a state of equilibrium, eventually.

For example, governments spend millions with good intention on wiping out all bugs in hospitals. TV advertising persuades you to do the same in your home. This kill-all policy creates (attracts) superbugs that kill in return. Health authorities attempt to kill every bacterium that could possibly harm you (and every helpful one, as a consequence) by washing your hands in some kill-all lotion, every time you enter or leave a hospital ward. (Personally, I prefer natural soap and hot water but that's my decision not yours. You make your own choice freely.)

Native Americans knew that bacteria had as much right to live as humans. They didn't attempt to kill of all the harmful bacteria. Instead they would remove a portion of it from, for example, a wound to allow an injured person's body to heal itself naturally, i.e. co-habit with bacteria. They sought to build a balance with their environment through natural immunity.

Either strategy, 'kill all' (separateness) or 'live with' (oneness), has consequences.

Despite good intentions, when you act out of shame, anger, sadness and fear, you attract a negative holding pattern. One part within you experiences what another part does not. You create a separateness, a divided self that invokes repeating negative situations in the outside world, until you act out of not shame, not anger, not sadness, not fear and not separateness; until you act out of love, compassion, truth and oneness.

Either through oneness or separateness, many of us try to attract material things which we feel will make us happier or more secure;

things we don't have. When we get those things, do we feel happier and safer? Yes, we might. But is that enough? For me, no it hasn't been - not yet anyway. I haven't attracted enough wisdom and spiritual experience. I have not yet found my *true self.*

I seek more than the material world has to offer. Why? Because, a few years ago, I realised that I wouldn't find my sense of fulfilment in a job, a family, financial security and good health. These represent many of the wonderful things I desire but they don't represent the end of my journey.

Because you say, "I have amassed a store
Of wondrous riches, and need nothing more",
And know not that of all the powers of mind
You are the starveling, piteous and blind.
From *Message to the Hierarchy of Selene,* the opening of the Crown (7th) Chakra, the Moon Goddess[39]

Little do ye know your own blessedness; for to travel
hopefully is a better thing than to arrive, and the true
success is labour.
From *Virginbud Puerisque* by Robert Louis Stevenson

Let me stress, if you want any or all of these things (and why not?) then go for them. If, as and when you want more, go for that too. You choose what you populate your *Desire World* with.

According to ancient wisdom, the *Desire World* operates in a higher vibration than the Physical World – the domain of our *dense* and *etheric bodies.*

Your feelings make an 'impression' in your *Etheric Body* of what you desire to have (for example: health, wealth, fame and fortune) and what you desire to have not (for example: poverty, isolation and

---

[39] Ref: *The Restored New Testament, The Hellenic Fragments,* by James Morgan Pryse, published by The Theosophical Press.

suffering). When you do something that 'feels right', It makes you feel fulfilled, even if the task is something as mundane as keeping a tidy house or doing the washing up. You also have another category of tasks; those governed by fear.

When you perform a task borne out of fear, you feel more relieved than fulfilled. You may be hugely successful and repel that which you fear.

For example, you work hard in your job to avoid poverty or getting fired, or you work hard in a relationship to avoid someone you love perhaps leaving you. You focus and work diligently with good intent. You succeed enough to cocoon your fear. You may feel financially independent or that your relationship is on an even keel. But even with the best intention...

Decisions and actions borne out of fear, even the most successful ones, never erase that fear.

More than anything else, fear holds you back from becoming your *true self* and stepping into your true power, to serve your fellow hu-man - which, I suggest, is what life as a species is ultimately all about.

This means you have to discern and choose between the duality of fear and not-fear to progress.

You can't know anything in life without knowing its opposite. You can only know if something is wet, for example, because you know what not-wet, dry, is. Hot and cold, joy and sadness and so on, everything in life has its opposite, including fear. You learn love by understanding what not-love is. In an indirect way, learning fear eventually teaches you to appreciate fully what not-fear is. When you *feel the fear and do it anyway*[40], you act as if you are fearless. The opposite of fear, not-fear, is not courage though; it is love.

Use Love to Invoke the *Law of Reversibility*:
You learn love from not-love. This is connected to the *Law of Reversibility*. You can choose love (or not-love) in any decision you

---

[40] Ref: *Feel the Fear and Do It Anyway* by Susan Jeffers

make. All you need to do is imagine the outcome of your decision borne of love, as if it has already happened in the here and now. Be honest. You must ensure that what you imagine is really what you want and borne of love. Imagine the feelings you associate with the outcome fully, be honest, have faith and be patient.

Your outcome exists already, here and now - as does its duality, i.e. not your outcome. This is how the *Law of Reversibility* differs from some definitions of the *Law of Attraction*. The definitions I speak of are an approximation to the *Law of Reversibility*. They omit a key point:

> *What you seek is already present. You invoke it through your imagination and love[41]. This is the essence of sorcery. Love invokes white magic that manifests what your soul truly seeks.*

As you journey towards love, the closer you get, the more you realise that each of your fears, one by one, are a self imposed illusion. You have to allow your fears into your consciousness and let them be, to see through them.

Allowing fears to be, neither fighting nor feeding them, takes courage. When you allow your fears to be, they diminish - albeit slowly at times. As each fear subsides you start to appreciate what fearless means.

> *'Fearless' <u>might</u> mean courage.*
> *'Fearless' certainly means void of fear.*
> *'Fearlessness', on the other hand, means wisdom.*

You create a void where each fear used to be. But with what do you fill the void? Fearlessness? - No!

Fearlessness is, by definition, the absence of fear - and you can't fill a void with absence. You can only fill it with 'es-sence'. You fill the void with the essence of life, love. As you look back, you realise now that

---

[41] You invoke 'not-it' through 'not-love'.

your original fear was illusory. You transform your feeling fearless (i.e. courageous) into fearlessness. You transform from a warrior into a magician.

Experienced magicians, seasoned travellers within, who've taken many *spiritual steps*, are not brave - they have no need to be. They see the illusory fears they stepped through for what they were. They've experienced fearlessness that we can all experience as we take each *spiritual step* towards love.

The feeling of fearlessness indicates you've mastered the level (or taken another *spiritual step* towards your truth) you've been working on. It also informs you (i.e. you do not know) that you don't yet know of the fears you may have to face at the next level, on the next stage of our journey within.

When you master one level, you become a blithering idiot at the next, at the same time.
Dr Thomas Maughan, Chief Druid, The Druid Order, London, 1964-76

Part II: How to Get What You Want from 'Defrag your Soul'

Purpose of this Book...

Some say the purpose of life is to feel truly happy. They're right. Although you can omit the word "happy"; the purpose of life is to feel truth, your truth, your true nature.

Allow me to twist the words around: the purpose of life is to feel happily true. For your true nature is a state of joy and happiness. I've written this book to...

1. Help you accelerate the pace you take on your *life's journey* to find, open, become and express your *true self* - and thus find true happiness from within.

2. Equip you with the know-how and exercises to:
   - Quicken your journey.
   - Gauge better where you are.
   - Know you're heading in the right direction.
   - Read the map and the signposts.
   - Find what you're here to seek.
   - Awaken to new possibilities

3. Make you aware of pitfalls (many of which, I've fallen into) so that you will hopefully manage your way past them or at least recognise and know how to deal with them effectively.

I won't be telling you what you will find when you're 'there', at your journey's end, because...

- I haven't found 'there' yet for myself (hopefully I've made progress!).
- It is your journey and yours alone.

BUT...

You will get help to....

a. Increase your sensitivity to certain feelings, specifically fear and fearlessness, so that you know what to do when you feel them.

b. Obtain a clearer picture of your purpose in life.

31

c. Work with your purpose at a deep level to find and open the contract you made for this lifetime

d. Understand the next steps you need to take to keep to your contract.

e. Choose the courage to take these steps.

Oh, and by the way, there's no 'there' anyway, only further.

Is this Book for You? Perhaps....

I meet more and more people of all ages who seek something more than a 'normal' conventional life.

Many chase after and enjoy the same amusements as I have done in the past to varying degrees: alcohol, social drugs, sex, TV and travel. These days, we enjoy relatively new phenomena such as the Internet, Social Networking and a vast array of 'apps' for mobile phones.

Nonetheless, I see less desire in the younger generation to follow the conventional post-war, 'baby boomer' lifestyle that I took on, once I'd passed through the 60's hippie era. The idea of seeking stability, starting a family and acquiring a mortgage that you can only just afford, does not appeal as much anymore.

Perhaps the young see through the emotional pitfalls of saddling themselves with long term debt. Perhaps they feel the price of property is out of their reach and not worth the hassle. Perhaps the lack of confidence in the property market in recent years has made it unattractive too? Perhaps the trustworthiness of financial institutions has plummeted so much that the young no longer have any faith in them. Or is it something simpler?

Perhaps the young seek freedom. Freedom from the biggest shackle that conventional society seeks to bind them with – DEBT! Instead they seek freedom to go their own way. Take gap years out. Party.

Granted, some still take the conventional route. Others beg and borrow from their parents to do their own thing. Others merely drop out and busk their way through life. But no matter which route they opt for, more and more young people seem to be turning inwards for answers. I've over 20,000 followers on Facebook, most of them in their twenties, asking for something more than the latest apps and parties. They're interested in things beyond the realm of what the outside world has to offer. They haven't rejected convention, materialism and sensual pleasures but do sense that these things have limitations to finding fulfilment.

Perhaps still in the minority, they seek relationships that have a deeper meaning than having lots of mates or 'someone special' to love. They seek relationships or groups that will help them to grow spiritually.

They've moved on from the lust for wealth of *Generation X*[42] and the cosy and conventional nature of *Generation Y*[43]. These young people are sometimes times called *Generation Zero*[44] – because they carry the hope of a new start for humankind. They seek help. They are not alone.[45]

For there are also a growing number, still young at heart, from the *Generations X, Y* and *Baby Boomer* generations (like me) who have also started to look within. We all seek deeper meaning and purpose to our lives. Some of us (including me) only really got going in the last few years. Collectively, there's a quickening of spirit in the world.

The quickening requires us to shed faster much of the programming and influence of traditional and rationalist thinking. Leading yourself

---

[42] Generation X is attributed to people born between 1965 and 1980, approximately. Generation X came of age in an era of two-income families, rising divorce rates and a faltering economy. Women were joining the workforce in large numbers. As a result, Generation X is independent, resourceful and self-sufficient. In the workplace, Generation X values freedom and responsibility. Many in this generation display a casual disdain for authority and structured work hours. They dislike being micro-managed and embrace a hands-off management philosophy.
Ref: http://legalcareers.about.com/od/practicetips/a/GenerationX.htm
[43] Generation Y: were born in the mid-1980's and later. They are attributed as being: 'tech-savvy', family-centric, achievement-oriented, team-oriented and attention craving.
Ref: http://legalcareers.about.com/od/practicetips/a/GenerationY.htm
[44] Etymologically connected to the term *Ground Zero*
[45] Kids these days are getting smarter and smarter. We are giving birth to a '*Generation Wow!*'

to a vision of something new, beyond the context in which you live, takes courage.

Are you at that stage where....

- You feel life is more than what happens to and around you?
- You want to find or move more quickly towards the purpose of your life?
- Many of the things you try that used to work, no longer do?
- You're unsure of which direction or steps to take in life?
- You are making decisions borne out of fear as opposed to those that feel right?
- You're fed up with the 'winner takes all' attitude of the conventional society we live in?
- You see through the propaganda you are fed to justify wars for oil and wealth?
- You're starting to realise that happiness is not found without but within?
- Shame, anger, sadness or fear stops you finding or feeling self-compassion, self worth, self-trust, love for the child within you, love for yourself, for who you are, as you are?
- You want to put an end to the negative emotions that affect you physically, emotionally, mentally or spiritually?

***Defrag your Soul* reveals how you can free yourself from those things that hold you back in life and move on the path to find, open, become and express your *true self* - one *spiritual step* at a time.**

Adopt an Open Mind...

I ask that you....

1. Believe nothing I write. Instead I ask you to imagine.
2. Ask yourself
   a. "What if what I read holds true?"
   b. "What are the consequences for me, if it is true?"

    c. "Might my life make more sense if it did hold true?"

    d. "Can I see myself living a more fulfilled life, if it were true?"

    e. "Am I prepared to find out if it is true, <u>for me</u>?"

3. Build the self esteem and trust to have faith in your own experience, using the exercises contained herein. Find your own truth, your own purpose, and should you choose - your own life's contract, that (even though you might not know it yet) you've already committed to deliver.

4. Find, open up, become and express yourself. When you do, the opinions of others (especially those who see you as outside the comfortable norm) will matter less. But stay tuned with them, for they may change their views when they see the change in you. If they do, they'll seek your help.

5. Prove what I say for yourself. I, at some level, have experienced it to be true for me. I know it to be true for me. I don't need anyone else to verify my experience. Some might vilify what I write. I'm ok with that because I'm ok with that part of me that has had the experience. I continue to learn to put my trust in and love myself more and more. I'm no self-sycophant. There are plenty of things I've done that I'm not proud of. We are all a work in progress.

I'm not perfect, far from it. My friends tell me there are loveable and good parts to my character. There are some not so good parts too. So I have something to build on and work with respectively - huh? When you work through the exercises, you will find those good and maybe not so good parts of yourself too, if you haven't found them already. You'll get a much clearer view of your own *life's journey*. You'll travel. Your journey will differ from mine but it will have the same characteristics: risk, adventure, uncertainty, successes and setbacks – but most of all, wisdom.

One must take the path of wisdom eventually - because all the others lead to it.

Henry Miller[46]

---

[46] From the Foreword titled, *The Wisdom of The Heart* to *The Mind of the Druid*, by E Graham Howe, Sompong Press Ltd., Thailand. A later, UK version,

The path will take you to your *true self*, to oneness and the love of it, starting with yourself.

You don't have to find perfection to love yourself. If you're uncomfortable with the notion of loving yourself wholly, start by loving your inner child - which is synonymous with your shining self. Exude care and compassion for those parts of you that you are maybe not so pleased with. More than anything, trust yourself to give and receive self-love.

(Looked at another way, if you cannot trust yourself, you cannot trust your feelings. If you cannot trust your feelings, you cannot trust the feeling of love, whether you give it or receive it.)

Sometimes that self-love (cocooned in shame, anger, sadness and fear) is encased in a shield of armour. Some childhood experience or trauma forces your unconscious mind to lock away your self-love.

This book will help you shed that armour. When you do, you find inside all the shame, anger, sadness and fear - created by a child who did not have an adult mind that could cope. The child was never equipped in the first place to deal with the traumatic experiences it underwent. So the child's unconscious mind wrapped the experiences and emotions away to protect itself. It may have made a pact with itself that no longer serves a useful purpose in your life and hasn't done since you entered adulthood.

Here's the good news. When you see that childhood shame, anger, sadness and fear with an adult mind, from a safe distance – you will find its irrelevance to your adult context. In that instant you can start to release it. What remains is your *true self*, part of that inner child who seeks to grow and experience life to the full. The inner child willing to take the *spiritual steps* to achieve its purpose in life and deliver the contract it made for this lifetime, after your last lifetime.

That's what I've been able to do for myself and what I do for my clients. I've learned how to take *spiritual steps*. Some have been baby steps; others, especially the one I'm working on now, have been in front of me since I was a child. I know better now, how and where to head in the right direction, even if I don't always take that direction.

---

published by Skoob Esoterica, has an equally insightful Foreword by David Loxley, Chief Druid, *The Druid Order*, London.

Either way, I try to be fully accountable for the steps I take. I encourage you to do likewise, if you are not doing so already.

Defrag your Soul attempts to help you optimise your route to your true self, to give you the maximum growth from minimal and courageous effort.

Why an Open Minded Approach is Important

Open mindedness does <u>not</u> mean believing in something. Closed mindedness <u>does</u> mean not believing in it however.

We can share the wisdom of insight but the experience and perhaps more importantly, the application of that wisdom, is a personal journey. *Spiritual insight* comes from a place deep within.

For example, suppose you are meditating or practising yoga. You focus your attention within. As you go deeper and deeper, the mind slows down and eventually comes to a standstill. It forgets your past and any troubles ailing you. It 'parks' any fears you have about the future. It resides at rest in the present moment, moment by moment - the *present tense*.

Deep within, you find yourself on the 'shoreline' of your unconsciousness (*Atma*). You can tap into the infinite wisdom that your unconscious self holds. It is here that you can hear without listening. It is here that you can receive wisdom without asking for it. You can rest without sleeping. Here on the 'shoreline' you are at that place of inspirational creativity, intuitive awareness and heartfelt peace.

It is in this place of (even momentary) stillness that many written words, works of art, scientific breakthroughs, solutions to mathematical puzzles and *spiritual insights* are experienced.

Spiritual insight can be described as an egoless[47] connection with a point inside of us that says "as best I know, this is <u>the</u> truth about a situation". It may not be the whole truth yet it is a richer awareness of the truth of the situation you are focusing on. Making this egoless connection requires an open mindset, free from all influence (positive or negative) that we have been subjected to in the past.

I ask you to keep an open mind to experience fully what I write about in this book. I share clients' and my own experiences, anecdotes, case stories and research. I share how <u>I</u> have found that life works. I present exercises to help you share that experience for yourself.

As you complete the exercises, trust yourself and have faith in your own experience. You can feel that experience to be true or not. I don't attempt to prove it to you. You have a laboratory in which to experiment and experience the exercises first hand. It's called 'your world'.

Upon completion of the exercises, gauge for yourself the validity of the connection and learning you receive from your inner self. In the meantime, trust what the little voice inside of you says. Trust your intuition - always.

You already have the answer to every question that your mind could ever ask.

Tune into the Answers Within

Who taught you...

- What love is and is not?
- How to love someone, anyone?
- How to listen to and use your intuition?
- How to be sensitive to other people feelings?
- How to make decisions wisely?
- When to use patience, when to hurry?

---

[47] By egoless I mean "devoid of our false ego". It dwells in the dark shadow that fills the gap between our personality and our *true self*. Ref: page 112, *Learn to Love and Be Loved in Return*.

- When to assert yourself and when to remain silent?
- How to deal with a crisis?
- How to deal with unwanted and abrupt change?
- How to deal with shame and resentment?
- When and how to forgive yourself?

As I read the above list, I can think of more errors than not-errors that I've made in my life. The biggest errors occurred typically when I ventured into a situation in which I had little or no 'hindsight' experience AND didn't seek the advice from an expert when available. Instead I learned how to deal effectively with such situations through trial and error.

Perhaps the biggest error of all was not learning from errors the first, second and in some instances many times around.

For example, if I became agitated by an event and remained so after it was over. I would keep attracting similar events and repeat the same agitation over and over until I learned how to respond to such an event differently - in an uplifting way, instead of getting upset.

Joy does not manifest itself out of sadness. Sadness attracts more sadness, shame attracts shame, anger attracts anger and fear attracts fear. We remain clouded in our emotions until we learn how to 'park', if not release, such negative emotions and piece together the true picture of what our *life's jigsaw* could hold for us. We clear the foggy cloud that deep-felt negative emotions cause.

No longer clouded by our emotions, we see that which was previously unknown to us. We enable ourselves to use insight - the peace and wisdom of egoless truth.

We see more clearly how to piece together solutions to problems and answers to questions - from a still and peaceful place within. At the same time, we develop a 'feel' for the right solutions and answers.

This feeling comes through the third chakra, the *Solar Plexus* in the abdominal region, the 'power chakra', ruled by Mars. According to ancient wisdom...

"The Solar Plexus is a receiver of intuition from the spirit worlds and Higher Self. Many people will recall occasions when they have thought about something and have instantly received a strange feeling in the area of the lower stomach as a direct result. People often refer to having

such experiences as having a 'gut feeling' or other sensation in the area of the stomach. This is an inner communication by way of intuition and impressions originating in the inner realms or from the Higher Self, and is a confirmation or warning about a thought within the mind."[48]

With practice, you can develop the 'right feel' for what to do when you face the unknown. You can see what the situation needs. You reduce the need for trial and error.

Not only can you see all the jigsaw pieces available, you also see how they fit together, to make a more desirable picture.

Tip[49]: If you're feeling really 'freaked-out' about something, find a place on your own. Recite to yourself <u>seventeen</u>[50] times, out loud, the lines in italics below.

"I place the word 'stillness' in my mind.
I place the word 'peace' behind my heart.
I place the word 'power' in my abdomen."

Even though you're upset, act as if you mean the words spoken as best as you can. Allow the energy of the words to fill your body.

Ω

In addition, I found a number of videos of tapping techniques by Brad Yates on YouTube that helped me through a very shaky period in my life. I practised them every morning for several weeks and noticed they had a beneficial effect on my feelings compared with those days that I wasn't near a PC. I particularly liked: *Fear and Panic Right Now - EFT Tapping with Brad Yates* and *Clearing Fear and Worry - Tapping with Brad Yates.*[51]

---

[48] Ref: http://www.ourultimatereality.com/the-heart-chakra-the-solar-plexus-chakra-the-sacral-chakra-and-the-root-chakra.html
[49] Given to me by Jeanne Ayling, Spiritual Mechanic, Hove, UK.
[50] Refer to the Glossary, The Major Arcana card number 17of the Tarot, *The Star.*
[51] Ref: http://www.youtube.com/

The Jigsaw Puzzle of Life

My father raised me as an only child. He ran a pub and so was very busy at weekends. I spent most Saturdays and Sundays at my Cousin Mike's home nearby. In dry weather, Mike and I would be out playing football, cricket or tennis depending on the month of the year. If it rained, and it rains a fair amount in North East England, we'd stay in and play board games and the like. In our very early days, there was only one TV channel, BBC, in black and white. The Internet, mobile telephones, computer games and 'apps' were a thing of the future. If you nodded your chin from side to side, or had the gall to say something like "Whatever!" - you'd get a clip around the ear. It was 'well early' before such slang would edge its way into everyday life. We children were taught to converse politely in the language of our parents. I recall saying "please" and "thank you" to every request and for everything given to me, respectively. I would not be allowed to leave the dinner table before saying "I've had sufficient, thank you. May I step down please?"

Fun and games were a face to face phenomenon, in which the whole family engaged. Adults and children would pit their wits or luck against one another and sometimes we'd collaborate over something creative.

"Aunty Rita", Mike's grandmother, loved jigsaws. We would often join her to put together a gargantuan, 1000+ piece jigsaw puzzle, usually a landscape painting. Aunty Rita would get Mike and me to sort all the pieces that had a straight edge. The straight edges, when connected, set the boundary, outside of which we need never venture. Next we'd sort the jigsaw pieces into piles that had the same colour or texture. Fields would be lush green. Trees would, hopefully, be a different shade of green and contain wooden branches. There might be a building, like a church, made of grey stone. In order to piece together the bits that made up the church, we'd start with its outline first. That is, we'd look for pieces that had a bit of grey with a straight edge that looked like the outline of a building. We pieced together the outline of the church. To create the church, we had to discern between the pieces that were the church, not the church, and the pieces which, when connected, defined its outline.

This technique, 'start with an outline and then fill it in', worked very well, area by area. Buildings, roads, signposts, people, trees and meadows were connected, piece by piece, as the picture came to life. All went well until we came to the last area, the sky; a vast swathe of cloudless blue with no discernible features at all.

Blue Sky, Nothing but Blue Sky

When faced with blue sky, our 'fill-in-the-outline-first' strategy, to complete the picture, no longer worked. We had to revert to visual trial and error. We didn't have the nous to get a 'feel' for where each piece slotted correctly, the first time around. We'd pick up a piece that looked the right shape and test it one way then the other. Sometimes we'd see if the piece in our hand fitted in a number of vacant slots.

On occasion, we'd try and force a piece, which looked very nearly right, into place. When we realised the error of our ways we'd extract it. We needed to be careful because if we removed the offending piece quickly, out of frustration, we would drag up some neighbouring jigsaw pieces with it. We would then have to reconnect the pieces we'd torn from their sockets. We learned to stay cool when things didn't fit into place the way we wanted them to.

Fitting 'blue sky' jigsaw pieces together, proved a good analogy for my trial and error approach to getting my own way as a child. If I gave out a howl when I didn't get my own way, I soon got to know about it. (I immediately felt the discomfort of trying to insert an ill-fitting jigsaw piece to my 'blue sky'.) If I tried to force the issue (i.e. the wrong piece in the wrong place), I'd 'rip out' any 'credits for good behaviour' that I carried at the time.

Hissy fits were not tolerated. I found out at a very young age how to discern between acceptable, polite behaviour and the opposite. I found out what being a 'good boy' meant partly through the responses I got when I was 'naughty' - and how being a 'very naughty boy' could result in a very unpleasant reprimand.

Like many kids I tested the boundaries. How far could I go with 'naughtiness'? What could I get away with? Where would I find the line not to cross? Where and when did I need to temper my behaviour to get what I want and avoid punishment?

Howling and carping on about things I wanted to happen didn't work but neither did keeping quiet. How could I let people know what I wanted if I didn't speak out? So I instinctively learned how to temper my approach to influence others. I learned about temperance.

I learned temperance from other sources too, *Goldilocks and the Three Bears*, for example. *Goldilocks* chose porridge that was neither too hot nor too cold.

What about other 'blue sky' feelings such as love and security (never mind the shame, anger, sadness and fear that can ensue when we don't get love and security)?

We hopefully provide our children with love and security. I can think of no happier sight than seeing an innocent child, smiling and living life to the full, knowing that they themself feel completely safe and secure.

This begs questions, When do we set them free to stand on their own feet? How will the child learn about insecurity (not security) and not-love? When do (or could) they start to learn about shame, anger, sadness, fear? How will they cope with trauma?

The answer is, "Do what feels right. They will call these experiences for themselves when the time is right regardless".

It's only recently that I've realised the dualistic metaphorical jigsaw nature of how you learn about life. For example, to appreciate love, you need to learn what <u>not</u>-love is. Otherwise how could you discern when you love (or are loved by) someone? And to fully understand the term 'unconditional love' you need to learn what 'conditional love' is.

Furthermore, the picture in the metaphorical jigsaw is not static. It's a movie that changes with life's ebb and flow of breath, days, years, relationships and so on. What creates success one day can create a setback another and vice versa.

Times change. People change. Contexts change. Nature demands change. You evolve, if nothing else, to survive. You learn from successes and setbacks. For example, if you consistently show the same anger to different people, you probably won't get the same response or outcome. You can also find yourself continually fitting a piece of anger to a situation where only patience will fit. There's 'a right fitting piece' to every situation you attract in life but it might require great subtlety, instinct or sensitivity to find it - for there are many pieces to choose from.

Life's Jigsaw has an infinite number of pieces. It evolves into a lifelong movie that you get to act in and direct (sometimes partly and sometimes wholly) for yourself. And the most challenging parts to act and direct tend to be the 'blue sky' pieces.

So the art or perhaps science of life is how to reduce the trials and errors that can cause upset and piece together its 'blue sky' pieces more efficiently. How do you respond to those situations that happen to us all and only a few know how to handle effectively - the 'blue sky' pieces - the known unknowns?

Knowing you don't know is learning in itself. It is the first step up from not knowing what you don't know or *unconscious incompetence*, life's starting place. Training professionals call this first step, *conscious (of) incompetence*. Through practice, experience and ideally having a role model to copy, you can become *consciously competent*, i.e. you know what to do but you have to think about it. For example, when I was learning to drive I was told to change gear every 10mph. So I used to know which gear I should be in by reading the speed gauge consciously.

Eventually, you get a feel for what needs to be done. You attend to what's needed intuitively. This state is called *unconscious competence*. You do what's needed without thinking about it.

Through experience and maturity you hopefully learn how to piece together 'blue sky' pieces to *Life's Jigsaw* - such as love, decision making, patience or coping with trauma. What about when you attempt to go beyond the puzzle's edge? Here you find the unknown unknowns - for example, buried emotions or childhood pacts you made with yourself that you didn't know you carried around with you. Here you find yourself back where you started life, *unconscious incompetence*.

Case Story: Bradley's Unconscious Pact of Loyalty

I spent some time with Bradley helping resolve a number of relationship issues that had reoccurred throughout his adult life. After two attempts we still had not got to the bottom of one particular issue. Bradley had remained in an imbalanced and deeply unhappy relationship that he knew he had to let go of or at least change his feelings toward. Bradley wanted a level of commitment that his partner was unwilling to give. He had broken the relationship off three times. Each time, he and his partner subsequently got back together. The breaking ups and getting back togethers had gone on for over a year.

During this period, Bradley had tried in vain to use generosity and persuasion to get what he wanted. When that failed he'd use anger, sadness, shame and fear to try to control the relationship. All his attempts came to no avail. Yet he and his partner would still come together every few days because they missed one another's company.

On our third emotional healing attempt, I took Bradley back to his childhood. He was three years old. Bradley's parents were at loggerheads. Bradley's father had been having an affair with a woman who had become pregnant by him.

There was one specific heated moment when Bradley's mother attacked his father in frustration. Bradley's father pushed his mother away and she fell awkwardly on the carpet floor. Bradley witnessed this.

In that instant, Bradley's unconscious mind detected that his mother, in desperation to be free from the situation, regretted ever becoming pregnant. Bradley sensed his mother's rejection.

It was at this precise moment that Bradley, with good intention, made an unconscious pact between himself and his mother. The pact went as follows, "Mummy, no matter what happens, no matter what you think of me, no matter what daddy does, no matter what you do to me, I will never leave you Mummy". The three year old Bradley buried his pact deep in his unconscious mind's cellular memory. Fearing desertion and isolation, the three year old child was willing to do anything to avoid his mother leaving him. Furthermore, he blamed himself for his mother's feelings of regret which invoked another unconscious but nonetheless profound feeling of low self worth.

Bradley now realised that he was re-enacting this same pact with his current partner. He felt a deep need to keep his pact to avoid a huge and mostly unconscious fear of isolation and low self worth. Bradley had dug deep to find what he didn't know that he didn't know - *unconscious incompetence.*

Bradley realised the flaw in the pact he had made with his mother. How, in order to maintain the status quo, he effectively made himself as a doormat to be trampled on. Now he knew why he persevered with his unhappy relationship. Bradley now had something to work on.

Ω

It's only during the last five years that I have discovered childhood anger and fear I developed and locked away in my unconscious cellular memory. This buried anger and fear would drive me to be overprotective in relationships. I couldn't resolve my dysfunctional behaviours though until I found their source. I eventually chose to explore within, not just at a psychological level but a spiritual level too. I wanted to understand the nature of my unhelpful behaviour in the context of my *Life's Purpose and Journey* - outside the edge of the jigsaw puzzle of conventional life. To go beyond the edge, I chose to journey within.

Like Bradley and me, you step into the unknown-unknown here. You don't know what you will find. If you do find something (e.g. 'gems' of hidden wisdom, a forgotten childhood memory or notion of a past life experience), you have little or no proof of its validity. (In such instances I find myself relying on either the intensity of the experience or the profundity of the wisdom it reveals.)

Furthermore, linking inner experiences to what goes on in the outside world requires faith - first and foremost in yourself. It may take you some time to convince yourself that you have experienced a hidden truth. If your scientific experimentation is like mine, you'll go down a few blind alleys as well.

I refer to the science of the occult. It has many faculties or practices, such as the time travelling (spiritual healing) technique used in the case study I've just cited. Occultists may practice meditation (which means 'knowing something better'), shamanism, astrology, clairvoyance, mediumship, the Tarot and so on to get to the unknown unknowns.

Whatever practise you choose, your laboratory holds only one scientist, you. I can help you find the way to your laboratory but I can't enter it or conduct your experiments for you. That laboratory is vast however. It's called, *"Life!"*

After sufficient experimentation, experience and validation, you no longer require convincing. You come to know your inner world better - certainly not completely, at least I haven't.

You see farther within. You become a seer. In time you may choose to help others find their path in life - even though you won't necessarily know of what their path holds for them.

My First Trip Outside the Edge

Some of us insist on a hard and straight edge to our *Life's Jigsaw*. We refuse to go outside, i.e. contemplate our inner world. We stick with the world as measured by Isaac Newton, i.e. from the atom outward, not inward.

In my childhood, my *Life's Jigsaw* had a very firm straight edge to its boundaries. I can't recall ever thinking about any desire to step outside the commonly accepted time-space continuum taught to me in school.

Then came along *The Beatles, The Rolling Stones, Bob Dylan, The Byrds, The Small Faces, Pink Floyd, The Grateful Dead, The Kinks, Otis Redding, Jimi Hendrix, Captain Beefheart, Jethro Tull, Frank Zappa, The Who* and *Cream* (to name the first few of hundreds of '60s musical artists that spring from heart to mind). Their music touched my soul. It lit a heavenly flame within me that still shines as brightly as ever. It sparked my imagination that there was more to life than that which I experienced through the five senses.

I had my first 'inner cosmic experience' when I went to the *Bath Blues Festival* in the summer of 1970. At around 2am one warm Sunday morning, *Pink Floyd* came on stage and played a two hour set with full orchestra, choir and light show. It was a few minutes into one of my favourite tracks of *The Floyd's, A Saucerful of Secrets,* that I realised my consciousness was not of this earth.

A simple chord progression from Richard Wright's keyboards played out across the Somerset field which was filled with nigh on 400,000 people. Pink Floyd played tones of heaven. (This was before the days I experimented with recreational drugs. My mind was tired but otherwise it was clear.) *The Floyd* connected me to a celestial vibration. Those seconds have stayed with me throughout my life, as if they had only just happened.

From that moment on, the belief I had in something 'greater and good' took root. I became curious as to what there was about the universe and beyond that which my schooling and childhood did not teach me. I no longer felt bound by the norms of convention or the limiting beliefs it protects.

If you limit your beliefs, you limit your imagination; you limit your understanding of the universe. Truth lies beyond your imagination.

Defrag your Soul points the way to help you on your journey within - i.e. a part guide and part route map that takes you outside the edge of the *Life's Jigsaw* that most of us have been taught to piece together by our parents, teachers, scientists, clerics, mainstream media and politicians.

To journey within
To 'boldly-go' from where you once fell to earth
I wish you, "Happy trails!"

Part III: Experiencing Within (i.e. Going Outside Life's Jigsaw's Edge)

Consciousness does not obey quantum physics.
Consciousness is not made of material.
Consciousness is transcendent.
*........ The material world of quantum physics is just possibility. It is consciousness, through the conversion of possibility into actuality, that creates what we see manifest. In other words, **consciousness creates the manifest world.***
Eugene Wigner, Nobel Prize physicist

The Scientist and Mystic Meet and Greet, Part I

I spent three years in post graduate research in the field of statistics. I have experience in adopting well founded mathematical and philosophical maxims in business research from my years in corporate life. For example, four years ago, I completed a worldwide study, for one the world's largest Information Technology companies, to isolate what their top performers do differently from the moderate performers.

I have also spent the last six years journeying proactively on the path within to find my *true self*.

I am comfortable using my alleged analytical and objective left brain to setup and analyse data. I am comfortable practising meditation too, from the alleged creative and emotional domain of the right brain.

When I practice meditation, occasionally the analytical part (left brain) of me asks the emotional part (right brain) of me "Are you really experiencing something significant?" But as soon as it asks, the experience is gone. That's the nature of being in the present moment, the present tense. It can't be analysed by the brain or mind. (Although scientists at the *Large Hadron Collider*[52] are getting darn close to it.) I, for example, can't provide you proof of its existence. It can only be experienced personally. Verifiable proof is historically the bedrock of all traditional science. Quantum science (the study of possibilities as well as subatomic particles) is changing 'traditional' thinking.

Quantum theory has led the physicists far away from the simple materialistic views that prevailed in the natural science of the nineteenth century.[53]
Werner Heisenberg, a founder of Quantum Physics

Electrons are Mystical
While quantum physics may not 'prove' mystical teachings the fundamental reality which it describes is not incompatible with such teachings. For example: sub atomic particles (or energy) can manifest, de-manifest, and once they've become entangled ('got to know one another'), they can transmit information to one another outside the time-space continuum[54]. I describe some such experiments in 'entanglement' in *Part VI: Beyond the Time-Space Continuum*.
Furthermore, science and mysticism have much in common, in many of their foundations and maxims.

> *For instance,*[55] *while mystics recognize that faith is a significant part of a spiritual path, they also maintain that faith alone is not enough. In fact, according to the mystics, if faith solidifies into*

---

[52] Ref: The Large Hadron Collider is the world's largest and highest-energy particle accelerator. It was built by the European Organization for Nuclear Research (CERN) from 1998 to 2008, with the aim of allowing physicists to test the predictions of different theories of particle physics and high-energy physics. http://en.wikipedia.org/wiki/Large_Hadron_Collider
[53] Ref: Werner Heisenberg, *Physics and Philosophy,* (New York: Harper & Row Publishers, 1962), 128.
[54] Einstein referred to this phenomenon as *"Spooky action at a distance".*
[55] Ref: paraphrased from
http://www.centerforsacredsciences.org/publications/science-and-mysticism-in-the-twentieth-century.htm

dogmatic belief, it will actually become an obstacle to further progress.

In what concerns divine things, belief is not fitting. Only certainty will do.[56]
Simon Weil

As the wise test gold by burning, cutting and rubbing it (on a piece of touchstone), so are you to accept my words after examining them and not merely out of regard for me.
Lord Buddha

This is also why Sufis (the mystics of Islam) who have reached the end of their path are called al-muhaqqiqun, which means 'verifiers'. They, too, have examined the teachings and verified their truth for themselves.
Ω

Mysticism and science both begin with faith that there is truth to be found through experimentation. Both can only be successful when we prove that faith to ourselves.

Quantum or not, science is diligent and maybe there are some occultists who would benefit from more scientific rigour in their approach to discern truth from fantasy. I certainly would have benefitted so.

There's only one person who can discern truth from illusion, your heart's desires from *false-egotistical* fantasy - you!

---

[56] Ref: Simone Weil, *Waiting For God*, trans. Emma Craufurd (1951; reprint, New York: Harper & Row, Publishers, 1973), 209

Noticing, Qualifying and Working with Inner Experiences to Manifest your Heart's Desires

To connect with your inner feelings you need to notice them first - especially the subtle ones. Your feelings reveal your intentions, i.e. are your intentions borne out of love and compassion - or are they borne out of not love or not compassion, i.e. shame, anger, sadness or fear? Love and compassion point to truth. Not love or not compassion points to illusion.

Over time I have found the need to notice the thoughts and feelings I associate with all inner experiences (images, visions or sounds within). I do my best to notice thoughts and feelings - rather than attach myself to them without checking first where the inner experience, they portend to, came from or is heading toward. I (do my best again to) discern those experiences which represent my truth (what my heart truly seeks or desires) as opposed to those which are (false) egotistical fantasies.

I have **three criteria** to qualify any inner experiences, thoughts or feelings **to discern truth from fantasy**:

1. Is the experience, thought or feeling uplifting, i.e. does it raise my spirit or enthusiasm?
2. Does it raise my curiosity, creativity, consciousness or wisdom?
3. Does it bring joy? (If not will it hurt anyone?) Is it beneficial to all, a win-win?

When all three criteria are met, the experience, thought or feeling points to an opportunity to acquire wisdom and/or share joy with others. I do my best to act as if the opportunity holds true, i.e. what my heart truly desires. I am now willing to get in and go with 'the flow' of allowing those feelings and that opportunity to become a reality. Whether it becomes a reality or not is not as important as 'going with the flow'. Why? Well....

Any opportunity my heart truly desires will (by definition) look good, feel good, sound good, taste good or smell good - will it not? So far, so good - but there's often a 'but'.

'But' what about if I fear failure, being hurt or disappointment that I don't get what I desire?

Desires can raise fears. Some of those fears you know about, some you may not.

This is where the noticing of fears (and any other negative feelings) you attach to desires, comes in to play. The next step is to 'park' them - allow them into your consciousness and let them be. Practise non-attachment.

By acknowledging those 'parked' desires and fears, you present your 'truth in the moment' to the situation. You recognise that the fears are part of you - at least for now - and seek to release them.

So, neither focus on the form of the outcome (desire) you seek nor embrace the fear (or any other negative emotion) that stops you from fulfilling your desire.

Instead you place yourself 'in the flow' for spirit to manifest the outcome. Present your 'truth in the moment' and 'go with the flow'.

(This gets a little subtle to explain so please stay with me. It took me a while to figure out.)

This doesn't mean you don't work towards your goal, just the opposite. Do things borne out of love or compassion towards your goal and 'park' those things you might have done in the past, borne out of fear.

By practising love and compassion, you surrender to spirit.

Spirit knows what your heart truly desires, regardless of any fears (conscious or unconscious) that you may harbour. When you 'park' those fears, you allow spirit to get on with the job of manifesting - whilst you go with the flow in the 'free space' surrounding your desire, not in it. That 'free space' is your 'truth in the moment', wise but not attached to your desires and fears. Here's the magical consequence.

When you live in the space of truth, only truth can enter that space. You drive falsity out.

For example, let's say you are in a relationship that isn't going how you want it to be...

1.   Do you end the relationship?

Have you or any of your friends fallen into the habit of attracting the same types of relationship over and over again?

If you pack the relationship in, you may not have learned what you needed to learn when you attracted the relationship. You may well attract another just like it, to repeat the learning process.

2. Do you do nothing or divert your attention elsewhere and hope things turn out for the good?

   My advice here is simple. If you're waiting for a person or situation to change, they or it probably won't. If anything, the situation worsens because your soul is not getting what it seeks.

3. Do you try to control what goes on?

   If you attempt to control the other person's actions (e.g. threatening them, pleading with them, making them feel guilty) you are embracing your fear. You haven't 'parked' it.

   What the other person does or how they react is a reflection (mirror) of that fear. That's why you attracted them into your life. If you try to 'clean up' their act, you are polishing the mirror - which doesn't 'clean' what's in it.

If you look carefully, polishing a mirror might help see clearly what needs cleaning in its reflection but that's all. Cleaning the mirror doesn't clean what it reflects.

The more you try to clean up someone else's act, the more they will do, even inadvertently, to point out your own fears to you. If you find this happening - stop. Observe how what the other does is a mirror of some aspect of the relationship you have with yourself. Instead of admonishing them (this took a lot of faith when I did this) give forth (forth give ~ forgive) thanks to them for pointing out what you haven't learned yet about yourself.

If you want to change a situation, avoid trying to control it.

4. Do you 'go with the flow', to evolve the relationship to the good? This means 'stop trying to control the relationship' and attend to what's needed by 'presenting your truth'.

Truth attracts truth and repels falsity.

The other person in the relationship will thus <u>have</u> to present their truth to the relationship to stay in it. If they are unwilling to do this their falsehood will drive them away. They might stay, they might leave the relationship. Either way your heart receives what it truly desires - truth!

By 'presenting your truth' you may feel defenceless. At a *false ego* level you are BUT in truth you are mighty.

In truth, your defencelessness is your strength.

We defend ourselves through actions borne of shame, anger, sadness and/or fear. In this context, 'defencelessness' means you avoid such actions. Instead you place your trust in spirit and present your truth to the relationship.

Exercise: Presenting your Truth

Think of a situation you're in where you're not getting what you want right now. It might be a relationship issue, a project or something to do with work.

1. What is it your heart truly desires?
2. What outcome do you seek specifically?
3. What will that outcome bring you?
4. What fears might you have of not achieving that outcome?

Now imagine an atom. Place the answers to questions 1-3 (desires and outcomes) at the core of the atom. 'Park' your fears (answers to Question 4) and place them inside electrons that revolve around the atom's core.

Notice how the electrons pop in and out of existence. When electrons (fears) present themselves, let them be; neither embrace them nor push them away; allow them to circle the core of the atom as they will.

The core and the electrons make up less than 1% of the atom; the rest is 'free space'.

Now, 'go with the flow' and 'swim in the free space' of the atom. Attend to what the situation needs but do only things borne out of love or compassion. If an electron comes close, send it light and compassion. Otherwise let it be, <u>notice</u> it and let it float by as you shine light into its darkness.

If you get close to the core (the outcome you seek) <u>notice</u> it and remain non-attached to it. Send it the same light and compassion as you did the electron.

The dark energy in the electrons will start to brighten, as will the counterparts the electrons attract themselves to in the core. Eventually, their dark energy will merge with the light, which means that any counterpart inside the core that is not truth will merge with the light too.

What remains at the core is that 'zero point', called truth, your truth. As you merge with that 'zero point,' you swim in the sea of unlimited possibilities.

Summary Tip*:* Neither feed nor fight fears. Instead, shine light (compassion) on those fears. The brighter the light, the less dark they become - until eventually they merge into the light!

The Scientist and Mystic Meet and Greet, Part II

The more I know, the less I rely on beliefs, even faith. But the more I know, the more I find I don't know. I find there are far more pieces - unknown unknowns than I ever imagined – were I to know! At least that's my experience.

This maxim seems to work well for science too. The universe is still expanding. As it grows larger and larger, the more we find out about its behavioural nature and the mathematical validity of theories of how it was created, e.g. The *Big Bang Theory*. Scientists debate mathematical models and...

Philosophers and occultists ask the not-mathematical questions, such as, "What banged and why?" Some questions still appear beyond the remit of traditional science because they cannot be measured. Magic, by definition, is about transformation without perceptible physical intervention. That is, with no discernible exchange of energy.

Traditional (pre-quantum) science works on the reductionism principle of breaking something down to see how its parts work together. Quantum science is shifting the focus from reductionism to possibilities. We move closer to understanding how magic (the interaction of consciousness and matter) works at a subatomic technological level.

Any sufficiently advanced technology is indistinguishable from magic.
Arthur C Clarke.

Or put another way...

Magic is that which science cannot explain.

The word 'magic' doesn't sit comfortably with everyone. Some clerics denounce mysticism as irreligious; humankind is not meant to research into the ways of the divine. As long as we stick to particles and things we can measure, we are okay. But should we cross the line into consciousness, the functioning of the soul, the power of spirit – 'not-okay'. Some announce that going outside the edge of <u>their definition of your</u> *Life's Jigsaw* is the work of Satan. They attempt to use fear and shame, i.e. not-love, to threaten people.

I ignore them and ask for the grace of spirit within, to help me to find truth, love, light and wisdom – free from shame, anger, sadness and fear. I choose the courage to explore and experience the unknown of my existence, my existentialism – in harmony with nature and all humankind.

Existentialism:
Life's Jigsaw has a fixed number of pieces only if we
restrict ourselves to adhering to the maxim of fixity.
Life's Jigsaw has an infinite number of pieces only if we
allow ourselves to adhere to the maxim of infinity.

So what if you can experience the unknown for yourself? If you gain sufficient experience of interacting with the unknown, you reach a state of knowing how to work with <u>it</u>, without knowing what <u>it</u> is precisely. You experience enough to go beyond the point of reasonable doubt. You no longer need proof from anyone or anything else. You have gotten closer to understanding the universe that you live in.

You develop a much deeper awareness of your own existentialism. Others who have not had the same experience may challenge you. They may ridicule you. They may disparage you. They may ostracise you. They may even crucify you. But you are prepared to stand without the need of a conventional sword, shield and suit of armour (i.e. scientific proof) with which to attack others or defend yourself.

You stand in your truth securely. You have experienced oneness within sufficiently. You see the world differently now.

You see matter as crystallised spirit. Force is spirit not yet crystallised. Crystallisation is spirit becoming matter. Decay is matter becoming spirit.

Spirit Force

I can tell you as a result of my research about atoms this much: There is no matter as such. All matter originates and exists only by virtue of a force which brings the particle of an atom to vibration and holds this most minute solar system of the atom together. We must assume, behind this force, the existence of a conscious and intelligent mind. This mind is the matrix of all matter.

Max Planck, 1917

I chose this quote from a renowned scientist and not a religious or spiritual leader deliberately. Planck's research led him to understand that the creation we live in, all its wonders and miracles, the *'matrix of all matter',* is a function of the mind - as is duality.

Duality – You Can't Have One without the Other

Can you think of anything in life and not think of not-it?

Recap: to appreciate what 'wet' feels like, we need to know what 'not wet' or dry feels like. To appreciate joy we need to know what sadness feels like.

We compare everything: high-low, tall-small, curved-straight, one feeling that opposes another, tangible and not tangible or ethereal (get it?) – the list is endless. This phenomenon we call *duality*. It has deep spiritual meanings at the heart of many eastern religions and ancient wisdom. For now, let's stick with things that feature heavily in our lives - day in, day out.

Some abstract but nonetheless vital pieces to *Life's Jigsaw*:

- Purpose and not-purpose
- Truth and not-truth, illusion

- Love and not-love
- Health and not-health
- Oneness and not-oneness, separateness
- Real and not-real, ethereal (ether-real)

I cover certain aspects of all the above 'jigsaw pieces' in this book. Let's start with the ethereal.

I had a dream, a very realistic dream, as real as walking along the seafront promenade outside my flat, listening to the waves rolling in and out, talking with friends and hearing their laughter. I felt totally *compos mentis*, i.e. of sound mind.

I visited a world in which you could fulfil all your desires. Imagine heaven on earth. A world where everything happens exactly as, or how, you want it to. The ancients called it the *Desire World*. A world of magic, in which stands a castle.

The Castle

His face was solemn not grim. As tradition has it, he wore a long dark robe, but no scythe, no outstretched skeletal hand.

He came through the window. I stared up into the bowed, hooded face. I acknowledged his purpose silently.

"OK, let's go" I nodded.

My guide's face turned a polite friendly smile as he took me up into the night sky.

We travelled north. We reached Rothbury, the place of my birth, in the heart of Northumberland. It was a bright sunshine dawn, 31st July 1951, over 60 years ago. The time was approaching 7am - about thirty minutes before the time of my birth. Before us stood a castle, an ethereal castle, by the shore of the River Coquet, set amongst the Simonside Hills.

As we approached the castle's sandstone walls, a lady came walking, the other way. She shared a few pleasantries with my guide whilst giving me a knowing smile as she got into her green Morris Minor and drove off.

"Who is she?" I inquired.

"Oh, she's a Guardian Angel, heading to the local hospital", came the reply.

Somehow, I knew who she was. My guide knew I knew. She wouldn't appear visibly in my life until I was about forty years old. But that's another story..... My guide and I walked on.

"We are going to heaven aren't we?"

A big smile and a knowing chuckle was all I got.

We entered a courtyard, the size of half a football pitch. People were gathering, milling, and exchanging curious, friendly and nervous greetings. Before us stood a group of young women. One woman seemed familiar, like from a photograph.

"Kiss one another!" instructed my guide, to me and the woman who looked familiar, "see what happens!"

The woman and I smiled at one another. We raised our eyebrows, and after a short nod of mutual approval, we obliged. We embraced in a suitably affectionate kiss, not too short and not too long. We took a step back. A moment later – 'whoooooa!' It was like all the kisses I'd ever been kissed, packed into a ten second rocket trip.

The kiss was beautiful.

"Wow, this place is amazing!" I shrieked.

"It can be everything you want it to be", my guide replied. My guide and I walked on.

Passing a field, I noticed some beautiful, large, deep red and luscious fruits. A farmer with a silent tractor was tending the crop.

"Strange, to have tractors here (being uncertain where 'here' actually was); what about carbon emissions?" I asked. "And why is that farmer toiling?"

"That's no ordinary tractor", my guide assured me, "it runs on the continuous energy from the sun. Tending and sharing fruit is the farmer's choice. It's a labour of love".

"C'mon" he said, "let's get you to the (*Etheric Body*) hospital. It's been a long journey and your spiritual body's 'atoms' are still a wee bit out of kilter. You'll be as right as rain, by morning".

I awoke refreshed and chose to explore alone. I went into the depths of the castle where I found an exit door. Outside I found myself walking down a wide cobbled road with terraced housing that reminded me of ancient Rome. At its far end I saw an entrance to a dark cave. In the entrance stood a large lion, with a huge mane of black hair.

"Uh-oh", I turned to head the other way, only to notice a lioness walking toward me. I started to panic. I made my way into a house. I realised though that the window frames facing the street had no glass in them. I ducked under a table and hid motionlessly trying to calm my anxious breathing. Just then, my guide walked in.

"Come with me", he ushered me to follow him with a wave of a hand, "let's go to the changing rooms".

We went into a small building across the road and waited in the hallway. The building had an annexe containing shower cubicles and a changing room. Out from the annexe stepped a man and his wife. I recognised the black whiskered eyebrows they both had in common. Acknowledging my guide, they smiled me a friendly hello and left. "They have been shape shifting," my guide explained. "On earth they have been lions many times and enjoy the freedom. So they come here to be. Let's explore."

My guide and I passed through fields where we saw people at play. Finally we came to a field where two medieval knights were in combat, sword to sword. Eventually one knight dealt a crucial blow, felling the other. "Whoa" I said, "this can't be right, people slicing one another up?"

"That's no ordinary sword" my guide replied. "It's a spiritual sword of truth and those knights are spiritual bodies. A quick trip to the hospital and the fallen knight will be fit and ready to fight again. These knights are the guardians of the truth, *The Grail*. They have fought many battles on earth, to keep its secret safe from those who would abuse it. For only he who is borne of truth can know the secret of *The Grail*. (Only Arthur, borne of truth, could extract the sword from the stone.) The knights keep their skills sharp, retain their wisdom and practice battle symbolically – so they are ready when needed."

"It's time we went to the Assignment Room", my guide instructed.

Following, I entered what looked like a small, very old fashioned shop. On the wall inside, hung a huge and complex flow chart connecting people's names, events and outcomes. The parts could be moved around like a child's sliding puzzle. People, events and desired outcomes could be brought together at a specified time. The whole history and future of humankind was mapped out.

Administrators were constantly making adjustments – as they pushed around the parts, sliding them up and down into the right pattern.

There on a small plaque in the middle of the chart, I read my name, 'Paul C Burr'.

"Why me?" I inquired.

"You have a role to fulfil, a mission, a purpose and a contract. Now it is time that you return and fulfil that contract", the guide replied. "You agreed a *Life Contract* before you were born. Your time to fulfil it has come, on your return."

"But what is my contract?" I inquired.

"Continue to write. Your purpose for now is to heal and share wisdom. You'll find out your real mission and contract when the time is right", my guide replied.

"Go in peace!"

I thanked my guide for the wisdom and quest. As I headed back I suddenly realised the coincidence that my favourite band for many years was called *The Grateful Dead*. Coincidence? Maybe not......

When I awoke the next morning, back in the physical world, I knew that the time to complete my purpose in my life had come back, again.

What Purpose? What Purpose? What Purpose?

You will already have twigged that to find our purpose in life we must also know what our not-purpose entails.

If you'd asked me ten or so years ago "What's your purpose in life?" I might have said something like "To live life to the full". It's a bit of a fuzzy answer. Pressed harder, I'm not sure what I would have said beyond things like "do well in my career", "make money so I can be free", "have a loving relationship with my wife", "have a nice place to come home to", "do things to the best of my ability" and "oh yeh, and see Newcastle United[57] win something".

---

[57] I've been a Newcastle United Football Club supporter since being knee high. Alas, Newcastle haven't won an English domestic trophy since 1956 and the

Most of these items are fairly mainstream ideals. It wasn't until a pal of mine, Terry Elston of NLP World[58], kept repeating the same question, "For what purpose?"

Terry quizzed me in an NLP workshop question and answer session. The conversation went something like this.

Q: "What's your purpose in life, Paul?"

A: "To do well in my career."

Q: "For what purpose?"

A: "To provide for those whom I love and to feel I've done a good job."

Q: "For what purpose?"

A: "Well, to feel that I've lived up to ideals that fit the world I want to live in?"

Q: "For what purpose?"

A: "I dunno, erm, maybe... maybe fulfil my full potential as a human being."

Q: "For what purpose?"

A: "Arghhh, help me – and don't say for what purpose!"

(Silence)

A: "Er, ok, to be my *true self!*"

Eventually, I had come up with something, albeit somewhat abstract, that resonated inside of me. Lights went on. A feeling of tingling energy shot up my spine and outwards through the extremities of my body. I call these 'A-ha Moments'. They're difficult to describe to you fully unless you recall one of your own and relive it, right now.

I recall a Grateful Dead concert at RFK Stadium, Washington DC, in July 1994. Towards the end of the second set, the Dead played *Standing on the Moon*. A sixty foot high video of lead guitarist, Jerry Garcia, became the focal point of a spiritual connection between the band, the music and audience. Jerry's soft and slightly croaky voice sung out into the summer night. Verse by verse, what felt like huge fire-balls of energy rose up my spine and filled my entire body. Those around me shared

---

European Inter Cities Fairs Cup in 1969. I'm still a season ticket holder, despite living over 360 miles from Newcastle's home ground, St James Park.
58 www.nlpworld.co.uk based in Hove, East Sussex, UK. Terry Elston is a great NLP trainer.

the same experience. We shone. I tingle now as I write this paragraph (late addition - I tingle again as I proof read it).

Can you recall a moment in time when energy rose up through your spine and spread throughout your body?

Fun Exercise: Re-live an 'Ah-ha Moment'
- Think of your own 'Ah-ha Moment', right now, keep it in your head and pause briefly.
- Close your eyes and recall that moment.
- Travel back in time to it, as if it's now.
- Step into the picture or movie of it.
- Look through your own eyes. See the people and what's going on around you.
- Put in any sounds, smells or tastes.
- Breathe in and out purposefully. As you breathe in, take in that feeling again. As you breathe out, relive it to the full. Shine!
- Hopefully, right now, you are all a tingle. Enjoy!

So What Is your Purpose in Life, in One Sentence?

<u>Your</u> purpose in life is a journey -
to find, open up, become and express your true self.[59]

I have spent most of my life <u>not</u> finding my purpose in life; such is the nature of duality. It took me 55 years to get an inkling of what my purpose was. I started to get the message from within that I was to become a writer. After much self analysis, it took me a couple of years to raise the willpower to start the process of writing. I wrote *Learn to Love and Be Loved in Return*, which transformed from a book about relationships into one about finding your truth. It was my first attempt

---

[59] If you haven't already, you might want to read my first book, *Learn to Love and Be Loved in Return*. I write about how truth, and not-truth, make or break relationships, including the ones we have with ourselves.

to express my truth, at whatever level I was at, by March 2010. I now know there's far more for me to open up.

Becoming and expressing myself as a writer was/is a stepping stone towards becoming my *true self*. I feel very blessed to have found my purpose in life and am committed to going for it. But not everyone feels like me.

Many people choose not to journey within. Some fear it, others deny its possibility. I still possess a healthy degree of scepticism. Even when I had my own personal 'Ah-ha moments' in life, I wasn't always comfortable speaking about some of them, or my journey. For example, pub mates would say, "you talking your mumbo-jumbo stuff again Paul?" I bit my lip a few times but there was (and still is) no going back for me. Wisdom beckons and my soul demands it – as does yours.

When you honour your soul's quest, you honour yourself. The journey takes you down a path. You'll need to discern when you are not on the path. I still find it a challenge. I have veered far and wide from the straight and narrow, perhaps more often than not – oops! But I'm on it or near it now and commit to staying this way.

The path takes you to your *true self*. The 'not-path' takes you to your not-*true self*. The path for me has been and still is a long journey. As you journey down your path your truth unfolds itself slowly, one *spiritual step* at a time. But before I talk about *spiritual steps*, let's cover some things that get in the way. They block or divert you from your path.

When Things Block or Divert You from your Journey

Imagine a pathway that leads to your *true self*, as you proceed through life you always have the choice to journey down it. If you choose to veer away, you always have the choice to return to it. The fact that you are still breathing tells you so.

And should you choose to take the path, you may still meet things that thwart you. These come in the form of 'events' (situations and people) that you respond to with shame, anger, sadness or fear. These 'events' keep coming until you change your response and release the negative emotions that you allow these 'events' to evoke. Until then, you don't feel good because you allow these blocks to:

1. Divert you away from the path, so that you go around in circles. Life loops.
2. Drain your energy or leak away your life force.
3. Slow you down through unnecessary burdens.
4. Stop you in your tracks.
5. And, possibly worst of all, block your view from the path ahead, so that you lose faith in yourself and your journey.

I've met all the above patterns. Some are blighters to figure out. I still allow a few things to manifest the symptoms in 1, 2 and 3. Such is my spiritual awakening. I've also felt myself to be at 4 and 5, a complete standstill, a few times. (As the Elton John song goes, whether I feel that way again or not, "I'm still standing!")

Recognise that which holds you back, is <u>not</u> the event, <u>not</u> the situation and <u>not</u> the person. It's your negative response that you cling on to, born of stuff I once heard someone refer to as *head-trash*.

Head-Trash, Hey-ho, Let Go!

Let's focus on the contents you can find in your *head-trashcan* and what you can do to release them.

Look at some of the major decisions you make and have made in life. Which of them were/are borne out of fear? Such decisions, borne of fear, help you avoid unpleasant feelings such as poverty, loneliness, looking incompetent to others, and so on. You make these decisions with good intent but decisions borne out of fear don't take away the fear.

Case Story: Fear in Business

I coached a UK General Manager of a large global software firm. He'd been in his post for just over a year. He was very experienced and excellent at corporate account, business-to-business, selling. In the current economic climate he felt exhausted. He told how he spent the vast majority of his time chasing 'big-ticket sales contracts' personally. He feared that if he didn't make his company's sales targets then he would be fired. So he took it upon himself to engage personally in selling the really big deals, whilst his salespeople stood and watched from the side.

He didn't allow himself time to focus on strategic changes he wanted to make, so that the company would become more competitive in the long term. Come the end of his first year in post, the UK company made its sales target. But, the General Manager felt unfulfilled. He was using "less than 5%" of my creative skills". He felt he had no option but to get up and do it again. He feared if he left the selling to others they wouldn't do the job properly. He feared to let go. So the coaching we went through focused on releasing his fears.

Ω

Fear is the main source of superstition, and one of the main sources of cruelty. To conquer fear is the beginning of wisdom.
Bertrand Russell

I respectfully add the following...

Fear is not conquered through courage; it is released.

Life's journey is a continuous stream of decisions and choices. One choice you make all the time is courage or not courage. You choose courage when you allow your fears into your consciousness and let them be - so that you can release them.

If you over-embrace your fears, you hold yourself back. If you repress, deny or push them away, you do not have them to release - and face the consequences, the repetitions.

The fear you embrace holds you back. The fear that you deny in yourself, attracts the thing that you fear.

When you learn to accept that you are human; prone to errors, prone to successes and setbacks, you ready yourself to move on in *life's journey*.[60]

Feel the fear and do it anyway!
Susan Jeffers.[61]

Find and Boost your Passions

You learn very little from things that come easy to you; stuff you are good at. The soul seeks new wisdom and experience. When you do something creative that you feel passionate about, you feel fulfilled. And in order to bring more creativity and passion into your life, you need to let go of (or reduce the number of) those things that distract you. So, what do you let go of?

By way of example, here is what I am up to today, Saturday:

1.   Watch TV/ Surf Internet
2.   Go for a run*
3.   Wash dishes and tidy up home*
4.   Write*
5.   Read some non-fiction*
6.   Meditate*
7.   Drink a few Saturday night beers with friends

I have placed an asterisk (*) against five tasks because they give me a sense of fulfilment – even the washing up! The percentage of 'fulfilling' tasks today, comes to (5/7=) 70% approximately. Now if I were to weight the amount of time I allocate to each task, I spend approximately 50% of my available energy doing things that make me feel fulfilled.

---

[60] Brené Brown: *The Power of Vulnerability* - a wonderful, light hearted and hugely informative video about self worth on *YouTube*. I've watched it many times and still watch end to end when 'I lose it'.
[61] *Feel the Fear and Do It Anyway* - a best seller by Susan Jeffers.

Tip to self: go for 70% or more. The more creativity I apply to my work, for example, the higher the sense of fulfilment I feel – both during and after completion of whatever I am doing.

Passion for what you do is vital.

Here are my passions, i.e. the things in life I am most curious about and/or enjoy the most:

- Raising human consciousness, by translating ancient wisdom into modern day parlance and crafting simple practical tools, for everyone - starting with me
- Love and relationships
- Writing, coaching and healing
- Newcastle United Football Club
- Music, lyrics, poetry and going to gigs
- Running along the promenade outside my window, enjoying the sea view and breathing the salty sea air
- Global movements, such as Occupy Together and Zeitgeist Movement.

When you clarify what you are passionate about, you know where you will apply most curiosity. And curiosity leads to imagination, which leads to creativity, which leads to wisdom and in some cases, magic.

Passion → curiosity → imagination → creativity → new associations between things → wisdom + magic → satisfied soul (especially when you share that wisdom with others) → connect with other people → shine and share → oneness

Or

Not passion → not creativity[62] → stay where you are → dull repetition → boredom → lethargy → depression → your light dims.

I speak of passion and the actions that take me down the path to my truth. Some of the other stuff, I do for fun. They don't necessarily take me to truth any faster - but hey, life's about having fun too, isn't it?

"All work and no play makes Jack a dull boy."[63] On the other hand, *"All play (distraction) and no consciousness development entraps Jack in illusion".* Embrace everything that's fun, necessary or creative. If it's neither necessary nor creative, acknowledge its fun value. Feeling good mixed with a strong belief in yourself is the fastest route to fulfilment. Make fun a sustainable part of your daily repertoire. Avoid excess and abstinence. Practise passion, fun and balance in your life.

A fulfilled life is a life filled full of fulfilling experiences.

Tip: Practise Balance (or Temperance)

Temperance does not mean 'do without or prohibit'.
It means balance.

I return to the importance of and provide an exercise in practising balance or temperance in *Part XIII: What Does it Take to Make Spiritual Steps Toward a Fulfilled Life?*

Tip: Act like a Child.
When a task is important and not that exciting to you (e.g. washing the dishes is a boring chore for me) *act as if* you are a child playing a game.

---

[62] Remember, to learn what creative means, we need to learn not-creative too.
[63] *Proverbs in English, Italian, French and Spanish* - James Howell, 1659. http://en.wikipedia.org/wiki/All_work_and_no_play_makes_Jack_a_dull_boy

Just this morning, I watched two children who pretended to be UK's Prince William and Kate Middleton on TV. They approached a third child, dressed as the Queen. They bowed and curtsied to 'her majesty' respectfully. All three focused completely on playing their roles, without distraction. Every step, every movement was made with precision and timing (like in Tai Chi). Nothing around them could distract their attention. They were focused completely in the present, moment by moment.

Act like a child at play when you do even the most tedious things. Be curious. Make every movement deliberate.

Fun Exercise:

Every morning, as you put your socks and shoes on - notice the feeling of each sock as you put it on each foot. Notice the difference between the feeling on the skin of the foot that doesn't have a sock on to that which does. Repeat the exercise as you put on your shoes, in addition focus on the feel of the laces as you tie each shoe up. Focus on everything slowly and deliberately as it happens, one step at a time. You are now mimicking spirit. Use this step by step approach to all your daily chores for a week. See how much more you notice about what was routine life.

The better you act, the better the time will pass and the more fulfilled you will feel.

Self-help Tool: Increase your Day to Day Creativity

Increase the fulfilment you feel from your day to day life.

Write down all tasks that you already have done or will do today, outside of your normal work. [If you find your work to be creative and fulfilling, you (like me) are blessed.] There may be some exciting things and there may be boring ones too. Boring stuff can be important though.

I'm not that keen on washing dishes and clearing up. Who is? But when I'm done, I do feel a small sense of satisfaction at having a tidy kitchen.

A kind of mini-version of the same sense of completion I have when I've completed a four mile run. I feel fulfilment.

Put an asterisk (*) next to all those tasks which when completed give you a sense of creative fulfilment. Here are some of my examples: writing, reading, singing, researching. What percentage of the tasks, in terms of time and energy spent, have an asterisk?

Gather a week's worth of data. Make a conscious effort to raise the amount of time you spend on creative tasks by say 10%. Once you have embedded the increased level of creative actions into your day to day life, do it again. See how high you can go. (We all need to eat, sleep and poop!☺)

Keep a log of the changes you attract in your life, as a result of say a 10% increase in your 'fulfilling-creativity' time. When you've achieved that, do it again, go for another 10%. Don't overdo it all at once. Keep fun and laughter in your life! ☺☺

The next page contains an example table, a *Creativity Log* of the awake but not working part of the day (say, 6-7 hours).

The activities **highlighted and marked with an '*'** in the first column are those that I feel I get a sense of creative fulfilment out of. When you complete you own log, use your own definitions.

Example of a Creativity Log
Time spent in minutes on activities day to day.

Activity/Days →	1	2	3	4	5	6	7
Go for a run*	60	0	0	60	→		
Watch TV/Surf Internet	20	120	40	0			
Keeping the home tidy*	40	20	0	40			
Write*	40	0	0	60			
Read some non-fiction*	40	60	0	60			
Go out for the night	0	0	240	0			
'Chit-chat' or socialise with friends	40	60	0	0			
Listen to music*	0	40	0	40			
Meditate/relax without interruptions*	40	40	20	40			
Purposeful discussion*	40	0	0	20			
Routine things: e.g. dressing, eating, driving, bathing, going to the loo etc.	80	40	60	40			
Total minutes:	400	380	360	360			
Time spent on creative and fulfilling things	260	100	25	320			
%age of time spent on creative activity	65%	26%	7%	88%			
Average over four days:	46%						

(Tip to self: run every two days instead of three. Spend at least one hour writing every day. Go for 100% fun and creativity. See how high you can go Paul!)

Tip/Exercise: **Do Routine Things Differently and Consciously**.

Change the way you do the daily routine things. For example, if you watch TV whilst you eat, switch the TV off and focus your attention on chewing and tasting your food.

This is also where acting as if you have the curiosity of a child can improve the experience of what otherwise might have been a routine act. Focus on doing one thing at a time very consciously, like in the 'socks and shoes' fun exercise earlier.

Stay in the present moment. Make a note of what you notice or learn as you do routine things differently. Keep a log. See if you can change every routine habit[64] in your life at least once.

> *If you seek a new life you will probably need to go beyond your habits and look for something new with which to replace them.*

Tip: **More is Less**

Rather than focus on what you want to cut down on in life e.g. snacking, watching mindless TV, idle chatter - focus on doing more of the things that will help you achieve what you seek, e.g. eat more healthily, exercise more, tidy up more as you go around the house, read more.

By doing more of the things that will help you get what you want; you do less of those that don't.

---

[64] I'm not talking here about routine habits to protect yourself from harm, such as looking both ways before you cross the road.

In the Bigger Scheme of Things What Do You Want to Keep and Let Go Of?

Recap: *4 seeds of negative karma* hold you back in life:
1. **Shame**

There is no shame in failure but failure is endemic to shame.

2. **Anger/Resentment**

Resentment is like poisoning yourself whilst waiting for someone to die.

Better still,

Holding a grudge is letting someone live rent-free in your head.
Sourced from the Internet.

3. **Sadness/Hurt**

I've cried, and you'd think I'd be better for it, but the sadness just sleeps, and it stays in my spine the rest of my life.
Conor Oberst

4. **Fear**

F. E. A. R. = False expectations appearing real.

These four negative emotions serve a purpose. For example, when you have learned all you need to know about shame, you have readied yourself to appreciate not-shame - i.e. to feel good about yourself. To appreciate a high vibration fully, you need to know about its exact opposite.

Such is duality:

- Shame → not-Shame → e.g. feel okay, feel good, self compassion, caring for self, trusting self, self worth, self liking, self love, love
- Anger → not-Anger → e.g. composed, relaxed, fondness, love
- Sadness →not-Sad → e.g. joy, happiness, serenity, expansion, wisdom, love
- Fear → not-Fear → courage, faith, fearlessness, stillness, wisdom, love.

The opposites of all *four seeds of negative karma* lead ultimately to love. When you release shame, anger, sadness and fear, you journey towards love, borne of oneness, borne of the divine.

Where does life's journey take me?
To truth, your truth, love, oneness, your divine self.

Duality: anything that is not truth, not love or not oneness is not divine.

Everything evolves to the good...[65]
David Loxley, Chief Druid, The Druid Order, London

(I add one word.)   *...eventually!*

---

[65] Since I joined the company of The Druid Order, London, in 1996, I have only been asked to hold one belief - *everything evolves to the good.*
In a post script comment, David Loxley, Chief Druid, pointed out that I'd missed the idea that everything is good in the first place. We created the not good out of it. Eventually, it will return like the prodigal son back to its original goodness. There is no such thing as original sin or error. Life being circular, the bad is drawn back to where it came from, back to the good. Redemption is a return home to goodness.

Fearless versus 'fearlessness' – The Difference between Courage and Wisdom

If you ignore or remain in denial about situations or people that you allow to invoke negative feelings within you, you learn little if anything at all. The situations fester and pester.

For example, if you cannot acknowledge sadness, you cannot release it. This makes logical sense, does it not? By 'acknowledge', I mean, be willing to accept your sadness exists and learn from it. Should you detach yourself from sadness, you detach yourself from not sadness, i.e. joy.

(I recall a few years back when a relationship I was in broke up. I took myself to the pub at night to inebriate myself, from the fear and sadness of spending lonely evenings on my own. It took me nine months before I readied myself to acknowledge the sadness and fear - and start to move on in life.)

When you ignore or deny fear, you deny not-fear – i.e. courage. And it takes courage to allow your inner issues into your consciousness. In fact, all issues are inner issues. It's not what's happening around you, it's how you respond that can cause you a problem. The more courage you choose to face your inner issues, the more you learn about them.

There are two paths we can take when we face our fears.

1. Some of us wise up to our fears and manage them. We take control of them. We can become warriors, even heroes, "Hail, the all conquering hero!" But this path does not take us necessarily to our journey's end. We may have missed a fork in the journey's path – the path of acknowledgement, the path less travelled or not taken at all.

I shall be telling this with a sigh.
Somewhere ages and ages hence:
Two roads diverged in a wood, and I,
I took the one less travelled by,
And that has made all the difference.
From *The Road not Taken* by Robert Frost, 1920

2. Acknowledge your fear, let it be. Accept your fear for what it is. Send it love and light from within you. Allow yourself to experience the stillness or void outside your fear – whilst still accepting its presence. I speak not of an intellectual process but of imagining the feeling of being outside your fear whilst accepting it within your consciousness. Be still. You start to realise that the issue you faced was attracted by and to your fear. You brought the issue, perhaps unknowingly and unwontedly, on yourself. In return, the issue brought your fear to the surface. Observe it and let it be - so that you can release it and evolve to the good. This is fundamental to the game of life.

As within- so without...

What you don't sort out within you, keeps repeating in your outside world until you do sort it out. Face it. Neither feed it nor fight it. Observe it. Let it be. Allow it. Send it love. Sit in the feeling of being outside of it but with it. Be patient.

When your fear is fully out in the open, you can see through it. You wise up to the habits, behaviours, patterns, the *false-egotistical* fantasies and stories, no longer helpful that manifest that fear. You find the root of those habits and patterns in an early experience in your conscious memory.

If the root does not become obvious, it is hidden within your unconscious memory. In which case, you can elect to get professional help to unearth the connection - for example, I've visited NLP Therapists, Hypnotherapists, spiritual surgeons, Tarot readers and astrologists to help me unearth unconscious sources of my fears. I've sought out seers.

When you bring into conscious memory (in the vast majority of cases, from your childhood) the 'connection' between your fear and its source, you appreciate much more the impact it has had on your life. (The 'connection' may be a single event or a series of events.)

You discern more clearly all the major decisions you have made since the event(s), borne out of fear - as opposed to those that 'feel right' (and take you down your *life's pathway)*. You see the illusory nature of the negative habits and holding patterns that you allow to hold you back. You put yourself in the position to now release them, along with the fear.

You begin to realise you had nothing to fear in the first place. At this stage you are no longer fearless, instead you experience fearlessness.

The Role of the Seer

Maybe you only see a few steps in front of you. Maybe you see many. Maybe you see all the possibilities in life open to you. You become a visionary, a see-er, a seer.

A seer doesn't see the future, a seer sees within. They can see inside themselves and see the steps they need to take on their own *life's journey*. They see the consequences of inaction. They see the consequences of inappropriate or unhelpful action. They see the best course of action and take it.

The more accomplished a seer becomes in mapping and taking their own journey, the more they can help others too.

A seer teaches you to see for yourself. A seer helps you to see the choices (and consequences) you give yourself. Seers help you to become a seer yourself.

They don't need to be perfect. They don't need to have grandiose qualifications; they just need to be wiser at it than the people who come to them for help.

The seer's role is to lead others to be as good if not better than they are at Love. Once they've accomplished this feat, their job is done. Ω

The warrior or hero does not ignore or deny fear. They manage and control their fear. The master or magician dissolves fear. They shine light into fear's darkness. Magicians are not brave. They have no need to be. They have known fear for what it was, a very realistic illusion.

Fearlessness tells you that you have completed a *spiritual step* on your pathway. Only two types of people experience fearlessness – 'masters' and 'fools'. When you become a 'master' (i.e. have total mastery) at one stage of your journey, you instantly become a 'fool' (totally uninitiated) in the next. You become both master and fool at the same time.

Note the two purposes of fearlessness:

1. It indicates you've achieved mastery at one level.
2. It gives you the encouragement to tackle the next *spiritual step* in your journey.

The path to your *true self* lies before you always. You might have veiled it from view but it's always there. You walk it when you release: shame, anger, sadness or fear.

Fear is usually the last, the biggest and most challenging, of these four emotions, to release.

Example 1: Big Picture Fear

In the early part of the last decade, I became angry at all the lies spewed out of the mouths of war mongering politicians who sent brave soldiers to kill and be killed under false pretences.

The Western so called democratic governments were equally, if not more, corrupt than the oil-rich oligarchies whose lands we still plunder today. It became apparent to me that the world was a far more evil place than I'd imagined it to be. I resented the killing of innocent people by both sides - innocent bystanders going about their daily lives, in villages in Afghanistan and in office blocks in USA. I prayed to God for justice. I was angry, resentful and sad all at the same time.

Much later, I discovered all these feelings were fuelled by fear. A fear that everything my upbringing and schooling stood for was non-existent. I feared for myself and for humanity.

I feared that perhaps my life, in part, was worthless because I couldn't see what to do to right all the wrongs. I knew that violence couldn't win. But what could win? How could justice prevail? I didn't have an answer - until much later.

Example 2: Personal Fear

I've had a number of relationships which I've attempted to hang on to because of fear. In my young adult days I was involved in a relationship that was going downhill. I could see the relationship breaking up. I became terrified. I obsessed over the fear of feeling unwanted and unneeded - a fear that stemmed from my childhood days. So I asked the woman to marry me and have children. Marriage and parenthood seemed the only way to turn the ailing relationship around. Fortunately, she declined.

With another partner, I hid my true feelings of unhappiness and dissatisfaction with our relationship. I'd become attracted to other women. I didn't have the courage to speak my truth, about my thoughts of infidelity and lust. At the same time, I felt guilty for not living my truth. But what stopped me most, from acting out those thoughts or speaking my truth, was fear. Fear of hurting someone so badly that they would leave me. Fear of being on my own - again.

I can see those fears more clearly now, the shame still lingers a bit, because I regret not being strong enough to speak my truth. I feel guilty for allowing fear to rule the relationship. When fear rules, you're on the road to nowhere.

Was I selfish? In part, yes. Fear can cause us to be selfish and fear can protect.

Fear Protects, But....

Common sense fear protects you from foolhardiness. You look both ways, hopefully always, before you cross the road safely. Most of us live with this fear comfortably. We're okay with it - or as they say in the USA, it's a 'no brainer'. But, if you over-embrace fear, you would never cross the road, metaphorically speaking.

When fear rules a relationship, it can become the driving force, instead of love. The relationship eventually stultifies, withers and rots - physically, emotionally and spiritually. Ignoring or denying the fear (for example, by refusing to talk about it) damages the relationship as well. In both instances, allowing fear to rule or ignoring fear, you cut yourself off from the love and the life experiences your soul seeks.

Client Case Story: David, a Rock n'Roll Lifestyle, Borne of Fear

David played keyboards in a rock band. He led a rock n'roll lifestyle. He had a diet of Wild Turkey Bourbon and Coke, to wash down things that would keep him rocking. Aged seven whilst attending boarding school, David lost his parents in an aeroplane accident. He had grieved for over thirty years and his grief had taken its toll on several relationships and his life overall.

David couldn't countenance falling in love. He chose not to express love for, or with anyone, or anything. He couldn't face the fear of losing someone or something so close and precious to him again. David was a lovely, gentle and kind man. But he'd forged a huge shield that protected him from loving – especially himself.

It seems to be a faculty of childhood that when a significant, unexpected, emotional event happens to you (e.g. violence, abuse, divorce or the death of a loved one), you blame yourself. As a child, your conscious mind can't deal maturely with the trauma that's happened. So your unconscious mind locks the feelings of shame, anger, sadness and fear away in your psyche and protects you from them. The compensatory behaviours and decisions you make as a consequence can stay with you through your adolescent and adult lives.

They continue to hold you back in your *life's journey*. Until you choose to do something about them.

Ω

Summary:

When you isolate yourself from your emotions, you cannot be selective. Should you isolate yourself from fear, you also isolate yourself from joy, happiness[66], fulfilment and love.

> *We can easily forgive a child who is afraid of the dark; the real tragedy of life is when men are afraid of the Light.*
> Plato

> *Our deepest fear is not that we are inadequate.*
> *Our deepest fear is that we are powerful beyond measure.*
> *It is our light, not our darkness that most frightens us.*
> From *Our Deepest Fear* by Marianne Williamson[67]

You serve yourself best when you accept your fears. You live with your vulnerabilities and choose courage to deal with the bigger fears appropriately and truthfully. When you see the fears that lurk behind the other negative emotions: anger, sadness and shame – you give yourself the choice to act truthfully. Do something differently.

Fear is part of the human condition, it serves a purpose. When you appreciate fear, you ready yourself to appreciate not-fear, Love.

---

[66] Ref: www.ted.com/talks/lang/eng/brene_brown_on_vulnerability.html by Brene Brown.

[67] Ref: http://www.hidden-wealth-keys.com/our-deepest-fear.html

Love, Not-Fear, and *Karma*

The opposite of love is not hate or anger. Deep down, it's fear. To put it another way...

The opposite of the wisdom of love is ignorance, fuelled by fear.

I've noticed that behind every negative feeling - of anger, sadness and shame - I have ever had, lurked fear.

For example, I recall getting angry at a partner who'd sworn an oath of love for me. I gave up a relationship I was already in and a comfortable lifestyle to be with this new partner. Within a few weeks she changed her mind and left me. I felt angry at her for letting me down but more so - I was angry with myself for being so naive.

Within days I realised that what really upset me, behind and more fundamental than the anger, was the fear of being on my own - isolated, unwanted and unloved - the fuel of my ignorance to the real issues I faced - that I didn't have the willingness to love myself.

When you ignore the wisdom of love; when you block the expression of compassion (i.e. you allow fear to rule your actions), sooner or later, you invoke a *karmic* response (i.e. the basic *Law of Consequence*, cause and effect).

Negative karma responds when you veer from the path. You attract people and events that block your way or slow you down. Sometimes your pride kicks in and you continue veering away from your *Life Path* doggedly. And when you really 'go off course', *karma* can kick you hard (e.g. through drug addiction); you smash into a metaphorical brick wall. After which, you pick up the pieces, sort yourself out, maybe do some backtracking, and start again – only wiser, hopefully!

Life can sometimes be like going off an elevated road in *Mario Kart Wii*™. You plunge into the darkness. A few seconds later some ethereal machine cleans the kart, lubricates the moving parts, tightens up the nuts and bolts and you're off again. The only difference is, real life hurts and can hurt hard. The 'cleaning, lubricating and tightening up' period can take years and prove cathartic. You go through a *dark night of the soul*.[68]

Illustration 6: Behind Shame, Anger and Sadness Lurks Fear

---

[68] *Dark Night of the Soul*, a mystical poem, written in 16th Century, by St John of the Cross, a Carmelite monk who wrote of hu-man's spiritual journey. It is the dark passage we all must take allegedly at some stage.

And what about when you aren't even aware of the path your soul seeks? What if it's not part of your daily conversation? You don't think about the concept. You keep your head solely in day-to-day stuff through choice, ignorance, anxiety or indifference.

Here's a tale of two people who chose to ignore fear.

Case Story: Behind Anger, Sadness and Shame lies Fear - Henry and Vivienne's Karmic Brick Walls

Henry had been married for 20 years. He and his wife had three children whom they both loved very much. Henry and wife had drifted apart emotionally and their sex life had dwindled. They no longer enjoyed one another's company particularly but they stayed together for the sake of the children.

Henry had a few extra marital flings whilst his wife remained faithful to the marriage. With each fling, Henry's unhappiness with his marriage, and more importantly with himself, intensified. His sadness plummeted to new depths after the breakup of a particular relationship that had transformed into a full on affair. The affair had lasted more than a year. Ironically, the woman - with whom Henry had the affair - decided that she couldn't trust Henry. She broke their affair off.

Henry's ensuing depression took him to the brink of separation with his wife but he held back. He never quite plucked up the courage to speak his truth, face his fears or attempt to resolve his marital problems. Instead, he continued to seek the company of other women.

Enter Vivienne, 25 years Henry's junior and also in a very unhappy relationship. Vivienne was entranced by Henry's good looks, his eloquent conversation, his mature and gentle nature, not forgetting his exquisite taste for good food and wine. But as Vivienne and Henry's relationship intensified, she began to feel guilty. Vivienne felt shame over the lies and trickery through which she had deceived her own partner. She felt guilty that Henry's attachment to her could break up a marital home. Vivienne never pressed Henry to leave his wife.

The day came when Vivienne felt she could no longer carry on with the relationship with the partner she already had when she started seeing Henry. She chose to leave her partner but at the same time she knew that her feelings were not as strong for Henry as he felt for her. Vivienne told Henry how she felt. She attempted to break off her affair with Henry but didn't follow it through 100%.

Henry felt powerless. He was desperate not to lose Vivienne, who was now single and free. Henry came clean with his wife and they separated. He begged Vivienne to be with him. Vivienne's shame returned but this time it was for the hurt that she was going to cause Henry.

Vivienne and Henry came together as a couple briefly. As Vivienne's shame lingered, far from happy, she started to back-track her emotions. She realised that the relationship with Henry had started out of boredom at home. She'd used Henry and felt guilty about prising him away from his family. Eventually though, she realised that shame was a front for her own fear of being alone, bereft of any relationship at all. Vivienne started to acknowledge her fear. Her feelings for Henry grew weaker. After less than four weeks, Vivienne finally broke off with Henry.

She felt dreadful for hurting Henry but Vivienne realised that she had to face her own fear of loneliness in order to move on in life. She chose to hit her metaphorical brick wall and determined to pick up the pieces alone. Henry was now emotionally destitute.

He had damaged his relationships with his children severely. His wife wouldn't have anything to do with him and he had lost the woman he thought he'd loved. He slammed into his metaphorical wall whilst still in denial of fear. Alone, Henry hurt badly, very badly.

It would take Henry three or four more short lived relationships and a further two years to find his fears - and start the process of releasing them. Eventually he saw how he had allowed his fears of loneliness and not being needed to drive his behaviours for years.

Ω

To recap, *karma* serves a purpose. Its feedback tells you when you are and are not on the 'path' your soul wants you to take.

When I'm on the 'path', I've found things have a way of falling into place. And when I 'lose it', life (*karma*) has a way (thankfully) of kicking me up the backside – sometimes very unpleasantly. So I then attempt to turn *The Wheel of Fortune* back to its starting point. I turn it by changing myself, hopefully for the better...

Illustration 7: *La Rove de Fortune* **(***The Wheel of Fortune***)**
Major Arcana card from the Tarot of Jean Dodal, 1712.

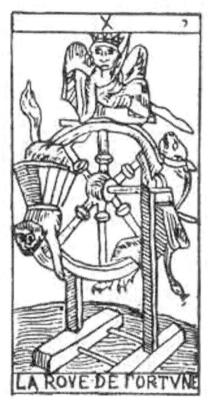

Unpleasant karma precedes the change in me that invokes pleasant karma - eventually!

As *the wheel* turns, it spirals. You choose which way - up or down!

You can go anywhere in the world that you want your false-ego to take you - apart from up!

Paul C Burr

Part IV: Escalating the Spiral Path

Spir(itu)al Steps

Life's journey might be one big spiral pathway. It makes sense - especially if you have done any *Past Life Regression* work. Everything you start or do, spirals through developmental stages from start to end, only to start again - like the days of the week.

> *We shall not cease from exploration*
> *and the end of all our exploring*
> *will be to arrive where we started...*
> *and know the place for the first time.*
> T. S. Eliot

By 'everything', I mean every project, every relationship, every team's progression you participate in, every phase of your life, every bowl of washing up, every *spiritual step,* as well as the whole *Life Journey* your soul seeks to experience. When you complete a spiral (as T.S. Elliot's words inform) you are by definition wiser; you know (more about) your starting place. You see it from 'above', wiser with the benefit of hindsight. That wisdom is the platform to help you as you begin your next spiral.

> *The spiral in psychology means that when you make a*
> *spiral you always come over the same point where you*
> *have been before, but never really the same, it is above or*
> *below, inside, outside, so it means growth.*
> C.G. Jung

A *spiritual step* can take a few weeks, years or maybe a whole lifetime. Each step is, in itself, a spiral within a spiral - which is in turn a spiral within a grander spiral and so on.

Suppose you step off your path. The steps back to your path present themselves; they are always there but perhaps not so clear to see. You encounter some form of karmic feedback; *karma* tells you that you have veered from your path. You can enlist a seer to help you (e.g. a counsellor, coach or therapist) for that's what a seer does. They help you see the way back to your path.

You are empowered moment by moment to choose your path or not. It takes good insight, intuition and self-awareness to stay on the path. You can attract a potential upset at any moment. If you allow that feeling of upset to take control of you - that's feedback in itself; that you're NOT checking yourself to STOP - AND... the thing that you allowed to upset you will keep coming back in some shape or guise until you take control of your response; instead of it controlling you.

It took the sceptical me a little time to acknowledge the influence my thoughts, intentions and feelings have over what I attract in life. At some level, I found this very liberating. At another, I found it scary. I'm still working on how to detach myself from my stream of thoughts and 'edit' them from a higher place.

You are not your thoughts but your thoughts and feelings are the vehicle of your magical power.

You manifest what you think and feel about most. There is no such thing as random, only choice. You have the power to choose what you think - which affects how you feel. Changing your thoughts or interpretation of events, i.e. changing your mind, is at a very simple level - your willingness (power) to change your point of view.

You can choose power, and when I say power, I mean choose passion for your spiritual journey. And when I say passion, I mean passion and compassion. And when you put passion and compassion into action you choose Love.

Love = Passion + Compassion
- first for self, then for others, in thought and action.

Sometimes we choose to ignore our power. Some of us deny it exists; that we have no vibrational influence over what we attract and repel in life. Some of us fear it.

Some of us tread spontaneously and ignorantly, like *The Fool* in the Tarot, which I discuss later in this chapter. Spontaneity has many positive qualities but if you deny, ignore or are ignorant of your *life's journey,* your *spiritual steps* will probably take a lot longer because you'll be taking them unconsciously. You'll subject yourself to *karma.* And if you choose to ignore the cause and effect of the karmic responses you attract, there can be a tendency to put such responses down to randomness - which they aren't; their purpose is to inform you that you are off beam.

Nonetheless, your next *spiritual step* will still be within your grasp. Every hour of your life contains an infinite number of moments, each called *The Present Tense.* Another meaning for 'present' is gift. Each moment is a gift that offers you the opportunity to follow your *Life Path.*

If you want to get on with your spiritual journey in life, look for your next *spiritual step* and go for it, proactively and consciously.

Seek and ye shall find.
Matthew 7:7

You can represent a *spiritual step* with a simple phrase or truth about yourself that you are in the process of finding, opening, becoming and expressing. For example, I've had clients whose next *spiritual steps* have been...

- *I am free*
- *I am beautiful*
- *I am divine*
- *I am released....* and so on.

You may well need help to arrive at a phrase as simple as those listed above. In years gone by I've used NLP methods, hypnotherapy and meditation to access intuitive answers. These days I use a channelling technique that I've found to be more effective and requires less effort.

Over the last two years my *spiritual steps* have included:

1. *I am discerning* (...able to tell the difference between truth and egotistical fantasy.)
2. *I am grateful* (My soul is grateful for the cathartic experiences I've created over the years, despite the hurt caused and received.)
3. *I am brilliant* (...at learning how to shine.)

The sequence of *Spiral Steps* is not necessarily linear; they can overlap. New spirals can start up in parallel and there are, no doubt, more variations.

Let's revisit the words of Dr Thomas Maughan, Chief Druid, The Druid Order, 1964-76. *"When you achieve mastery at one level, you become a blithering idiot at the next level up, at the same time."*

The term *"blithering idiot"* might seem a tad harsh. The first major Arcana card in a Tarot deck depicts *The Fool*. A merry young man, staff in hand and knotted bag over his shoulder, gazes upwards into the sky. He steps forward fearlessly. He doesn't notice the dog at his feet clawing at his trousers. It's difficult to discern. Is the dog a savage or a guide? Is it attacking *The Fool* or is it clawing at him to grab his attention and warn him of impending danger? Either way, the naive young knave has his head in the sky. He doesn't notice the dog or the dangers he may be about to face.

Life is like a computer game. When you master one level, you ready yourself for the next level up. Sometimes you play a number of computer games in parallel. You will often find they all connect with one another.

For example, consider the *spiritual steps* listed earlier: *discerning, grateful* and *brilliant*. It seems logical that one needs to master discernment and gratitude, in the contexts given, in order to become a blithering idiot (or *Fool*) at shining? I don't want to paint too rosy a picture about my own personal struggle with pesky habits and negative holding patterns - and my ability (or sometimes lack of it) to discern truth from illusion. (You'll find out how and why in the next chapter.)

Illustration 8: Le Mat (the Fool)
Major Arcana card from the Tarot of Jean Dodal, 1712.

As I write, the world has entered an astrological phase in which your power to discern truth from illusion is critical.

About Discernment - Neptune Plunges into Pisces, 3rd February 2012 to 2026

Neptune is at its most powerful swimming in waters of Pisces with its fishes. According to many astrologers, Neptune is the most spiritual planet and the most illusionary at the same time.

Pisces is an emotional and dreamy sign – so you can think you are swimming in the seas of fun and good times without realising the 'sharks of *karma*' – shame, anger, sadness and fear lurk in the depths below.

The 'sharks' await to see if you swim in truth or fantasy. Do you swim in spirit or *false ego*? Do you swim in and with the divine or manipulate the ethers for your own sensual pleasure, at the expense of others?

The key to lasting success is DISCERNMENT.

Separate that which:

1. Feels right, to take you down the path to find, open, become and express your *true self* from....
2. The *false ego* fantasises - but deep down renders a fear created by it.

This can be very tricky, especially in affairs that are close to your heart and uncomfortable in the head. And it's almost impossible to decipher when you're split 50/50 between head and heart.

* *Do I love her? Do I not?*
* *Shall I go for this job? Shall I not?*
* *Am I being true to myself? Am I not?* – This is the key question.

Discern between oneness and separateness.

Live with your vulnerabilities. Neither deny nor over-embrace them. Let it be okay to have them and let them be at the same time. They/you are human.

And....

1. **Trust yourself.**
2. **Trust spirit.**
3. **Trust the Divine.**

Take Conscious or Unconscious Steps. You Choose!

When you step consciously, you develop a sensibility to the decisions you take. The key factor, mentioned earlier, is to discern which decisions you make out of fear from those that take you down the *Life Path* your soul seeks.

Illustration 9: Decisions that Take You Down your *Life's journey* versus those Borne of Fear

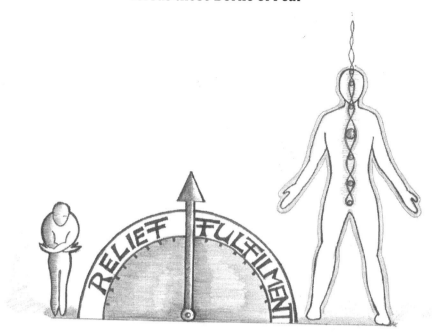

If you choose not to step consciously.....

Unconscious Steps Take Longer

We wander through life with a set of habits. Some serve us well, for example: keeping fit, eating healthily, working hard and caring for others. Some, although enjoyable, serve us 'less-well' perhaps. I cite some 'less-well' type habits I've had in the past - for example: going to the pub, watching mindless TV, recreational drugs, pornography or gambling. Neither category will kill us necessarily. As long as we avoid excess.

Being healthy, working hard and caring for loved ones are undoubtedly worthy causes. In excess however, each can lead to unpleasant side effects. You operate with tunnel vision. You limit your overall learning.

I've worked with several workaholics devoted totally to furthering their career and providing financial security for themselves and loved ones. Alas, they often didn't have a home life to go home to. They lived a separate life from their families even in the same household. They had chosen work at the expense of family life throughout their career. The small amount of time they did give to family life had not felt, and still did not feel, fulfilling. They neither gave nor received 100%.

When you give something 100% commitment, you fill the time and energy you put into it fully. You fulfil your experience. You feel fulfilled, for example, at work, with family, in health, at leisure, managing finance and so on. Fulfilment requires variety, balance and temperance as well as commitment.

Take away variety, commitment or balance and you limit your learning. Should you avoid temperance; not only do you limit your learning, you can do yourself harm – physically, mentally, emotionally and spiritually. If and when you put a limit on your learning, you get bored – eventually.

Case Story: Not Taking *Spiritual Steps* Consciously

Temperance is not a quality that has come easily throughout my life.[69] I have tended to put my foot down hard on the accelerator or brake pedal in life. Living in cruise control has never been my chosen lifestyle, until recently.

1997-9, my life was good by traditional standards. I had good business coming in. I was in a good relationship. I had a lovely flat to come home to. I jogged regularly and felt in pretty good shape. My football team was doing okay. What else could I possibly want for?

I grew an addiction for computer games. I played *Championship Manager*[70] just about every day. I can recall one weekend, when my partner was away. I played it for two days with very little sleep. How obsessive is that?

I'd simulate football season after season, some games went 25 years into the future. My team would win the Premier League and international contests, year after year. I'd take a team from the lower leagues and get them into the Premiership. Eventually I 'maxed' out. I

---

[69] I'm a Leo (essence of real me), with Leo ascending; the sign on the eastern horizon at the time of my birth.

[70] A life-like game where you elect to become the manager of the football team of your choice.

had nothing left to learn, I got bored with playing but still kept plugging away. I developed a sense of moroseness. The habit no longer satisfied my hunger to learn but I still wouldn't give it up. I began to regret how much time was wasted.

Eventually, I took my partner on holiday and left *Championship Manager* at home. During those days away I saw through the illusory power that the game held over me. At the same time, I began to realise that I'd allowed my gaming to become an addiction for a deeper reason - a lack of fulfilment. I was grateful for all the wonderful abundances I had in my life - but at the same time I did not feel fulfilled by them. Success and good fortune, in a traditional sense – job, partner, home and financial security - was not enough. I wanted something more, something ethereal.

I used the computer game as a mirror to look at my 'real life'. I realised eventually that fulfilment, i.e. finding the real me, was not going to be found through the physical world around me, in isolation from the inner world within me. I felt blessed that I had just about everything I could ask for. I had many things to be thankful for. *But I still hadn't found what I was looking for.* I focused much energy on developing a new coaching business. I put a lot into the normal things in life, but still felt I was drifting a bit. I carried on taking, by and large, unconscious steps for a further six years.

Pause, Recap and What Next?

So far I have written about many abstract ('blue sky and beyond') jigsaw pieces of life, for example:

- Love
- Oneness
- Passion
- Compassion
- Self worth
- Temperance
- Courage
- *True self*

- *False ego*
- Forgiveness
- *Etheric Body*
- Spirit
- Soul
- Conscious and Unconscious Mind
- Shame, anger, sadness and fear

I have covered how each influences the pace of your *spiritual steps* in your *life's journey.*

Each affects your emotions, intellect and consciousness awakening. Next let's see how these jigsaw pieces can affect your physical and mental wellbeing.

Part V: Health = Mind and Body at Ease. Not-Health = Dis-ease.

Let me start by announcing:

1. **I have no medical qualifications whatsoever.**
2. **Before you make any decision about your health, you should seek advice from an appropriately qualified health practitioner.**

I have researched 'alternative' or what is now starting to be called "Integrative Medicine". My main sources of reference are listed because they are thoroughly research-based and recommended as important reading, experiencing or viewing.

- *The Healing Psyche* by Rob van Overbruggen: a layperson's guide into the beneficial effect of therapies worldwide on cancer patients. It is an illuminating read and you don't need to be an expert to understand its wisdom. When a pal of mine died four years ago from cancer, I gave my copy to his wife. Later she told me the book helped her greatly during the deepest periods of her grieving.

- *The Secret of Cancer and all other Diseases* by Susanne Billander: a ground breaking book that describes what Integrative Medicine is and how it works.

- *The Biology of Belief,* book and DVD, by Bruce Lipton, Ph.D.: Dr Lipton is one of the pioneers of understanding the function and connection between body cells and the *Etheric Body.*

- *The Genie in your Genes* by Dawson Church, PhD: explores the function and purpose of genes ignored by many traditional bio-scientists. Dr Church shows the pitfalls that some scientists have fallen into by labelling most DNA as "junk DNA". More importantly he reveals much about the innate 'intelligence' of human genes and how you can work with this 'intelligence' to improve your health and wellbeing - another great read for the layperson, like me.

- NLP Practitioner notes and exercises, from NLP World[71] approved by ABNLP and ANLP.
- *The Living Matrix, The Revolution in Alternative Healing,*[72] DVD: another ground breaking piece of work, in the form of a video that summarises scientific investigations into the human energy field referred to as *The Living Matrix*, known by the ancients as the *Etheric Body*.
- *Zeitgeist, Moving Forward,*[73] DVD by Peter Joseph, amongst many pearls of life-changing wisdom, this film (The Zeitgeist Movement - TZM) breaks many myths about genetics and disease currently held by the majority of traditional bio-chemists. TZM reveals the significance of how pre-natal and childhood experiences influence our susceptibility to ill, physical and emotional, health.
- *Dr Bruce Lipton explaining how cells tune into memory in the Matrix, Parts 1 and 2,* film clips on YouTube.[74] Dr Lipton presents the bio-chemical connection between the material world (the cells in our physical body) and our spiritual journey to our true selves (our *Etheric Body* or *Living Matrix*).

My interest in the mind-body connection to physical well-being really took off in 2006 when attending an Introduction to Meta-Medicine® course facilitated by Susanne Billander[75]. I submitted myself to and delivered (under supervision) basic therapy sessions. I found out first hand that there was something to the relationship between mind, body and the environment we live in.

Thousands of client case studies of the 'mind-body connection' causes of ill health have been researched. The links between significant emotional events (singular points in time triggered by a traumatic or near-traumatic experience) and the diseases that can ensue as a result

---

[71] Ref: www.nlpworld.com
[72] Ref: www.thelivingmatrixmovie.com
[73] Ref: www.zeitgeistmovingforward.com
[74] Ref: www.youtube.com
[75] Susanne Billander, META-Medicine® Master Trainer, META-Health Coach, Master Practitioner of NLP, Time Based Technique, Vortex Healing®, Soulrealignment® ref: http://www.metamedicine.se/

are well established. The International Meta-Medicine Association®[76] (IMMA) now offers training and certification as an Integrative Health Consultant in mind-body healing. Integrative Medicine is still not regarded seriously by many of the mainstream scientific, medical authorities, healthcare and pharmaceutical industries. Interest is growing though, thanks to people like Rob Van Overbruggen, Susanne Billander, Dawson Church, and Dr Bruce Lipton.

Professor João Magueijo[77] writes how science has an *"argumentative tradition"* and *"has no shortage of very clever people who love to show off"*. In fairness, Professor Magueijo extols how such an environment has merits. It increases the rigour and diligence by which new science sets out to prove its worth. But... (and this is a deliberate <u>but</u>)

There exists a conflict of interest, especially a financial interest, between Allopathic (conventional) and Integrative (alternative) Medicine. One cannot help but suspect that 'very clever people' (scientists, marketers and politicians) are using their talent to defend against, if not attack, Integrative Medicine - and corner the supply of herbal remedies to the public in the UK. In the name of 'science', they seek to protect and expand the financial and illusionary sacrosanct 'turf' of multi-billion dollar industries in pharmacy and healthcare.

Meta-Medicine®, in my mind, is now a well grounded science.

The nub of the scientific research reveals that <u>all</u> disease is linked to significant emotional events in our lives. The onset of every disease is preceded by an unexpected, unwanted, deeply upsetting event.

Put another way, the ontology of this research implies that all disease (= dis-ease) begins in the mind - which means: to heal we first need to put our minds at ease, i.e. we must change our interpretation of the significant emotional event that we attracted before the onset of our disease.

In practise we are often unwilling to talk about significant emotional events or the symptoms of the disease.

---

[76] Ref: http://www.metamedicine.info/
[77] *Faster than the Speed of Light,* by João Magueijo, cosmologist and professor in Theoretical Physics at Imperial College London. He is a pioneer of the varying speed of light (VSL) theory.

- The event may be so traumatic that we refuse to acknowledge it. We literally blot it out from our conscious thinking or, at very least, we refuse to talk about it.
- We may feel shame about the event. It weakens or destroys a self image that we dearly wish to hold on to, and project on to others.
- We may feel shame about the 'weakness' we would reveal by talking openly about our malady. We feel embarrassed. We don't wish to be seen as a second class citizen.
- We may fear the consequences of being told that we have a serious health condition. We fear possible 'future fear'. We fear a possibility that we don't want to happen. We ignore early symptoms. We stick our head in the sand, metaphorically speaking, and hope the symptoms go away.
- We may even lack the self worth needed to call out for help. We may feel we don't deserve others' attention. We don't want those that we love and care about to worry about us. We place their emotional wellbeing before our own.
- We may be in a Machiavellian environment (for example, in corporate business or politics) where problems translate into weakness. Where there lurk many, envious of our power, who will seize the opportunity to brings us down, and hopefully gain our power.

If there is one piece of wisdom to counteract all the above, it's this:

Love and care for yourself wholly so that you can love and care for others wholly too. You cannot give to others that which you do not give to yourself first.

Quick Exercise: Repeat the following affirmation out loud, seventeen times, first and last thing, every morning and evening, for seventeen days.

"I now release all that is unlike love.
I love myself wholly and unconditionally."

If you find the above affirmation a little challenging to say, imagine you are speaking to the inner child or divine spirit within you. Spirit doesn't need to hear it. It's you saying it that counts. You speak and the body (your DNA) listens.

There's a deeper logic as to why love, care and compassion start with the self.

You cannot share what you do not already have or experience.
In sharing you demonstrate the 'how to' of it.
Jeanne Ayling

To do so, you must be open to learning from your feelings of vulnerability. When you acknowledge (= acceptance and willingness to learn from) a significant emotional event, you have already started the self healing process. You choose courage to find, open, study and restructure the information in your *Etheric Body* pertaining to the significant emotional event.

Your brain transmits all the latest relevant information available from the *Etheric Body* to your nervous system and endocrine system. This new information can impel new bio-chemical reactions that power your return to emotional and physical wellbeing.

When you replace the unhelpful information (that triggers shame, anger, sadness and fear), in your *Etheric Body*, with helpful information (for example: calmness, abundance, self-acceptance, care,

compassion, courage, wisdom and love) you change the bio chemical reactions in your body. You empower your ability to self heal.
Study the following reframes.

Disease serves a purpose. It reveals that you hold unhelpful information about yourself. You have not cleaned it up yet. That information is found in or below your deepest conscious feelings.
Paul C Burr

Rather than focusing on the genes and the body's chemistry, which is the myopic focus of conventional allopathic medicine, the new physics and the new biology reveal that we should be focusing on both the physical signals and the energetic signals, which include thought.
Bruce Lipton

Dr Lipton's reframe opens up a new dimension, maybe more, when we ask the question,
- "At what speed do thoughts transmit their signal and with how much power?"
And were we to go beyond thought....
- "How fast does consciousness travel and how far does it travel?"
Both the above questions beg a further question,
- "Who or what can decode these signals and for what purpose?"
The answers to these questions, as we shall see in the next chapter, point to a convergence between modern science and what ancient wisdom has been telling us all along.

Part VI: Beyond the Time-Space Continuum

Bluebottle, "What times is it Eccles?"
Eccles, "Urrrrrr, the time is now!"
"How do you know it's now?"
"Urrrrr, I got it written down on a piece of paper."
"What do you do when it's not now?"
"Oh, I don't it read it then."[78]

Where Time Doesn't Exist

Should you google 'retrocausation' on the internet you'll get a whole whack of stuff on this phenomenon. Most of it is scientific speak so I give my simplified version.

Retrocausality means, under certain circumstances, a human being can influence something that happened in the past. Now if this is possible, it infers that at some point in the future we can influence what happens now. Either way, it means that for me to cause an event that happened yesterday, last week or even last year then 'I,' in some way, can travel back in time, or put another way, at some level, time doesn't exist. To prove this I use some simple scientific evidence.

I started reading Lynne McTaggart's works in 2005. I first read *The Field, The Quest for the Secret Force of the Universe* followed by her subsequent book, *The Intention Experiment*, as soon as it was published. McTaggart's books accelerated my interest and understanding of Quantum Physics immensely. They are written lucidly by a self-professed non-scientist (an investigative journalist) for a non-expert reader, like me. One scientific revelation, from the many cited, baffled me more than any other. I cite the experiments of Helmut Schmidt, a 'far-out' physicist who made a remarkable discovery about man's relationship with time.

---

[78] Inspired by a sketch and the characters Bluebottle (voice by Peter Sellers) and Eccles (voice by Spike Milligan), from the *Goon Show*, a series of the hilarious and iconic comedy radio and TV shows in the 50's and 60's.

Schmidt[79] rigged a computer program to send clicks randomly to stereo speaker/headphones. As randomness suggests, 50% of the clicks were heard out of the left channel and 50% were heard from the right. Schmidt then ran the same computer programme and recorded the results on tapes. He copied the master tapes to 'slave' copies, ensuring no one knew of or had access to the tape's contents.

Later, he asked students, picked at random, to listen to samples from the library of slave tapes. Before they listened, they were instructed to focus on receiving clicks through their left ear. Each student would be the first person ever to listen to the contents of the tape assigned to them. Guess what?

The tapes produced a 55% bias towards a click in the left ear. The slave tapes matched the master tapes perfectly. Control tapes, recorded and locked away at the same time, revealed the expected 50/50 left-right balance of clicks. Schmidt conducted over 20,000 trials. Let me scream – "Wow!"

Let's put aside the time factor for the moment. A 55% bias over thousands of trials is way outside the tolerance levels of the results of such a bias happening randomly. Let me put it another way.

If you go to Las Vegas to play roulette and gamble with the certainty that red is going to come up 55% of the time, and if the table has only one '0' slot (bank takes all money on the table) on the wheel, amongst the numbers 1 to 36, the bank has a 1 in 37 chance of winning all bets on every spin of the ball. The bank has a 3% say (rounded figures) chance of winning all bets on the table, in a single spin of the wheel. This is how the casino makes its money over the long term. You have a 97% chance of the roulette ball landing on red or black. And of that 97%, you have a 55% chance of the ball landing on red; 55% of 97% = 53% approximately.

Which means, on average, if you laid down 100 x $1 bets, one after the other, on average, you will lose 47 x $1 bets to the bank. You will win 53 x $1 bets. You will end up with $53 from your starting stakes and $53 in winnings. You end up with $106. You make a $6 (or 6%) profit.

---

[79] If you want to read fuller details about Schmidt's experiments I refer you to *The Intention Experiment, Chapter 11: Praying for Yesterday.*

108

Now just wait a minute, before you all pack your bags and fly to Las Vegas. This is statistical logic and an unproven hypothesis. I am <u>not</u> advocating that you gamble. Why? There are 3 reasons:

1. If you gamble for real then you have something to lose - which introduces fear. When you introduce fear into the equation you disturb the vibrational frequency of the intention you emit. Which means the power of your intention is compromised by 'eddy currents' of fear.

2. Let's say you go ahead anyway and gamble on the roulette ball landing in a red slot. If a large number of people are gambling (i.e. sending out intention) on black, the collective intention of your fellow gamblers may disturb the signal that you transmit to influence the outcome of the red you seek.

3. If now is the time for you to attract wealth, you will have already done something in the past to attract it, so that wealth will come your way.

Should you want to try an exercise for fun, flip a coin a thousand times. Record the number of heads and tails you flip, like so....

Heads	Tails
ĦĦ ĦĦ ĦĦ ĦĦ	ĦĦ ĦĦ ĦĦ III

Focus on heads before each throw. Count how many 'points' you end up with in each column. If you create a result in line with Schmidt's findings you'll end up with around 550 points under heads and 450 under tails. There's more to Schmidt's research than this simple experiment that runs in 'normal' time.

Schmidt's experiments remove the time dimension. In total, his experiments demonstrate two things:

1. Through intention, students could influence the outcome of a computer programme that, in essence, models the tossing of an ordinary coin.
2. Students could influence the outcome of hitherto unwitnessed computerised 'coin tosses' that happened in the past.

I struggled with these two concepts when I first looked at them and tried to think through their implications. I asked myself, "What if this rings true for you or me?"

1. You have the power to influence the arrangement or flow of electrons and atoms, inherent in a computer programme (or a coin[80] for that matter) whilst it is running (or being spun in the air, in the coin's case.) You have the power to influence the probability of a result, an outcome in the form of matter, i.e. something you can see, touch, hear, smell or taste.
2. You are capable of witnessing the effect of sub-atomic influences on sub-atomic structures in matter. How Quantum Mechanics (thoughts) influences Newtonian Science (matter). Are we nearer a unified theory?
3. You have the power to increase probability of the specific result of something that happened in the past, as long as no living thing witnessed it or knows the result of the event before you do.
4. There exists a dimension, which you are unconscious of through your five senses, where time does not exist.

What about going forward in time? The *Law of Attraction* implies that the thoughts and intentions that you send out now, can influence a result in the future. By tomorrow, you've already sent the intention out and its effect has already started. Its influence may be already going to happen unless you send a counter thought. Whether you get what you intend or not, where are the energies/electrons pertaining to your intention? Can you see them hanging around? No - because your thoughts have transferred to the timeless *Desire World*. Their effect will filter into the now and materialise when the time to receive them is right for you.

---

[80] Millions of trials, using real coins, have been conducted in normal (I almost wrote 'real') time.

The corollary to this is that you can influence things that you choose now to have started, happening to you unknowingly, in the past. Contemplate something consciously now, for the first time, something ethereal that you want to have started in the past, even a second ago. Make sure what you desire is uplifting for everyone. Expand your beliefs around what is possible and that which you desire.

Repeat the following incantation seventeen times, *"Spirit is my prospering power"*. Focus on that which you desire. Allow its image to fill your body. Imagine. Now sit in the feeling of having already achieved that which you desire for a further seventeen seconds. When you do this, you bring the future into now.

Where Space and Time Don't Exist

Let's begin with a simple definition.

Hypercommunication: the ability to transfer information from one point to another outside of time and/or space.

For example, in ant colonies and beehives, when a queen is separated from her colony/hive (and regardless of distance)[81] the workers continue to build and construct the colony/hive. In both cases, if the queen is killed then all work in the colony or hive ceases, instantaneously. In either case, upon death, the queen's connection to her group's consciousness ceases. We can thus refer to these forms of hyper-communication as quantum consciousness ('quantum' in this context meaning 'discontinuous across time and space'). Let's switch our attention to human consciousness.

Human DNA-spirals expand when your consciousness is relaxed, happy and peaceful. They vibrate and emit bio-photons of light in coherent wave patterns – i.e. in tune with one another. When you are at peace, your DNA 'sings' in tune with the universe - and the opposite? Your *DNA Spirals* contract when you feel stress, sadness and depression. The wave patterns emitted lack coherence, your DNA no longer 'sings'. In extreme cases, *DNA Spirals* contract, close down and cease to emit light. Your DNA clams up, literally.

---

[81] Ref: www.hermes-press.com/number_frequency.htm

You can find an abundance of scientific research on how consciousness transcends space and time. Many traditional scientists somehow ignore it but an experiment by the United States military blew me away, metaphorically. I refer to a particular experiment, conducted by United States Army Intelligence and Security Command (INSCOM), on human DNA.[82]

In 1993 INSCOM researchers took DNA samples from test human subjects and placed them in measuring devices in another room of the building. The subjects viewed various video images of loving peaceful settings, as well as war scenes, tragedies and erotica. When a test subject was having a particular emotional response, both the DNA samples in their body and the other part of the building gave the exact same response synchronously.

The researchers stretched the distance of the remote DNA samples to a location 400 miles away from the test subjects. They repeated the test, and the results were exactly the same. The remote DNA was affected by the subject's emotional responses over distance without any lag in time whatsoever – instantaneously, faster than the speed of light.

What does this mean?

Your consciousness transmits information instantaneously, from one place to another, outside of your day-to-day space-time continuum. The information travels through a conduit-dimension where time and space do not exist.

Are you willing to accept the notion of, 'A dimension where time and space do not exist'? If so, let's add a further building block, which connects everything to everything.

Everything Connects

Something is deemed 'intelligent' because it is capable of processing intelligible data (or information) coherently.

---

[82] Ref: INSCOM experiment www.becoming-alactic.org/presupp4.html; www.inspirationsofthepast.com/InspirationsMain/GreggBraden.html

Were you and I to talk, we would be able to 'connect' in the same language. By 'connect', I mean 'transmit and receive information (dialogue) coherently'. This implies 'intelligence', in the:

1. Sender (you) able to codify your thoughts and transmit information (words)
2. Receiver (me) capable of receiving and decoding such information (your words), processing it and thus acting upon it (i.e. understanding).

What of human's capability to 'connect' with other species of animals and vice versa? Can you connect with plants as well? Yes you can!

Dolphins Save Flotilla's Crews in 2004 Tsunami[83]

On the morning of the Indian Ocean Earthquake, scuba diving instructor, Chris Cruz's boat along with a number of fellow diving boats were moored at sea, just off of Khao Lak, north of Phuket in Thailand. Cruz recounts how the lives of many divers were saved that day because they followed dolphins to safety.

At around 10.30am, local time, the flotilla found itself caught up in a sea of whirlpools. The boats' ropes had become entangled. The captains agreed to cut themselves loose from their respective anchors. All of a sudden dolphins appeared right up close to the boats and started to jump in front of them. In the two years he'd been there, Cruz had never experienced such intimate or excitable dolphin behaviour.

He and his fellow captain's sensed that the dolphins were warning them of imminent danger. They chose to follow the dolphins. Far out at sea, the flotilla surfed safely over the oncoming, unbroken, tsunami waves. On their return, they found their shoreline camp had been devastated. They realised that had they ignored the dolphins, they would all have been swept tumultuously by the breaking tsunami waves on to the shore. The dolphins knew before man of the impending doom.

The dolphins somehow had the ability to read the signs from their environment of the oncoming tsunami. This implies a collective intelligence in tune with the earth, in this instance, far more so than

---

[83] http://www.hawaiidolphinretreat.com/DolphinsTsunami.html

man. It also implies dolphins' collective compassion and intention to help humankind from harm.

Ω

A Whale Thanks its Rescuers with an Acrobatic Display

This amazing video on YouTube[84] features a whale showing its thanks to the crew of a small boat who had saved its life. The whale was caught up in fishing nets. It took the crew nigh on two hours to free the whale. When the whale had recovered sufficient strength, it shared its joy with a personal display of thanks to its rescuers. The video reveals that these beautiful mammals have the capacity to acknowledge grace and kindness from their fellow species.

Ω

These two stories exemplify humankind and fellow mammals applying/ sharing wisdom to help one another. What about plants? Are they intelligent, i.e. capable of decoding information? Can plants read our thoughts?

Plants Read Minds

Cleve Backster started his career as an Interrogation Specialist with the CIA. During this period, he was one of the foremost authorities on lie detection technology in the CIA.

In 1966 he hooked up a polygraph lie detector to a cane plant in order to work out its rate of water consumption. (Polygraphs test for physiological responses in humans when they feel stressed or threatened.) He got a huge surprise. The plant showed human-like responses.[85]

Backster only had to think about feeding the plant with water and his thought produced a physiological response in it. Later, when Backster thought about setting a plant's leaf alight with a flame, he got another

---

[84] Ref: Search for *Saving Valentina.6.8.11.h264.mov* on YouTube
[85] Ref: Primary Perception: Biocommunication with Plants, Living Foods, and Human Cells by Cleve Backster, published by White Rose Millennium Press. There are several videos of Backster's experiments on YouTube.

reaction. *"The pen on the lie detector jumped right off the top of the chart."*

From this point on, Backster started a succession of experiments which showed that the plant was in tune with human thoughts, images and even emotions. He could leave the plants alone for a length of time and sit in a bar, talking with friends and the polygraph test would measure the ups and downs in the conversation that Backster was experiencing.

Furthermore, when Backster poured boiling water down a sink, killing all of the microbe life (bacteria) that lived there, the plants responded vehemently, reacting to the death of the bacteria. The bacteria seemingly emitted signals that were interpreted coherently by the plants.

Ω

The studies and stories, in this and the previous chapter, illustrate that DNA has far more function and purpose than scientists first thought.

DNA: the Biological Internet of the Universe

Russian scientists have demonstrated in scientific environments how DNA can be influenced and reprogrammed by words and frequencies.[86]

Only 10% of our DNA builds proteins, many scientists label the remaining 90% as "junk DNA". Science though has made some revolutionary breakthroughs into the function and behaviour of this DNA. (The sources I've read are at the limit of my technical nous so this isn't very technical!)

Russian linguists found that the genetic code in DNA follows the same rules as all our human languages. Russian biophysicist and molecular biologist, Pjotr Garajev, and colleagues discovered that living DNA in living tissue will always react to language modulated laser rays and radio waves when coherent frequencies are used. Not only that; we

---

[86] Ref: *DNA can be influenced and reprogrammed by words and frequencies. Russian DNA discoveries* by Grazyna Fosar and Franz Bludorf, http://soulofdistortion,nl/dna1.html

can influence the wave vibrations our DNA emits simply through the words, phrases and sentences we speak - and perhaps more significantly, the feelings we express.

This shows that DNA is intelligent. Every DNA strand acts, in effect, as an organic computer; a solitonic[87] data processor that regulates each and every cell in our body.

The Russian scientists built devices that emitted radio and light frequencies, modulated suitably, to influence cellular metabolism to repair genetic defects. Garajev's team managed to repair, for example, chromosomes damaged by X-rays. Also, they were able to capture the information patterns of a particular DNA and transmit it onto another; thus reprogramming cells to another genome.

One experiment astounded me. It involved the transmission of DNA patterns of the embryo of a salamander into the embryo of a frog. What started life as a frog, grew into a Salamander without any side effects or microsurgery required; without a single gene being cut out or replaced. The scientists transmuted the embryo of one life form into another by vibration alone.

One can imagine how shape shifting could possibly take place in the physical dimension. Now that _is_ alchemy!

Pure Speculation on My Part:

Scientists can repair genetic defects in malfunctioning cells. They can transmit information patterns from one cell to another. Does this mean that one day we may end up with non-invasive cell therapy, instead of surgery or cell destroying radiation for all diseases including cancer? Instead, we could impress the information from a healthy cell on to an unhealthy cell. Wouldn't that be a wonderful thing? Imagine.

---

[87] Soliton: a quantum of energy that can be propagated and does not dissipate, a standing wave. So a solitonic computer stores its data in a formation of photons, the most miniscule particles of light that man has discovered, yet.

'Under the Hood' of the Law of Attraction

- Moment by moment, you respond to the people and circumstances around you. Your mind emotes language patterns which impress your *Etheric Body* with information. The nature of this information (e.g. happy or sad, peaceful or angry) influences the pattern and vibration of your DNA.

- DNA can be influenced by the information presented to it in the form of light and sound as well as language.

- DNA acts as a computer and regulates your body cells accordingly.

- When that information is coherent, you feel peaceful and relaxed.

- DNA transmits signals of its vibration across the universe, outside the space-time continuum.

- Your body cells are influenced by the information they receive from the mind. You use your mind to respond to the people and circumstances around you. Be you engulfed in peace or chaos, you have a choice. Do you respond through spirit (uplift) or animalistically?

- How you respond to your environment, be the environment peaceful or chaotic, regulates **the vibrations you send out** - which **govern what you attract in life**.

How you respond consciously to events you attract, transmutes into what you project unconsciously. **What you project, you attract**. Thus we see how the human mind is the fulcrum of your Spiritual Constitution. Your mind governs the signals you transmit; the "vibe" you put out to attract what you get in life.

As you choose courage to climb the spiral path toward your *true self* (choose spirit), you raise your vibration – and thus you raise the vibration of what you attract. All this seems a fair enough deal for adults, but what about children?

Unborn and young children haven't developed responses to deal maturely with information (events or situations) they don't expect or want. Part VII covers some of the challenges we as children can face, knowingly and unknowingly, as we develop our *Spiritual Constitution*.

Paul C Burr

Part VII: The Early Years, 0-14: Kidding Is No Joke

Kids take in everything. Only recently have I discovered the extent to which parents influence their children's whole lives, way beyond the age they leave home. Kids accept and live the *Law of Attraction* with full accountability and responsibility.

A child seeks love, security, warmth and touch. When a child receives <u>not</u> love, <u>not</u> security, <u>not</u> warmth or <u>not</u> touch, that child accepts full responsibility for <u>not</u> receiving what they want. Furthermore, it blames itself for having neither the physical nor the intellectual strength to deal with untoward behaviour in a mature adult fashion. It doesn't know how to channel the negative emotions (shame, anger, sadness or fear) that arise within. How could it?

The child feels helpless about how to cope and so locks away the negative emotions in a shield or 'bubble-wrap' of etheric energy. The child develops compensatory behaviours (e.g. remaining silent, denying/blocking negative thoughts about others, blaming self) that shield its conscious mind from the negative emotions hidden within its shadows.

This is not a mature decision and it's not exclusive to children. How well do we adults react in such situations? Ask yourself, "How often do I...

1.   ...hide my hurt or sadness to avoid confrontation?"
2.   ...resort to anger to get what I want?"
3.   ...manipulate someone emotionally to get what I want?"
4.   ...use brute force to get my way?"
5.   ...harbour ill feeling?"

None of the five strategies are mature acts, I suggest. Let us look at Strategy 1 because that is how many people I know deal with confrontation to begin with. Many adults, including me, when faced with controversy, let things be and say nothing. We either do not have, or choose not to employ, an effective strategy to deal with unwanted or inappropriate behaviour. Instead, we remain silent. We hope the issue will die down, go away and all will be forgotten in time. Let us not confuse weak with meek.

- When weak, you put yourself second, you subsume yourself to someone else with disregard for your own feelings. You place their feelings above your own and you hide behind a veil but the negativity lingers. You feel shame from not speaking or being your truth. You feel shame because you choose not the courage to be meek.

- Meek, I suggest, is putting your honour on an equal status with those around you. You do not need to use brute force to get your point of view across. You do not resort to conflict, anger or threatening behaviour. You do not manipulate or seek to instil anger, sadness, fear or shame in others either. Instead you seek to put your point across constructively, positively and truthfully – so that others understand the impression they make on you. Your seek parity, not to win outright. You speak or act according to your truth. You choose courage to be meek.

If we act 'not-meekly', i.e. weakly, how can we expect children, to whom we set an example, to choose courage? Furthermore, kids not only take in every conscious thing that's going on around them, they take in all the untold, unsaid things as well. They absorb, at a subliminal level, all the endemic family moods, trouble and strife. They register the negative vibrations from their environment and store the information in their *Etheric Body*. They/we develop compensatory behaviours; one or more of the five strategies cited earlier to cope.

Kids blame themselves for all the feelings of insecurity they endure. They make themselves fully accountable and responsible for the untoward behaviour of their parents, for instance. They convince themselves that they caused it and therefore they blame themselves accordingly. (The very morning of writing this paragraph, a lady who had suffered child abuse appeared on the BBC1 TV morning show. She described the complexity and paradox of how a child can still love a parent who abuses them.)

In her wonderful and insightful book, *Your Secret Self*,[88] Tracy Marks explains the subtle logic of this childhood dynamic. If the child were to

---

[88] Ref: *Your Secret Self*, by Tracy Marks, *Part Three, The Psychodynamics of Twelfth House Conflicts* and *Part Four, The Process of Integration: Twelfth House Liberation.*

blame their parents for untoward behaviour and place themselves as completely innocent (which they are) without the intellectual or physical ability (which they do not have) to change their environment; they, in effect, relinquish all power (to change things) and hope for their lives.

On the other hand, if they consider their untoward parents or carers to be normal loving people and blame themselves for everything that happens – then at least they give themselves hope. They give themselves the ability to 'rectify' themselves in the hope that their parents will show the love and security they seek.

Faced with a no -win situation, the child blames themself, wraps away the negative emotions in their subconscious mind and develops compensatory behaviours. They hide their feelings away. In denial, they pretend that all is okay with their parents. But they can withdraw from wanting or expecting love. Their self worth plummets.

A damaging behavioural subroutine sets in. It can stay with the unloved, insecure child into their adult lives. In their adolescent years they may well seek escape. Their susceptibility to drug addiction and, in extreme cases, self harming increases.

Child abuse can be categorized in two forms:[89]

1. **Things that should not happen that happen.**

   This category is considered much more damaging by society at large. I know of no greater sorrow or sense of injustice than to see an innocent child suffer, either physically or emotionally, by the hand of man. Here are two case stories.

   i. Caroline suffered along with her sister from the seemingly random behaviour of being brought up by a paranoid, schizophrenic father and submissive mother. She cowered in her bedroom in fear frequently throughout her childhood. She couldn't have other children visit her because her parents would not allow it. In early teenage years she became an outcast from the 'normal' people around her.

---

[89] Ref: *Zeitgeist: Moving Forward* - available on DVD or viewing and free download from www.zeitgeistmovingforward.com. If you feel you can afford it, buy one.

She escaped to a life of drugs and self harm amongst fellow outcasts. Caroline became radical and lived outside the flock of normal society. She developed a reticence of allowing herself to become close to anyone for a prolonged period in her life.

It took Caroline many years to begin the process of bringing the shame, anger, sadness and fear to the surface. She found ways to express that buried energy through martial arts and Tai Chi, amongst other well-being activities.

Over time, Caroline found the care and compassion she feels for all humankind and started the process of applying these feelings toward herself.

ii.   At the age of 4, Rachel was molested on several occasions by her teenage uncle. She feared the unknown consequences of telling her parents. Why? Because she had enjoyed the physical gratification and had told her uncle so.

She feared the abhorrence her parents would have of her and her behaviour. She also felt enormous shame for enjoying the sexual contact. This combination of fear and shame affected Rachel deeply, well into early adulthood. She could not absolve herself of the profound shame she felt from her childhood memories.

From the age of 16 Rachel enjoyed sexual contact but suffered an innate paradox about sexual relationships. She could not reconcile sex with love and thus felt "dirty". She was a bubbly and good looking girl who attracted many would-be, but eventually short-term, suitors. Rachel would frustrate herself and her suitors with an unwillingness to express love, fed by childhood shame.

Through therapy and much self work, Rachel slowly released the negative emotions to find, become and express her beautiful self.

2. **Things that should happen that do not happen.**

This category deals with children who receive <u>not</u> the love, affection or security they seek. Their parents may be very well present in body. They provide their children warmth, clothing, shelter, nutrition and a good education. The parents give everything but that of themselves, their own spirit.

For example, I have one client, Charles, whose parents were both complete workaholics. He was 'spoilt' as a child. Charles got everything he desired apart from the emotional attention and physical contact from a loving parent. Charles was inadvertently taught how to take, take and do nothing but take. But he was rarely asked to share or demonstrate the love he held for his mother and father.

At the age of 17, Charles possessed every toy, gizmo, piece of clothing and accessory a young man could ask for - but had little conscious experience of how to receive or give love. Charles had not done well at school. He had no academic qualifications of note with which he could accredit himself. Charles had become withdrawn and shy of conventional society. Charles felt hugely unworthy.

Seeking acknowledgement, Charles joined a gang of youths where he got whatever esteem he could grab through petty crime and miscreancy. Although highly impressionable, Charles was innately a gentle soul and found the malevolent behaviour of the more violent of his gang fellows impossible to deal with or condone. The gang leaders spotted this 'weakness' in Charles. They victimised him. Their threats worsened. Charles tried to isolate himself by staying at home. His parents became aware of the threatening phone calls he received. They sought to find out all the 'misdeeds' that Charles had been up to. They threatened to call in the police. Charles cowered. He felt emotionally destitute. He almost attempted suicide.

In the end, Charles' parents moved away from the area with the hope of setting up a new life for, and with, Charles.

Ω

I have hopefully been successful at transforming many of my weaknesses into meeknesses. During this transformational period, I discovered that I am more than a conscious *Dense Body*. I discovered that I am more than the generous soul that people say I am. I discovered much more about the central import of my mind and the illusory tricks it can fall foul of. More than that, I discovered ...

> *We are all spirit flowing in a human form but not restricted to it.*
> Jeanne Ayling

Part VIII: Mind, Body, Soul and Spirit

The Spiritual Constituents of Adult Hu-Man

You invoke the *Laws of Attraction and Consequence* through the machination of your mind, body, soul and spirit. These elements and the connections between them make up the framework of your inner world's (conscious, unconscious, emotional, intellectual, physical and spiritual) constitution.

Mind - the Decision Making, Gateway Computer:

The mind functions as an intelligent gateway computer between spirit, soul and body respectively. It makes decisions influenced by the emotive responses you give the environment around you. The mind receives, filters and regulates the flow of information from and to spirit, soul and body.

Information of which you are aware flows through and is processed by the conscious mind. Likewise, information of which you are unaware is processed by your unconscious mind. In both cases a complete journal of your mind's 'data-processing' activity and outputs is stored in the *Etheric Body*.

Let's recap some glossary terms.

Unconscious mind – passes the beliefs held and decisions made by the conscious mind to each and every cell in your body along with information of which you are not conscious. The unconscious mind protects you from information that it feels you cannot cope with. All the information is stored away in your holographic *Etheric Body*. Each and every body cell is a fractal (the whole is contained in each fractal) of your *Etheric Body*'s hologram.

Body cell – Each and every body cell contains your whole life history, your memories, feelings, reactions and actions, everything that's happened to you knowingly and unknowingly. It is placed in cellular memory.

Illustration 10: Spiritual Constituents of Hu-Man Mind, Body, Soul and Spirit[90]

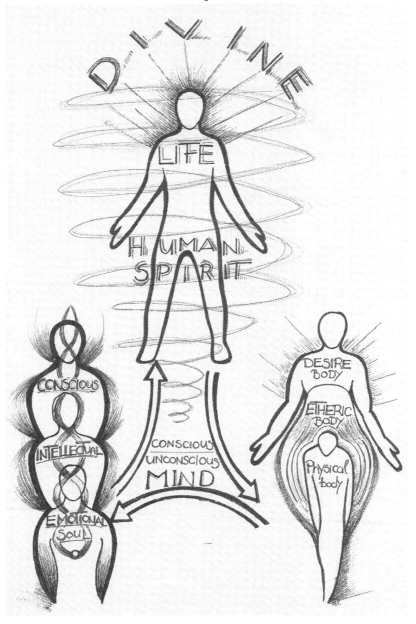

---

[90] Ref: *Chapter III, Man and the Method of Evolution,* of *The Rosicrucian Cosmo Conception Mystic Christianity,* by Max Heindel, 1922.

Vibe – is the vibration that your DNA sends out to the universe. You can increase the power of this vibe by acting as if you already have what you seek to manifest.

DNA – is your transmitter to the universe. It transmits your signal of how you are feeling in the moment – your vibe. Its signal is governed by your unconscious mind. DNA sends out to the universe via spirit[91]. DNA is synchronised with spirit via the mind. And DNA regulates the function of the body cells within your physical body. So how is this information transmitted between the mind and body cells?

Physical Body:

In the context of your *Spiritual Constitution*, the glandular system and the nervous system regulate the flow of information between your mind and body. Specifically:

The Pituitary gland is located at the base of the brain. In Druid meditation, it is represented by the *Brow Centre/6th Chakra*, just above and between the eyebrows. It is personified by its regent, *Hermes*, the winged messenger of the gods.

Illustration 11: Pituitary and Pineal Gland

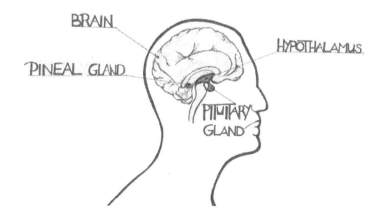

---

[91] Ref: As we saw in *Part VI: Beyond the Time-Space Continuum,* chapter, *Where Space and Time Don't Exist*

Illustration 12: The Pituitary Gland's Functions

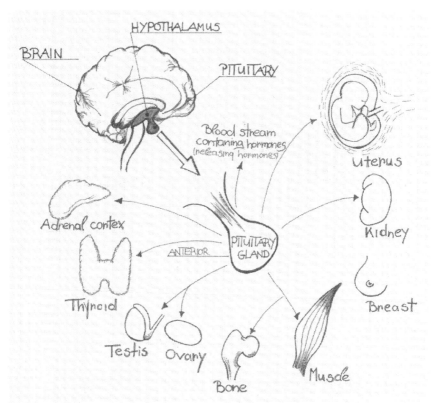

The Pituitary gland releases hormones into the blood stream that govern the functioning of major glands and parts of the body: the adrenal cortex, thyroid, testes or ovaries, bone and muscles, breasts, kidneys and uterus.

The *Brow Centre* locates where the physical body and *Etheric Body* meet as one. Information to and from the *Etheric Body* flows through the *Brow Centre*.

The **Pineal gland** produces the serotonin derivative melatonin, a hormone that affects the modulation of wake/sleep patterns and seasonal functions. In Druid meditation, it is represented by the *Crown Centre/7th Chakra*, in the crown of the head. It is personified by its regent, *Selene*, the moon goddess of emotions.

The Pineal gland (*Selene*) and the Pituitary gland (*Hermes*) together form a triad with the sun. *Hermes* is the ray, the messenger of the sun's etheric light, wisdom. *Hermes* also represents your personality which is shaped by the past, your memories and how you respond to them, the past tense.

The mythical *Hermes* was a thief and a trickster. He steals the sun's light (present tense) and in its place attempts to deal with *Selene* in the past tense. *Hermes* attempts to persuade *Selene* to reflect the sun's light in your body but clouded by the past tense (emotions).

The analogy can be strengthened metaphorically on a number of levels. When you attempt to stare at the sun you are blinded, you see nothing. Whereas on a cloudless night with a full moon (free from negative emotions from the past - hence the term 'clouded in emotions') you can see the stars; you see infinity; you see the full power of the reflected light of the sun in the moon (*Selene*).

Selene refuses to negotiate with *Hermes'* attempts to reflect the past tense into your body. The past tense is in effect at war with the present tense - a war the past tense cannot win if you seek your truth.

Hermes must surrender to the present tense willingly and share its prize with *Selene*. As your Pineal gland awakens, it reflects the glory of the sun's etheric light inside your physical body. The reflected etheric light energises the body for its spiritual journey.

That etheric light illumines your spine, muscles, tissues and every nook and cranny in your body. The present tense nurtures the *seed of the star* in your heart. In the same way that a seed in the ground is drawn to the sunlight at the surface each Spring season - so is that *seed star* in your heart. It knows not what the light will bring but places its faith in itself, its journey and its destiny.

> *That upon which light is shone becomes that light.*
> (Paraphrased from) St Paul

The seed in your heart becomes the light of the ray that *Hermes* presents unfettered for *Selene* to shine within you. You personify an everlasting star. You shine.

The Parasympathetic and Sympathetic Nervous Systems make up the Autonomic Nervous System. They regulate the flow of information from the neurons through and alongside the spinal cord between the brain and the eyes, head, lungs, heart, stomach, intestines, kidneys, bladder and anus.

The Parasympathetic and Sympathetic systems are symbolised allegorically in ancient wisdom by the caduceus.

In Greek Mythology, the caduceus is the staff carried by *Hermes*, the messenger of the gods. The caduceus is a symbol of negotiation between two realms in which balanced exchange and reciprocity are recognized as ideals. It is formed by two serpents entwined around a central staff, up to a pair of wings at the head of the staff.

Illustration 13: Caduceus

Illustration 14: The Autonomic [(A) Sympathetic + (B) Parasympathetic] Nervous System

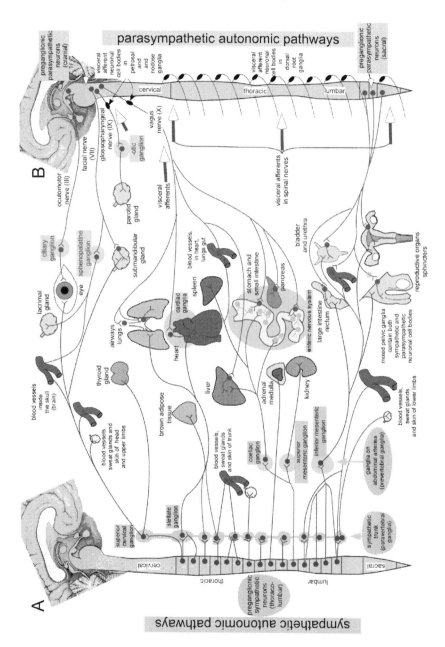

Preceding page:
Summary of sympathetic and parasympathetic autonomic neural outflows from the central nervous system. Figure drawn by the authors, incorporating material from Gray's Anatomy 31st Edition 1954, and from Cannon and Rosenblueth Physiology of the Autonomic Nervous System, 1937.[92]

One serpent (see Illustration 13, The Caduceus) represents the power of light, the other darkness; the light and darkness you embrace on your *life's journey*. In this context, the serpents symbolise the parasympathetic and sympathetic nervous systems entwined around the spine.

1. The Parasympathetic nervous system prepares your body to 'rest and digest'. In this context, 'digest' can mean food. It can also mean wisdom. In meditation, for example, your heart beat and breathing slow down and body temperature falls. The electromagnetic frequencies emitted by your brain decline from their normal Beta state (alert and working), to Alpha (relaxed and reflective), to Theta (drowsy and dreamlike) conscious state of awareness. If your brain drops into the Delta frequency, you fall asleep. On the shoreline between consciousness and sub-consciousness, the parasympathetic nervous system awakens your consciousness to the world within.

2. The Sympathetic nervous system prepares your body for 'fight or flight'. When activated, the Sympathetic nervous system releases *noradrenalin* (in USA, *nor-epinephrine*) to the heart, adrenal glands and muscles of movement. The adrenal glands release adrenalin into the bloodstream. Blood is diverted from the digestive system to increase the oxygen to all muscles of movement. The heart beats faster. Your body temperature rises. You perspire. You become angry, stressed or fearful. Your digestion system (supported by the Parasympathetic nervous system) closes down.

    If you're digesting food you can become sick, e.g. running straight after a meal. In extreme cases of fear, you can urinate or defecate uncontrollably. When the body is persistently in 'fight or flight', it gets no support from the parasympathetic system to 'rest and

---

[92] Ref: http://www.scholarpedia.org/article/Autonomic_nervous_system

digest'. This leaves the body susceptible to gastro-intestinal illnesses such as diarrhoea, stomach ulcers, Crohn's disease and colitis.

Illustration 15: Chakra System

3. The central staff is an allegory for the Central nervous (Chakra) system, protected by the spinal column. It rises from the base to the top of the spine, through the neck, around the back of the head, up and around the front of the brain like a shepherd's crook, to the *Brow Centre*.

Illustration 16: Shepherd's Crook. The Spinal Column of Light

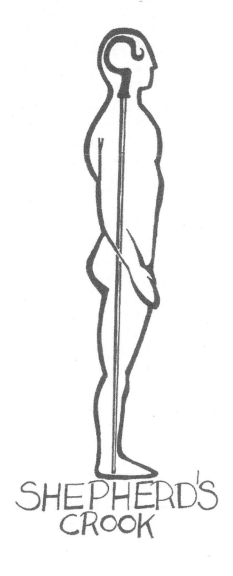

4. The top of the caduceus (see Illustration 13) containing the Crown (7th) and Brow Centre (6th) chakras looks like rays of light beaming out from a lamp. Combine the central staff to this image of a lamp. You see a lamp-stand, a *golden lamp-stand.*

Remember therefore, how from the heaven above
You fell to earth and with your zeal renewed,
Perform the first great works of sanctitude.
Lest I, when I am come, award disgrace,
And move your lampstand from its wonted place.
From *A Message to the Hierarchy of Chronos*
(Saturn), the Regent of the 1st Chakra[93].

Healthy body cells shine literally; they emit bio-photons of light. The cells throughout your body harmonise to emit light. Imagine each body cell as a musical instrument, combining sub-atomically and coherently, in a huge orchestra to play your tune, your vibration of health.

The German bio-physicist, Fritz-Albert Popp, discovered that the number of bio-photons emitted from the left and right hands of a healthy young person balance each other out[94]. Coherence and balance in the light you shine implies good heath; incoherence and imbalance imply the opposite. You can thus see how the body symptoms of ill health caused by extreme fear, for example, equate to havoc at the cellular level. Fear acts as a trap door to the light. Open 'the door!'

As you release fear, you step closer to becoming your *true self*. You create balance and achieve the harmony of opposites. The closer you become to and express your *true self*, the stronger the energy/light that flows up through your spine. You illuminate your spine – as symbolised in Druid meditation.[95] The seven energy centres (chakras) - up through your spinal column, crown and brow - align and glow their radiant colours respectively. Yet the illuminated spine and chakras symbolise more than the harmony of opposites, i.e. temperance.

---

[93] Ref: *The Restored New Testament, The Hellenic Fragments,* by James Morgan Pryse, published by The Theosophical Press.
[94] Ref: *The Field* by Lynne McTaggart, chapter, *Beings of Light*
[95] Refer to *Part XV, Case Story: The Cathedral,* for instructions on the Druid meditation process to illuminate the spine.

Temperance is a stepping stone. It affords you the insight to recognise that the serpents of darkness and light are equally important to the spiritual nature of your life and your physical wellbeing. As the serpents of light and dark harmonise their opposite nature, they become one serpent - as represented by the rod of the Greek god of medicine, Asclepius - the personification of a divine healer. Hippocrates worshipped Asclepius.

Illustration 17: The Staff of Asclepius

The harmony of opposites, the balance between the duality of light and dark however does not create non-duality. Harmony creates unity. Non-duality possesses harmony, balance and unity but it is none of these things, or anything. Conceptually, and I am at my conceptual limit when I write this, non-duality is an infinitely higher vibration or dimension. Non-duality is indivisible.

Summary: the oft used phrase, "Healthy in body, healthy in spirit", is an understated truism and fundamental to the functioning of your *Spiritual Constituents.* When you imbue truth throughout your mind, body, soul and spirit – you express your *true self.* **You shine.**

Etheric Body:

The *Etheric Body* as you may recall[96] stores the inputs, outputs and all information processed by your conscious and unconscious mind from the 'alpha to omega' of your life; every moment from the embryo to the moment you read this sentence – right now.

Desire Body:

At the lower levels, the *desire body* stores:
- Sensual wishes and passions of the *false ego*
- Impressions of others - those who have more wealth and fame, for example.

Most of us have striven, with good intent, to provide for our loved ones or have our "fifteen minutes of fame". Beware, when the lower level desires are fulfilled this can lead to indifference to higher level desires. When you have all the basics and luxuries of life, beware of idleness. In the past I have basked idly in the glory of success and occasionally seen many of its associated trappings disappear.

> *Because you say, 'I have amassed a store*
> *Of wondrous riches, and need nothing more'*
> From *Message to the Hierarchy of Selene,* the opening of
> the Crown (7th) Chakra, the Moon Goddess[97]

The higher levels of your *desire body* yearn for consciousness development, light, truth and to share what abundances come your way - oneness. When you share your abundances, these higher levels of desire feed your soul with the *right feeling*, a sense of fulfilment.

---

[96] Ref: *Part I: You Are All Magicians,* chapter, *The Physical and the Etheric.*
[97] Ref: *The Restored New Testament, The Hellenic Fragments,* by James Morgan Pryse, published by The Theosophical Press.

Soul:

Your soul seeks your life's quest to find, open, become and express your *true self*. It informs your spirit of progress at three levels:

1. **Conscious Soul**

   You act upon decisions borne out of courage and fulfilment. The decisions have the *right feel*. You raise consciousness. The *Conscious Soul* acknowledges progress has been made along the spiral path. Your *Conscious Soul* awakens your *Divine Spirit* to new possibilities. Spirit raises the vibration of the DNA in your physical body. You project and attract a higher vibration.

2. **Intellectual Soul**

   Your memories, studies, actions, thoughts, feelings and life experiences inform the soul of the wisdom you have amassed in this lifetime. Like the *Conscious Soul* as your wisdom grows so does your capacity to share that wisdom. You never lose that wisdom but it often takes willpower to choose courage (i.e. *cleanse the mind of shame, anger, sadness and fear*) and apply it, firstly for yourself. As you progress, your *Intellectual Soul* awakens your *Life Spirit* to share higher wisdom with all humankind. You enhance your capability as a seer.

3. **Emotional Soul**

   The desires and emotions of the *desire body* inform the *Emotional Soul*. Desires borne out of shame, anger, sadness and fear divert you from your emotional journey to your *true self*. As you release these *four seeds of negative karma* you can fill the void created with enabling emotions such as self worth, self compassion, joy and love. As you progress, the *Emotional Soul* increases the efficiency of *Human Spirit;* now less fettered by negative emotional blocks in the mind.

Spirit:

Spirit inspires. Spirit is the super-conscious force that manifests form.[98] Its power is filtered through the mind. In common parlance, you call your filtered spirit your 'character'. Consciously, character is how others see and describe you. But at a subliminal level it's the *vibe* of your character that people really tune into. Your *vibe* affects which people and events you attract, repel or merely pass by. More than any other factor, your character determines the nature of your journey to your destiny. The good news: you can reshape your character for the better at any time you choose. Treasures of knowledge, moments of light or miracles are available twenty four hours a day.

The Lodges all shall know that I am he,
Who searches loins and hearts to oversee.
All works creative and all works that find
Treasures of knowledge in the Cosmic Mind.
From *The Message to the Hierarchy of Helios*, the awakening of the Sun God within us, 4th Chakra, the heart.[99]

It will help to recap some laws of the universe and the tricks, meanderings and wiliness of the mind that can inhibit you from finding and applying such *treasures of knowledge*.

---

[98] For more information on the three levels of spirit (*divine, human* and *life spirit*) refer to notes, *About Spirit,* found in the preface of this book. Also refer to chapter, *Your Laws of Attraction and Consequence,* found in *Part IX.*
[99] Ref: *The Restored New Testament, The Hellenic Fragments,* by James Morgan Pryse, published by The Theosophical Press.

Paul C Burr

Part IX: A Collection of Blogs and Essays

About the Laws of Consequence and Reversibility

Much is written about the *Law of Attraction*. Beneath it lie two fundamental laws. The first is inescapable. It has many books written about it under the title of *karma*.

1. *The Law of Consequence*

When you choose <u>not</u> to shine light into the shadows
within your psyche, you attract people and situations
that mirror those shadows. They point, to help you return
to the spiral path your soul seeks. The path lies in front of
you always. Look for it. When the time is right, your inner
seer will whisper between your thoughts.
Listen carefully.
The seer speaks from the stillness deep down within your
body, not your mind.
Choose courage.
Heed the words.
Give them the acid test for surety.
Do they uplift your and others' consciousness?
If so, act upon the words given.
If not, be wary of the advice given for it is your false-ego
fobbing you.
Ponder.
You already possess the answer to every question you
ask.
Tune in.

The second is the fundamental law of manifestation or, if you will, magic:

2. The Law of Reversibility

Situations (events and people) affect your feelings. Imagining those same feelings will manifest the same events and people into your life.

Recognise that what you choose to manifest (by imagining the feeling) already exists in the here and now. As does what you choose not to manifest. Both exist side by side, untethered by time and space.

When you sit in the feeling of scarcity that's what you manifest. When you imagine the feeling of abundance, guess what? You receive what the feeling of abundance imagines.

These two laws form the basis of everything you attract in life. Whether you attract what your heart really desires or not is ultimately up to how you make up your mind. Your relationship with your mind has the power to submit to, dilute, distort or veto spirit's power to manifest. You choose your own fate.

You have a destination to reach, a map and an inner guide to point the best way forward. The path you choose though is up to you.

The remaining chapters in *Part IX* describe some of the detours your mind can take you. I attempt to share what it feels like when you take your spiritual journey. I use a client case story along with further metaphors to help you understand some of the most abstract *map reading* principles that I've come across.

Some of the concepts, although simple, took me a few years to get my head around. If nought else, I hope my explanations save you time. Happy trails!

You Rationalise

You cannot always trust your conscious memory. Were you able to access it, your unconscious memory though stores everything in minute and accurate detail. When thinking about a situation that I feel bad or shameful about, I try and remember to discern if what my conscious mind tells me is truth or illusion. I often recall the following phrase once spoken to me in a business context:

You can lose yourself. But you can't hide.
John Humphrey, when CEO of the Forum Corporation,
Boston MA, circa 1995.

Illustration 18: Shame

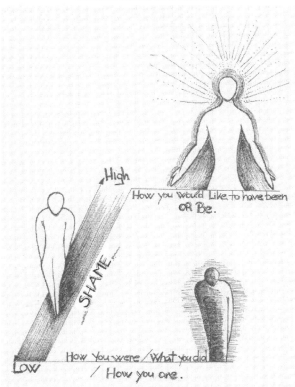

Let's say you fail to live up to the standards you expect of yourself. You let someone down or hurt them badly. You feel ashamed, fearful or saddened by the self image of yourself not behaving in the way you would have liked. Your behaviour pricks your conscience. You can tend to rationalise. You find a logical and tenable reason to bridge the gap between the vision of how you would like to be, have been or behaved - and your actual state of being (present or past) or behaviour.

You find an articulate way of rationalising (= rational lies) away or justifying your behaviour. You shift the blame subtly on to something, someone else or even fate. It needs to be fairly subtle so that you have a good story (not truth) with which to speak to your conscience. You 'duck and dive' your way from truth to illusion. When your 'ducking and diving' is good enough, you might even tell yourself that your conscience is clear.

Should you continue to repeat your illusory tale, it can become hardwired in your conscious memory. You, in effect, cut yourself off from facts and replace them with illusion. You base your subsequent thoughts, words and actions on illusion. You shape your character on illusion.

Actions to achieve sensual wishes (lower levels of the *desire body*) fuelled by your *false-ego*, can become misaligned with your heart's will (higher levels of the *desire body*: light, miracles, treasures of knowledge). You veer away from the path to your *true self.* You can get back on the path when you choose <u>not</u> to over-embrace or bypass the fear that caused you to rationalise in the first place. That fear however, can be subconscious.

Fear Bypasses your Conscious Mind

Sometimes the fear that drives your actions bypasses your conscious mind altogether. With best intent, you might do what you feel is good and proper, unaware that you are running a subliminal subroutine.

Case Story: Franz's Fear that Bypassed his Conscious Mind

Franz was a kind, generous and reasonably good looking man who loved to do everything possible for others, especially a new girlfriend. When he started a relationship he would wine and dine his partner lavishly. Franz would do all the little things when he and his partner were together: make the tea, cook, wash up, make sure his partner was comfortable always, provide a personal taxi service, splash out on gifts and so on.

Some partners welcomed this attention. But for some reason Franz didn't remain attractive to such partners for long. Most new partners, and there were several, somehow went off the idea of a long term relationship with Franz.

All were grateful for Franz's generosity. But something in Franz's vibe put women off a long term relationship; especially those he was the fondest of. They would leave Franz often distraught with loneliness and quizzical about what he had done wrong. Why did his kindness seem to put a series of women off him even though each relationship seemed to start off so well? Eventually, Franz sought my help.

I helped Franz trace the source of his relationship problems to his childhood. Franz's mother was, you might say politely, "of a flighty disposition". As far back as he could remember, Franz's parents had a quarrelsome relationship. They were a wealthy family so Franz was looked after by a series of nannies and housekeepers throughout his childhood.

His mother was not only absent emotionally, she would often leave the marital home and not return for long periods. Upon each return, little Franz would try and compensate for his mother's unhappiness by being kind and doting. He continued with this behaviour into his adult relationships. It took Franz nigh on thirty years to bring this sub (conscious)-routine to the surface.

I helped Franz to realise that his over-attentive behaviour was driven by fear as much as by love. As soon as he started a relationship, Franz's 'not wanting to be left on my own again' subroutine would kick in. The new partner would pick up on this. He and his new partner's collective vibe, which started so resonantly together, would start to lose its coherence. Their wavelengths would drift apart. The attraction would cease. The relationship would end.

Franz wished for a loving, lasting relationship but his overall character-signal contained a different vibration; fear of not-wanting-his-partner-to-leave-him. Franz's vibrations and wishes were out of kilter.

Even when he became aware of his fear strategy, it still took Franz some time to find the courage to allow his fear to be and put his trust in spirit. In doing so he slowly changed his vibe. He took a truthful and gradual approach to his relationships. He attracted a woman on his new wavelength. Their relationship developed the 'right feel' about it – truth and love. They both gave and received, happily together.

Ω

Franz's case shows how fear can sometimes bypass your conscious mind and become a *subconscious counter intention* that stops you from attracting that which your heart desires. You act out of fear but you don't know it. You attract the consequences of that fear (not love) from the world around you. Consciously or not, fear locks the door that bars you from the path to your truth.

Fear Locks Out your Conscious Mind

...All that happens is the result of character; the only manner in which the destiny can be changed is to change the character.....
the chart of birth....is merely a map of character.....
(and) can be markedly altered in any direction desired.
CC Zain[100]

[100] Ref: Chapter 4, *Doctrine of Nativities* from the book, *Laws of Occultism, Inner Plane Theory and the Fundamentals of Psychic Phenomena* by CC Zain, published by the Church of Light.

Whether you rationalise your behaviour and/or act out a subconscious holding pattern (as in Franz's case in the previous section), you shape your character to act on illusion.

You avoid what you need to learn from the energy in the dark shadows within your psyche. Consequently, you invoke the patterns that can cause shame, anger, sadness or fear to return to you. Why? Because the darkness within beckons light. It summons the situations, people and events to bring its existence to your attention. You attract, in effect, a mirror of that which is within. You avoid shining light into this darkness. You allow a locked *door* to bar your way and the *door's* lock is made of shame, anger, sadness and/or fear. The *door* locks you out from that which your soul seeks, the higher levels of your *desire body*. Outside the *door*, you can spend your time chasing *petty desires* (lower levels of the *desire body)*. But these low level wishes are out of kilter with your will (higher levels of the *desire body)*.

Outside the *door*, life loops. You end up going around in circles. As you keep looping you become sick and tired. If you still keep looping you become sick and tired of being sick and tired. You find yourself back at the *door* again. When you eventually knock, it will be unlocked. You can enter the *door* at anytime. The lock (fear) although apparently real was illusory.

As long as you attempt to avoid fear (unlocking the *door*) you may well succeed but successful avoidance doesn't take away the fear. Avoidance is not the characteristic required to allow that fear into your consciousness either. But the nature of duality means that when you have learned enough about avoidance you ready yourself to appreciate not-avoidance, i.e. allowing that fear into your consciousness so that you can release it to find the wisdom beyond it. That wisdom, the very nature of which raises your consciousness, transforms your character and thus reshapes your future, *spiritual step* by *spiritual step.*

This reminds me of the oft used phrase by NLP practitioners...

There's no such thing as failure - only feedback.

147

Feedback tells us when we have cleaned up our act. Cleaning up however requires us to notice and become highly responsive to helpful thoughts - and have the nous and willpower to bypass unhelpful ones.

The Responsive Mind Clothes your Thoughts

Thoughts can be observed as electrical storms popping up in your brain. Repetitive thoughts follow well trodden neural pathways. Thoughts are energy so their electrons must come from somewhere. Thoughts pop into the mind from the *World of Thought*, where you clothe them in accord with the *desire body* you seek to shape for yourself. You clothe thoughts in desire or repulsion.

Thoughts, like viruses, have no respect for the body they inhabit. Thoughts are neither good nor bad. They are neither correct nor incorrect. They neither work nor don't work - until you clothe them. Once clothed, some thoughts serve you well and some do not.

Should you let a thought dominate your mind, it transforms into a feeling. The more dominant the thought over time, the stronger the feeling over that same duration; the stronger the *vibe* that feeling emits; the more powerful it attracts that which is liken to itself.

The power of a thought (or feeling) is a function of its intensity and duration.

The mind also passes thoughts back to the *World of Thought* when it is done with them.

Herein lies a simple technique. If you're having an unhelpful thought, notice it and pass it back up to the *World of Thought*.

A Step-by-Step Guide to How your Mind Interacts with Higher Dimensions

Step 1: The mind selects/perceives a thought that it elicits from the *World of Thought.*

Illustration 19: *World of Thought* ←→Mind

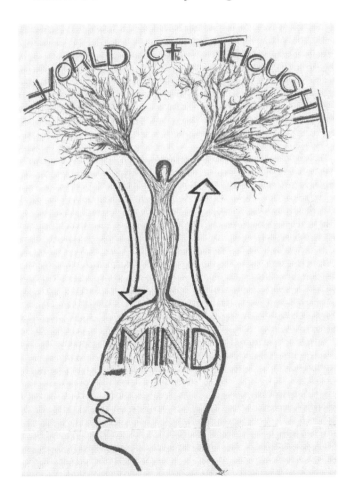

Thoughts are like streams of 'electrons'. They are 'downloaded' from a higher vibrational dimension known by the ancients as *The World of Thought.*

Step 2: The mind cross references the thought with memories, conscious and unconscious, stored in the *Etheric Body*. These include all past thoughts and life experiences.

Illustration 20: Mind ←→ *Etheric Body*

This is a very sensitive step. It is here where we meet (what Joe Vitale describes in his book, the *Missing Secret*[101] as) *subconscious counter intentions*.

---

[101] The audio book, *The Missing Secret*, by Joe Vitale contains a wealth of practical exercises to help you manifest what you desire, free of any *subconscious counter intentions*. I recommend it highly.

For example, in the *Case Story: Franz's Fear that Bypassed his Conscious Mind*,[102] Franz had two subconscious programmes (*counter intentions*) that read:

1. *"I am not worthy to give or receive love"* which manifests itself in the form of shame, sadness and perhaps anger too. AND...
2. *"I fear love"* because I have been hurt before and don't want to get hurt again.

The mind carries the positive intention of seeking a loving relationship along with the *subconscious counter intentions* simultaneously into the next step.

Step 3: The mind then refers to the will (heart's higher level etheric desires) and wishes (head's lower level sensual desires) of your *desire body*.

If there's one purpose to being a druid, it's to align your desire body's lower level desires with its higher levels.
Brenda Sanderson, The Druid Order, London

In Franz's case story, his desire for a loving relationship is thwarted by *subconscious counter intentions*, low self worth (shame, sadness and possibly anger) and fear.

On a wider scale I have had clients with similar *subconscious counter intentions* that manifested themselves in a number of ways:

- We attract a series of troublesome relationships with like-for-like partners who themselves feel unworthy of love or a willingness to love.
- We avoid getting too close in any relationship in case we get hurt. We keep our distance. We embrace our fear of love.

---

[102] Ref: *Part IX: A Collection of Blogs and Essays*, chapter, *Fear Bypasses your Conscious Mind*

Illustration 21: Mind ←→ *Desire Body*

- We indulge in distractions to distance ourselves further from that fear. On the surface these distractions can appear as healthy activities - such as keeping fit, charity work and caring for others. The underlying issue is that we engage in these activities to avoid facing that which we fear, in this case, love.
- We may indulge in not so healthy sensual pleasures (such as alcohol and drug abuse, promiscuity or gambling) to insulate our mind from acknowledging our fear of love.

We see how these *subconscious counter intentions* (the product of shame, anger, sadness and fear - usually from childhood) negate the power of your mind to manifest your heart's desires. Your DNA projects subliminal negative emotions to counteract the positive emotion your heart desires. You thus attract repeating situations, people and events for you to learn that which you have not learned yet from the shadows within.

The *missing secret* is to clean out these *subconscious counter intentions* that lurk in the form of lower level desires. Clean them out and replace them with intentions that align with and embrace your heart's desires fully.

The purpose of my life is to clean.
Dr Hew Len, Ho'oponopono Master[103]

Spiritual fulfilment thus requires a *"cleansing of the mind"*. You manifest that which will make you fulfilled truly, when you clean out all the negative information pertaining to any shame, anger, sadness and fear that lurk within. Should you miss something or 'try to hide something under the carpet', you attract a *karmic* response according to the *Law of Consequence.*

The mind is at the fulcrum. Each of the three worlds: *Thought, Desire* and *Physical,* interacts and only interacts through the mind. The mind chooses which path to follow. The mind selects the outcome it seeks to achieve.

---

[103] Ref: http://www.youtube.com/watch?v=OL972JihAmg

153

Illustration 22: Fulfilling your Heart's Desires is a Cleaning Process

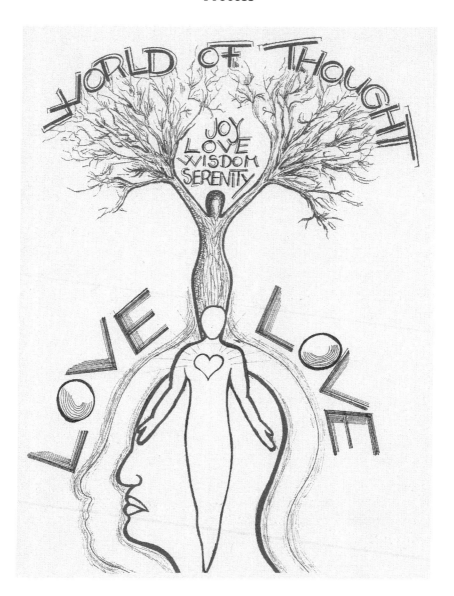

Because you say, 'I have amassed a store
Of wondrous riches, and need nothing more,'
And know not that of all the powers of mind
You are the starveling, piteous and blind.

A beggar, ragged near to nudity,
I therefore counsel you to buy of me
Gold, pure as Wisdom, tested in the fire.
That you may thus enduring wealth acquire,

And garments white as Truth, that you may clothe
Yourself in beauty, not in rags you loathe,
And magic salve wherewith your eyes to smear,
That you may share the vision of the Seer.

All whom I love I teach, but first confute,
Thus from their minds all errors to uproot.
For truth by biased minds is ne'er divined;
Therefore seek wisdom, but first cleanse the mind.
From *Message to the Hierarchy of Selene,* the opening of
the Crown (7th) Chakra, the Moon Goddess[104]

You can allow your mind to align your wishes (lower level desires) with your heart's will (higher level desires) or not. You can choose to create a new experience that fulfils your heart desires or repeat an old one, invoked by negative emotions. You can choose wisdom or you can choose ignorance until you choose wisdom.

It's like a light switch. When you switch the light (wisdom) on, you release the darkness (ignorance) - for it no longer serves a purpose.

---

104 Ref: *The Restored New Testament, The Hellenic Fragments,* by James Morgan Pryse, published by The Theosophical Press.

155

All along, at every step of the way, in every decision you make in life, **you have the freedom and power to turn the switch on or off at will**.

The Creative Mind and the Law of Attraction - and Other Laws of Nature

Clothes maketh the thought.

You see a beggar on the street. Do you, for example,
1. Help them out or give them money?
2. Walk on the far side of the pavement and hope they will not call out to you?
3. Tell them to clear off?

Your clothed thoughts influence your reactions to what you attract. In all three cases the beggar remains the same beggar. Your choice is how you respond, which in turn influences what you attract or manifest in the future.

When you latch on to new thoughts, you can attract new 'realities'. But thoughts themselves are not reality. They may appear real; especially those thoughts that are well drilled into your psyche by your programming and habits. Thoughts need not be fixed as long as you choose them to be otherwise.

You cannot change what you have experienced in the past. But you can change the thought with which you clothe the memory of that experience at any time. Remember, thoughts know no difference between the physical and non-physical. Thoughts are ethereal; they come from and return to the *World of Thought*. Choose heavenly thoughts and you can create heaven on earth.

The Law of Attraction: Heaven on Earth

A learned friend sent me a message that coincided spookily with an experience I'd had during the night before. Her message read,

If we do not desire something or feel a pleasant emotion about it, we do not strive to make it happen.
Passion is your power for manifestation.

Jeanne Ayling

Many of my friend's messages arrive when I need her wisdom most. Here's what happened the night before.

Before I went to sleep I pleaded with spirit that I'd had enough of my desire loops. I sought help. I wanted guidance because whatever I was doing wasn't working. I fell into a deep sleep but not for long.

I entered into a dream world of turmoil and darkness inside a huge complex ethereal machine. Cogs and wheels ground away but all seemed to work against one another. Parts kept stuttering and jamming. Then they would attempt to reverse out of gear to get going again – like the inside of a huge faulty printer trying to unjam itself. The machine had almost ground to a halt – almost, but not completely. I awoke.

An archangel appeared. We spoke of my desires and delineated those which belong to the upper echelons of my *Desire World* from the lower. She asked me to focus on that which I really wanted in my heart of hearts. At the same time she asked me to focus on all the shame, anger, sadness and fear I associated with NOT having what I desired.

She taught me to raise up to spirit all the shame, anger, sadness and fear associated with the one particular yearning I craved. I became aware that releasing fear came with a consequence. I would be obliged to choose courage. ....mmm!?!

Nonetheless I completed her instruction. But then came the surprise. She instructed me to now raise my desire to spirit and let that go too. I paused. I realised that releasing desire to spirit, especially the desire for something so important to me, wasn't easy. I badly wanted my wish to come true.

The angel waited patiently. 'Ah ha!' I awakened to the logic of the angel's instruction.

- Spirit can only manifest a desire if I release it to spirit and detach my mind from it.
- If I do not raise it to spirit explicitly then spirit has nothing explicit to work on.
- If I do not detach myself from my desire then my mind will fetter spirit's power to manifest
- When I submit myself completely to spirit, it will manifest what the higher levels of my *desire body* truly seek.

For the first time in my life I now understood, <u>in my heart</u>, the phrase....

A burning passion coupled with absolute detachment
(from the outcome) *is the key to all success.*
Gandhi

And...

Plant and nurture without desiring the fruit.
Jeanne Ayling, Spiritual Mechanic, Hove, UK.

I raised my palms upward above my head and raised my heart's desire to spirit. I said it forcefully and added the phrase, rather amateurishly, "and I really mean it!" I wanted to demonstrate commitment to my words.

I released my desire with all the heart I could muster. I realised suddenly how my desires had dominated my erstwhile thought world. Prior, when I yearned or felt fearful about not receiving what I yearned for, I was in a future dream world. When I became angry, sad or felt I must be unworthy about not getting what I yearned for, I'd been living a past memory. I'd spent little time in the present tense, the here and now, the path on which life takes place.

My passion for life was being held back. My friend's message made me realise some words of ancient wisdom that I'd pondered upon for years.

In order to journey the path, you must develop a passion for the path (life), not your destination. You become the path.

I thanked both my magical friends for the abundance I'd been blessed with – two angels, one in spirit form and one in human form. They'd taught me the secret ways of heaven on earth.

Not Knowing: a Key Milestone in the Journey

If you were to ask yourself, "What does spirit want for me specifically?" Over and above, "Feeling happy all the time", would you have an answer? Not that "feeling happy all the time" isn't a wonderful outcome (I wish!).

If you were to ask yourself, "In my heart of hearts, my very soul, what do I seek more than anything else in life?" Would you know the answer to this second question?

Perhaps you have an answer to one or both questions? The answer to both however is one and the same. In your heart of hearts, you are spirit clothed in a human form.

I ask these two questions because even when I do have an answer I find myself asking, "Do I really mean this?" When the answer is "yes", there arrives a second question, "Do I have the will and faith in myself to imagine it?" I sometimes have second thoughts.

Are you having second thoughts? Which is two thoughts too many.
Eckhart Tolle

It's at this point we arrive at what I found to be the most abstract and subtle discovery I've made since I started to take a proactive approach to finding my *true self*. It's simple but it took a lot of faith in self to start to understand it conceptually and experiment with it. It still represents work in progress for me. Nonetheless here lies one of the great paradoxes I've met on my spiritual journey - about security[105].

Security

The word *Mercury* can be thought of as two words. *Mer-* which is French for sea or seeing and *cury* or cure. The word *secure* is the same as *Mercury*. Your real security is in just seeing and understanding that you do not know what is of value or not, be prepared to understand that you do not know the truth - then you can see.

All thoughts are of the past or future. Even then, thoughts of the future are of memories replaying themselves. Thoughts and any subsequent feelings you have are thus based in the past tense. There is a gap. Spirit works in the here and now, outside of time and space.

Furthermore if your thoughts are swayed by even the smallest particle of shame, anger, sadness or guilt then they cannot and do not connect with your true nature - which is love.

This doesn't mean that what you think is truth isn't truth. It simply means that you do not and indeed cannot know what truth is in your mind.

You cannot liaise with spirit in your mind. You can experience spirit and hear its whispers but as you listen, what you hear is already in the past tense. The present tense gives birth to the past tenses moment by moment. And everything is possible in the here and now, present tense.

"Where's the security in this?" I asked myself.

Spirit, and only spirit, knows what your heart truly desires. **When the wishes in your head align with the will of your heart, you will get what you <u>think</u> you want, what you really wish for.**

When you don't get what you want and have presented (what to the best of your knowledge is) your truth to spirit - then spirit <u>will</u> always provide what's best for you. The courage in making yourself

---

[105] Ref: Extract from the druidic teaching *Learning not to Know: Mercury/Gemini/Pituitary*, Yew Tree Printing, UK.

defenceless to spirit is your strength - in accordance with the will of your heart.

If you haven't grasped this concept of security fully yet, I apologise. I didn't find it easy either so here's an example that will explain the security in *not knowing truth* further.

Case Story: Accepting that I Didn't Know Truth

Some time ago I fell in love with a woman who said she loved me but not in the same way. I wanted her by my side, physically, emotionally and spiritually. Our relationship yoyo-ed. She was attracted to me but when we got a bit too close, I'd not see her for days, sometimes weeks but she always returned as if nothing was wrong. I would get upset and angry during these periods of absence. I felt she was taking advantage of me. I resented that she did not return my love and I didn't have the strength to distance myself from her either. Later on, I looked at how our relationship mirrored that which I had with myself. I looked at me in the mirror.

I saw that it was me who couldn't love her the way she loved me. This woman had never lied to me. She told me that she was attracted to me but not in a physical way. She didn't have an issue with the way she loved me. I did. Why did I get so hurt and angry? When I found out, my bouts of resentment turned to shame.

I felt incapable of loving this woman without physical intimacy and monogamy as conditions. (Conditional love is not real love.) I also carried fears of isolation and not being wanted. These fears further fuelled my shamed pride and low self worth.

There was more to our relationship than lust but what was that inner connection? What was the truth that brought us together? At my request, we separated three times. On each occasion I wanted and welcomed her back with open arms. The relationship patterns repeated and I would later feel hurt, fear and shame again.

I felt that pushing her away was not the answer - at least not until I garnered the willpower to really mean it and the surety/wisdom that it was the right thing to do for both of us. I felt lost. It was at this point that I learned that not knowing the true connection (the like for like attraction) between us was a fundamental milestone in our journey together.

Coincident with this realisation of not knowing, a close and very wise friend asked a pertinent question, "What is it you see when you are with this woman and she's being affectionate towards you?"

After a brief reflection I answered, "I see someone with huge untapped potential who is capable of far more than she is expressing to the world right now. I see a *light-being* who keeps herself shrouded in a dark blanket. That shroud stops light and love getting out or coming in".

My friend then unearthed the hidden treasure in my subconscious mind for me, "You see yourself!"

It didn't take long for the gemstone to sparkle. I replied, "Oh God, that's it. That's the inner to inner connection between us. That's why we keep attracting one another. We're both allowing ourselves too many distractions from our real journey in life - and at a very deep level we both fear love".

My friend added, "The relationship is not about you and her so much. It's really about you and you. She is mirroring the relationship you have with yourself.

Since I've known you, you've attempted to love and be compassionate with yourself - and frequently allowed yourself to get sidetracked.

So this is not about you and her sticking together or parting company. First and foremost it's about you committing to care for and love yourself".

I needed to care more and look after myself first for the relationship (with me and then her) to evolve to the good. To do that I needed the courage to allow my fears, shame and low self worth be. I needed to neither feed (dwell on) nor fight against (repress or deny) them. I committed to a self development programme whilst at the same time I focused on allowing my fear into my consciousness so that I could release it.

Visualisation Exercise: Show Fear Compassion

Allow your fear into your consciousness.
If you embrace your fear tightly, you can't let it go.
If you push it away you do not have it to release.
Instead, place your fear in a bubble.
Attempt to neither hold the bubble nor prod it.
Let the bubble float freely.
Surround the bubble skin in light, compassion and love.
Be patient.
Wait for love's miraculous power of osmosis to weave its
magic.
Keep pouring more and more love into the bubble.
As you fill the dark bubble with light, in due course, the
fear will wave farewell.

At this juncture, I realised (real-eyes-ed) I also needed to imagine that the woman and I could be in a happy relationship on which I didn't attempt to place conditions or control. I needed to let my desires - as well as my fears - be.
I chose to be nothing and do nothing other than attend to what I felt I was personally responsible for. I did my best to acknowledge that I did not know the truth of how our relationship could be (despite many close friends voicing their opinions that I should turn my back on her - which is what I'd done in similar situations in the past).
I placed a void in the relationship space between us and filled the void with compassion. Imagining this was tough because I made myself vulnerable to being hurt again. It would have been easy to place a wall of anger and resentment around me to protect myself. I needed to

allow myself to become defenceless but I discovered that my defencelessness made me strong. By presenting my desires and fears into the void and letting them be, I presented my truth (to the best of my knowledge) to the relationship. The true vibration of who I thought I was, warts and all - with the self commitment to raising that vibration.

The woman could then choose how she wished the relationship to be with the 'real me'. I realised that if I evolved my vibration to the good then she might need to change her vibration too - if we were to stay in tune with one another. I didn't know. I resolved to trust spirit, having faith it would protect us both so that we could fulfil the purpose of our relationship together.

I trusted that whatever the outcome, it would be best for both of us.

Ω

When you wish to change a relationship or situation, avoid trying to control it. For when you do, you are acting out a past memory fuelled by fear. Instead present your truth, your defenceless truth in the present moment. Here lies your true strength. You allow spirit to attract what your heart truly desires and repel that which it does not.

When your Heart's Will and Mind's Wishes Become One

Most of us, most of the time, send out a signal to the universe made up of desires and fears. You broadcast your vibration. You attempt to attract that which you wish for. But who is it that makes the wish? Is it the real 'I'? Or is it a supplication of the *false ego*, 'me'?

Do you seek something tangible, for example, a life partner, money, a job, health or safety from harm – to which you attach a state of increased happiness?

Will what you seek truly fulfil you? Or will its energy be subsumed by the unlit darkness of the shadows that lurks within (fear)? Is it to fill a dark void you feel inside yourself with the light of a *false sun*?

Is what you seek more abstract - for example, to learn what's of real value, become your *true self* and fulfil your contract for this life?

This is the true art and science of discernment - to discern that which takes you down the path you've contracted to follow from *false-egotistical* fantasy.

When you <u>will</u> yourself to take the path to your truth, passionately, harmoniously and genuinely, the universe resonates. You attract that which you seek, your will and wishes become one. But...

When you seek to placate your *false ego*, you deviate from your path. You allow the shadows within to remain hidden. The universe responds and it disrupts your flow, it tells you there's something you've chosen not to learn about yourself. You ignore the glory to be found amongst your shadows. Consider the following symbolism.

Astrologers, ancient and modern, symbolise the sun in their charts as a dot in a circle. The dot (or point) symbolises the here and now, the present tense. The universe/infinity is represented by the circle. Its circumference represents a never ending stream of cycles in which you return continually to your starting place.

The point in the centre of the circle thus represents the vibrations you send out into the universe. They are a product of all the information you possess (from the past) and its impression on your thoughts, words and deeds to create a better future, your heart's will and your mind's wishes. What returns to you in the future is a product of your will and wishes right now.

Imagine a pebble tossed into a circular pool, as an expression of what you will and wish to happen. Everything you give birth to, all your thoughts, words spoken and deeds go out to the edge (of infinity) to return to you. On their return they meet the waves you project right now. When the returning waves are coherent with those outgoing, you observe a series of standing waves. Your individual wave formation resonates coherently with the universe. You tune into the greater good. Such is positive or harmonious *karma*.

This is fundamentally what the *Law of Attraction* offers you; the opportunity to resonate with the greater good. Yet this is not the end of the journey. But first, acknowledge yourself for coming this far.

Acknowledge = Accept + Congratulate + Reward + Consolidate Learning

We are not all equal in consciousness awareness. But we are all equal in honour. Acknowledge your power humbly and avoid over-lauding yourself. Your *false ego* reclaims lost darkness when you put yourself above others who haven't travelled as far as you.

What you attract is fettered by the mind. You thus don't necessarily attract what you wish for. Wishing is a relatively simple task but care needs to be taken that what you wish for suits the soul's passion for your *life's journey*.

Now imagine your journey as the pool of water in which you swim. You are at the centre where everything you desire is slowly moving towards you. If you disturb the water (i.e. get upset, annoyed or frustrated) you create waves. They flow to the edge of the pool and return only with greater force. The returning waves disturb the harmonious waves representing the things you truly seek to attract. You find yourself tossed and tumulted in a stormy sea. You struggle to keep your head above water.

In extreme cases you create your own personal tsunami. You can drown in your own shame, anger, sadness and fear. Such is negative *karma*. It's not about right or wrong. It's feedback that tells you that your life is out of balance and you've still got things to learn from the shadows within. It tells you to learn and act.

> **Top Tip:** Don't slap the water! ☺

When the returning waves counter-balance the outgoing waves, the pool becomes still. You become equally knowledgeable in connecting what goes on above the surface (the known world) with what's going on below (the unknown) it – and vice versa. You move freely between the seen and the unseen - secure in spirit, in the timeless present tense.

You discover that the opposite of life is not death but not-life, an illusion.
It doesn't exist. Birth is the opposite of death.
Life is eternal.
Derived from *The Power of Now*, Eckhart Tolle

You become one with all that is, non-duality. You live completely in the present tense, connected to the greater good, outside of time and space. You are now fully ready to apply the *Law of Reversibility*.

Recap: Your Laws of Reversibility and Consequence

They say that, one way or another, we end up paying a price for everything. They may be right. But that's not the whole story. Our every action earns us a reward. Our every decision leads to a consequence. If we always do our best to do the right thing for the right reason, we will invariably get a result we can be pleased with. Any price we ever have to pay for this will always seem small by comparison to the sense of satisfaction that we have been blessed with.
Jonathan Cainer, Astrologer[106]

---

[106] Ref: http://www.cainer.com

You attract or manifest form (things, events and people in your life) through spirit.

1. Spirit is a force that is unmanifested form. Nothing can be formed that is not from spirit. Every mineral, plant, animal and human was/is formed from spirit.

2. Crystallisation is the process by which spirit creates form, be that form mineral, vegetable, animal or human.

3. Form is crystallised spirit.

4. Spirit contains the essence of oneness between everyone and everything. It contains the essence of man's connection to one another - and every living, and mineral, thing in the universe. Spirit is the ethereal reagent of man to that which is all around him.

5. Every person has a spirit. Every homogeneous group, every nation, every continent, every planet and every solar system (and on...) has a spirit. Likewise every animal, species, plant and mineral has spirit within them.

6. Spirit requires a congruent mind to manifest what it wills. Put another way, Spirit requires a body in which to express itself in the day to day world we live in.

You invoke what the higher levels of your *desire body* seek when you subsume your mind to spirit. Trust the prospering power of spirit through oneness, truth and love. Trust not and things have a habit of not going so smoothly (trust me on this latter point, I know).

You attract. You repel. You sometimes live what seems a battle between the higher (will, spiritual desires) and lower levels (wishes, petty desires) of your *desire body*.

Four fundamental forces, negative emotions or vibrations hold you back from aligning your wishes with your will - the *four seeds of negative karma*: shame, anger, sadness and fear.

Through duality each *seed* presents you the opportunity when acknowledged (= accept + congratulate + reward + consolidate learning) fully, to appreciate not-anger, not-sadness, not-fear and not-shame, respectively. When you go into denial of or over-embrace each emotion, you lose yourself in the stormy sea of that emotion, you cease to learn. You react sharply. You may exact revenge, sometimes violently, animalistically, without a second thought.

Regardless of action, when you blame/resent someone or something, including yourself, you limit your learning and you make the matter worse. You thicken the shell between your thoughts (or words, intentions and deeds) and the wisdom within, of your *true self*. Eventually, when you journey within that resentment transmutes into shame.

Choppy or violent emotional seas imply that you are not learning something and not letting go of the negative emotions that created the storms in the first place. You have set limits to your learning about yourself outside the dark shadows of your shame, anger, sadness and fears within.

When you release that limitation, you remove the mental hands around your throat. You raise your vibration.

Solutions do not reside on the same frequency on which the problems they solve were created.
Jeanne Ayling, Spiritual Mechanic, Hove, UK

Tip: Watch your thoughts. Do not become them.

Conclusion
Take care and time to focus on that which you really wish for. Make sure it meets five criteria:
1. It is not borne out of shame, anger, sadness or fear.
2. It is borne of truth (as best you know).
3. It 'feels right' for your *life's journey*, purpose and contract.
4. When it is complete, it will give you a real sense of fulfilment.
5. You feel more passionate about the journey than the outcome.

When all five criteria are met, you are ready to manifest, i.e.
- Imagine the feeling of having what you want, as if it's happening now.
- Choose courage.
- Trust yourself and have faith in spirit.
- Be patient.

The universe will provide.

Part X: Love and Relationships - Update

Bookshaker[107] published my first book *Learn to Love and Be Loved in Return* in March 2010. This *Part X* covers what I've learned about love and relationships since then. *Learn to Love and be Loved in Return* had little focus on the nature and context of making love; an important jigsaw piece in most loving relationships. Neither did it differentiate between making love and having sex as a recreational activity.

Both making love (*spiritual sex*) and sex can be hugely recreational. They both re-create but they re-create different things. They recreate according to the nature and purpose of the relationship between two people.

Relationships

All relationships bring home the lack of love we have for ourselves in some shape or form.

Whether it's an imbalanced relationship or two people tuned into their love for one another, relationships act as a mirror. They reveal the things about yourself that make you feel good and not good - unless you remain in denial.

Relationships Exercise: Feeling Good or Not Good

Take a blank piece of paper and list all the people of significance who influence you or whom you have influence over. Hold the paper up in front of you. As you look at each name, think through the nature of your relationship with that person and all their behaviours. As you look at the whole list, you are in effect looking at the relationship you

---

[107] Ref: www.bookshaker.com

have with yourself. Look carefully and you will see all the things that make you feel good and not-good about yourself.

This is how and why two people come together: as lovers, friends, enemies, acquaintances or family members. You reflect the good and not good in the mirror of life. You can use the information in the mirror to evolve your feeling not-good to feeling good. This is not so much an in-the-head activity which can descend into moralistic judgement between good and bad. Instead...

Feelings are your guidance system. When you transmute feeling not-good to good; you immerse yourself in the common good; you transcend from separateness to oneness and enjoy the full power and meaning of companionship. One spirit, one human spirit, manifested through different personalities, with one common purpose:

Love yourself to love another.

By self, I mean you pay attention and practise self compassion whilst you seek your *true self*. You shine light into all the nooks and crannies within your psyche to ensure no darkness is hidden from your consciousness. Ultimately, seek out your innermost fears; those that lurk behind your most hidden motives. Conscious awareness of your deepest vulnerabilities eases the soul's work.

When you acknowledge your fears and vulnerabilities, the soul and conscious mind join forces. The power of the false ego attenuates.

Metaphorically, think of the soul and conscious mind combining forces to become a snake charmer. They play a harmonious tune that charms the serpent, the *false ego*, out of the shadows so that you may venture within.

It takes compassion, courage and willpower to process all the information found in the shadows within. To find all that there is to know about your *true self*, you cannot avoid the darkness through denial. Remember...

Darkness is as equally as important to human life as light. It is instrumental to life's purpose. If there were no dark squares or pieces on a chess board, you could not play the game.

You can seek help to know the game's rules. You can seek out masters who have played the game. Read their books, study their advice but ultimately, you choose the moves you make alone. Like Beowulf,[108] who descended into the abyss to fight the monster alone, you also must venture into the shadows within alone. Hopefully by reading this book you are better equipped for your journey.

To imagine that we are going to be saved by outside intervention, whether in the shape of an analyst, a dictator, a saviour or even God, is sheer folly.
Henry Miller

Understand the source and nature of your desires. See the impact they have on your life. Understand fully the 'what and how' of that which you allow to hold you back from your *life's purpose*. Spot the patterns or repeating habits that no longer serve to help. These patterns and habits reveal themselves in negative inner dialogues you have with yourself. Through self-compassion, courage and willpower, give these habits zero energy and replace them slowly with their 'alter-nature'. Here's a case story of a client, to illustrate what I mean.

---

[108] Ref: See Appendix *About Beowulf* and
http://doctapaul.wordpress.com/2009/03/04/about-beowulf/

Case Story: Jack's Unfinished Journey to Love

Jack is in his mid 50s, wealthy, good looking, intellectual and kind hearted. For one reason or another Jack remains a lifelong bachelor. Despite all the aforementioned attributes, he still hasn't found what he's looking for - a deep and lasting love.

Jack has had many loving, varied and dynamic relationships, all of which ended unhappily. I took Jack through therapy in which he 'walked along the timeline' of all the major relationships in his life. A number of repeating patterns surfaced.

In therapy, Jack stopped on his 'walk' to look at specific relationships objectively and non-judgementally from a safe distance. He recognised an evolving pattern of deep-seated negative emotions stored in the shadows of his psyche. He started to discern the lessons he had learnt and perhaps still needed to complete. Each stage of the pattern recognition provided Jack a vital clue about himself, his predilections and the barriers he allowed to hold himself back from giving and receiving unconditional love. Jack sought and discerned between the elements of love and not-love within his psyche.

Melinda (Jack's partner late 20's - early 30's): Jack gave Melinda every material thing she wanted: a huge house, fabulous jewellery, designer clothes and so on. Jack gave everything but himself. Melinda's one overriding wish was to have children, however that was not a responsibility Jack would commit to. Melinda and Jack managed to get through their disagreement about having children. They both threw themselves into their respective careers – both of which meant they spent less and less time in one another's company. Piece by piece, the glue of their relationship became unstuck over a five year period.

Jack agonised after the breakup of his long term relationship with Melinda. He felt a failure. In time, Jack learned that giving materially but not of himself, emotionally or spiritually, would place severe limitations on a relationship's purpose.

Jack's therapy confirmed what he had already learned, prior to our therapy sessions, about discerning love from not-love. Notwithstanding the need to harmonise, love requires giving of oneself: materially, emotionally, intellectually and spiritually. But what about receiving?

Sandra (Jack's partner mid 40s): Jack's only other long term relationship lasted seven years. Sandra was attractive, kind and completely devoted to looking after Jack. Jack saw Sandra as a capable and intelligent businesswoman. She excelled in relationships. Sandra was a natural leader.

When she met Jack, Sandra's career had hit a serious setback. Her confidence was at an all time low. Furthermore, Sandra had been cheated out of a significant amount of property. She was in debt, manageable debt but uncomfortable nonetheless.

Jack wanted to help Sandra. She duly accepted and returned his love and generosity with kindness and devotion. Jack and Sandra shared the same values:

1. A good job that brings in lots of money
2. A lovely place to come home to at the end of the working day
3. Security in their relationship: 'Love you today, love you tomorrow, God willing'.

Owing to a legal hitch, Sandra wasn't free to marry Jack. She would have gladly. Sandra wanted Jack to father her children. Jack, having learned or so he thought from his relationship with Melinda, put his all into loving Sandra. He acceded to having children.

The early years that Jack and Sandra shared were the happiest of their lives. Children though would not be forthcoming. Despite every attempt, Sandra was informed that she could not have children. She threw herself into work to compensate. With Jack's help, she resurrected her career. Promotion after promotion came her way. She and Jack, both now on six figure salaries, had "everything a couple could wish for, apart from children". They had good money, a lovely home and a secure relationship, until....

Jack became restless. There was something he wanted from the relationship that he wasn't getting. He didn't know what it was though. He felt Sandra had achieved everything he wanted her to have. Granted they couldn't have children. He felt very sympathetic toward Sandra about her medical condition. He would have given her the children she wanted so desperately. He would, in all probability, have been a great father too. But truth be known, he would have done it for "Sandra's sake not my own".

Five or so years later - despite all the love, kindness and generosity that Sandra returned to him - Jack once more had not found what he was looking for. After a few failed attempts to plan a new future with Sandra, Jack gave up. He felt the relationship no longer fulfilled him. They did not argue nor were they unkind to one another. On the surface their friends and family thought they made a happy couple. Behind closed doors however, boredom and monotony had set in. Eventually, Jack and Sandra shared the truth; their relationship was going nowhere. They separated. Much sadness ensued but recriminations were few and short-lived. They both knew that their time together was up.

Therapy revealed to Jack that to love, he needs to receive as well as give. In all the time he and Sandra were together, Jack focused on giving. But, he never asked a vital question of himself; "What do I really want from this relationship for myself?" Jack and I dug deeper as to why.

Jack discovered he had two basic negative holding patterns in the context of personal relationships. At a subconscious level, Jack possessed:

1. A low degree of self worth that prevented him feeling good enough about himself to love or be loved
2. A great deal of concealed anger that clouded his ability to give and receive love wholly.

Both these emotions stemmed from his childhood. They blocked or clouded out Jack's ability to send out a strong vibration to attract a lasting relationship.

Katey (Jack's partner mid 30's), Dani (Jack's partner late 30's) and Denise (early 50's): short lived relationships that shared a common theme.

Katey: ten years younger than Jack, looked up to him as an intelligent, very capable, 'business-savvy' and humorous man. She was also very capable. She held a first class honours degree from a top English university. Unlike Jack, Katey was very quiet in her public demeanour. In private however, she expressed her sexuality powerfully.

Katey met Jack on a riverboat disco. They spoke politely for two to three hours in the company of mutual friends. By chance, they both excused themselves to go to the unisex loo. They stood face to face at the end of a long queue. Out of sight, from anyone they knew personally, Katey and Jack kissed. The kissing became somewhat amorous.

As they queued, Jack asked a passing crew member if there was another loo available on the boat. He told them to use the crew's loo on the lower deck.

Katey went to the loo first whilst Jack waited his turn. When she came out, she would wait for Jack. He completed his ablutions and tidied himself up before opening the loo door. He'd didn't get through it however.

As soon as the door opened, Katey stepped in the washroom and locked the door behind her. There they began a sexually charged but fairly short-lived relationship.

Over the weeks that followed, Katey's desire for Jack grew. Restrained and demure in company, once the bedroom doors were shut, she would express her sexuality liberally and abundantly. Jack found the sex with Katey to be good but not great. Its novelty wore off. His lust for Katey dissipated. Love for Katey, unlike her feelings for him, had not entered his head. He found their relationship "convenient". They would go out and Katey would stay over at Jack's apartment once or twice a week. Jack did his own thing the rest of the time.

Jack knew intuitively that his feelings for Katey would grow no stronger. He viewed their relationship effectively as "a series of pleasant one night stands".

One day, Jack invited Katey to accompany him on an extended business trip. Jack's days were long and tiring. The nights they spent together were short and sexless. Kate expressed her disappointment. Feeling a lack of attention, she left the apologetic Jack earlier than planned to return home. He promised to contact her on his return.

Jack didn't make that call. When Katey subsequently called him, Jack told her "I feel it's best for you if we stop seeing one another" – end of.

Jack rationalised (= rational-lies) that he had not done "anything wrong" at the time. Jack knew from the off that Katey cared far more for him than he her. He had allowed her feelings of desire to grow unabated without sharing his truth. Semi-consciously, he had taken advantage of Kate's disposition. But he remained in denial of his innate willingness to demonstrate a lack of compassion until now.

Dani: Jack fell in love with Dani instantly. Unknown to Jack, Dani was secretly engaged to someone who lived abroad and was living in the UK temporarily whilst finishing a work assignment. Dani eventually revealed her secret to Jack with a complete lack of compassion. Jack was devastated. This time 'the shoe of lack-of-compassion' was on the other foot.

Denise: was over twenty years younger than Jack. She was "pennilessly charming", to quote Jack. Denise welcomed Jack's generosity. He paid off her debts and advised her to set up her own business. The relationship was less than two months old when, over dinner in a nice restaurant, Denise told Jack that their relationship was over. She had decided that Jack was "too old to enter into a long term relationship and too old to go clubbing" – end of, again.

In therapy, Jack visited several relationships that all ended up in a lack of compassion. In each, one partner had taken advantage of the other's generosity. Sometimes Jack had been on the receiving end, on the other occasions he had dished it out.

Jack's therapy helped him to discern not love (in the form of lack of compassion and denial of truth) from love. Once again though, the lack of compassion was a symptom of not love; it wasn't the cause. Jack and I dug once more.

Jack discovered a genealogical trait passed down from his grandfather to his father and on to him. Jack realised that he had used his charm and power to seduce women throughout his life to feed his self esteem. When he met a woman, he would attend to them with great care and attention. He would take them to swanky restaurants and buy fine wines. He would focus on getting them to feel safe and secure in his company. All the while, he believed in his conscious mind that his intentions were to give and receive love. Subconsciously though, Jack had been running a programme that countered those intentions.

At a very deep and subtle level, Jack was putting out a vibration seeking recreational sex. He would thus attract women who in return derived their self esteem from feeling sexually desirable. Jack began to realise that the driving force in his relationships was mutually superficial, between him and each partner. It wasn't love. It was sexual attraction.

If subsequently the woman rejected Jack's charms, he would feel "unloved and bad about myself". His pride would be dented. The *false ego* had him under control again.

On the other hand, when Jack and partner had achieved their mutual purpose to enjoy recreational sex, the relationship would often end abruptly too. Why? Because the relationship had achieved its subconscious purpose. It had nothing more to endure for.

More often than not, the relationships involving sex would end hurtfully for one or both partners. Jack and/or his ex-sexual partner would feel not good about themselves (shame, unworthiness) or not good about one another (resentment, anger). The *false ego* thus escaped attention because it managed to cloud the underlying issues. The Machiavellian *false ego* is one clever beggar.

Jack now understood the nature of the two unhelpful subroutines (low self worth and concealed anger) that had been running in his unconscious mind for all his adult life. He also saw his *false ego*'s strategy for covering up its trail of power and deceit.

Jack discerned that until he really knew himself better and shone light into the shadows within, he would not be able to give or receive love wholly. The therapy programme from there on focused on helping Jack take steps towards his *true self* by releasing the feelings of low self worth and concealed anger that held him back.

In the context of personal relationships, Jack succeeded in finding much information behind his: unhelpful behaviours, semi-deliberate actions fuelled by low self esteem, his concealed anger and fear. Jack found jigsaw pieces that, at the outset, he didn't know existed outside the jigsaw puzzle of his conscious life. He fitted them together and integrated them into the whole jigsaw. He wised up to the gestalt of the bigger picture. He readied himself to find the next pieces of his unknown.

Ω

Relationships are at the nub of every *spiritual step* you take, none more so than the one you have with yourself. If you allow them, they reveal all the elements of not-love you feel about yourself. Like Jack, as and when you see and work through what there is to find from your current *spiritual step*, three things occur; you...

1. Discover and see through the illusory nature of your shame, anger, sadness or fears.
2. See the true nature of yourself more and more, the same true nature of all humankind.
3. See more clearly how we are all stars, borne of one star.

Many couples choose not to venture beyond the material and emotional realm into the ethereal nature of their relationship. Nonetheless they get along together very happily as *kindred spirits*. Other couples engage in less happy and imbalanced relationships as *pacifists and tyrants*. Such relationships can endure for years. For other couples, the return to 'becoming your *true self*', is an integral part of why their souls attracted one another. They seem drawn together by some unseen strong force - sometimes happily, sometimes not so. We call them *soul mates*.

Kindred Spirits, Pacifists and Tyrants or Soul (Play-) Mates?

Two people come together through vibration. They share some of the same values, beliefs, ideals or sense of purpose. The abstract feelings that they have in common serve to make up a significant proportion of their respective characters. They attract one another at an abstract level as well as for any physical or material reasons. We call them *kindred spirits*; they delight in one another's company (vibration).

Character shapes the frequency and amplitude of the *vibe* your DNA sends out to the universe. The couple's vibrations are thus, characteristically, in 'synch'. They tune in together to create a single coherent 'partnership vibration'. They 'make music' together. And like a good musical duet, their combined *vibe* is greater than the sum of its parts, i.e. synergy, gestalt. Together they might even achieve that rarity, 'a perfect couple' and yet behaviourally, they can be quite different from one another.

One person, for example, can be shy and reserved whilst the other might be outgoing and gregarious. The two come together to learn from and perhaps develop (some of) one another's traits or behaviours. They can naturally come together for joyous practical reasons (e.g. to set up home and have children) and, were they to delve, more ethereal reasons too. Many relationships however start off or become twisted in the search for light.

Pacifists can attract tyrants and vice versa. Both have the potential collectively to harmonise and create a smooth relationship but by and large they don't. Because both parties have to release themselves from their *false-egos'* illusory needs to control/be controlled. Both have to let go. Their relationship was borne of shame, anger, sadness or fear. One partner, 'the tyrant', takes the dominant role and, over time, effectively controls the other; who gives up all their power to keep some semblance of stability. The 'pacifist' gives up their power because they didn't have the self esteem in the first place to make their own decisions independently. Maybe unbeknown to them, at a subconscious level, they were seeking to be controlled. They sought what they hoped would be the stability of someone else's guiding hand.

However any form of stability becomes fragile; upsets continue to interrupt both of the couple's happiness and conscious development. The giving and receiving is out of balance. The tyrant plays the role of a *false sun*. The pacifist (moon) has no light (because its counterpart is a *false sun*) to reflect back. Were both to focus on the darkness within their own shadows and help one another, they could become *kindred spirits* - or they might find that they are *soul mates*.

Not to be confused with *kindred spirits, soul-mates* have past life experience of one another in which they both separated from source (spiritual purpose) at the same time. They return in this lifetime to be with one another, to sort out unfinished business. They come back together because they are highly attracted to one another.

They return to be with one another because they share the same dark shadows within their psyches. They serve one another by shining light into each other's shadows. They come together to accelerate one another's consciousness development, faster than each would on their own.

Despite such a well intentioned bipartite arrangement, *soul-mate* relationships tend not to be easy. Both partners can remain separated from source (spiritual purpose) to indulge in the *false ego's* sensual pleasures of the lower levels of the *desire body*. On the outside, their relationship can appear wild and fun loving. It can also come at a cost in the form of conflict and upsets - especially if either partner allows their *false ego* to obsess about the relationship.

The *soul-mate* attraction is so strong that one or both can obsess over the other. If the obsession isn't conscious, they find themselves attracted to the other as if by magnetism. There lurks a big danger; the obsessor can obsess over the obsessee to the extent that they ignore all else in their lives, including their own personal livelihood and well being.

Discussions about hurt and anger can descend into blame and accusation. The couple need to stay in control of their emotions and keep a detached view of what's going on. They can find harmony consciously by[109]:

1. Recognising the sparks of attraction that first brought them both together – and the value that each brings to the other's table.
2. Being clear about the spiritual nature of their relationship.
3. Recognising that both share similar dark shadows within their psyche.
4. Acknowledging and showing gratitude for things they give one another.
5. Agreeing consciously, up front, the spiritual purpose of the relationship – as well as its physical, intellectual and emotional aspects.
6. Bringing complete truth to 'the table' with both partners acknowledging the sources of all:
   a) Shared joy and happiness that propel them in both their own *life's journey* and

---

[109]. If you want to learn more about how relationships come together, survive and thrive, through truth, please refer to my first book, *Learn to Love and Be Loved in Return*.

b) Shame, anger, sadness and fears by which they hold themselves back.

There will be unconscious truths, memories and negative emotions too; they're the reason the couple came together in the first place. When the couple first met, their souls recognised the struggle that each was having. Their souls made a pact – and perhaps each one's *inner child* recognised and wanted a new playmate. They chose to become *soul playmates* in the game of life.

7. The *soul-mates* keep 'the table' clear of hidden motives by each owning and releasing their own unresolved issues respectively. As time evolves, each speaks about feelings openly rather than dwelling on the events which cause upsets. They go back to the source of each upset and retrace their steps in the wisdom of hindsight outside the clutches of the unconscious mind.

There follows a story about two *soul-mates*, adapted from some anonymous client-couples I've worked with. The story is a fiction with roots in events that actually occurred.

Frank and Joe, a Tale of Two Epiphanies[110]

Joe (a female) and Frank met in a pub and became close friends quickly. Frank soon fell in love with Joe. Joe didn't return Frank's love in the same way. She told Frank that she felt a "special connection" with him, that she did love him, but that she didn't have feelings of a sexual nature for him. Nonetheless their friendship grew as they got to know one another more and more.

Frank pined for Joe but kept it fairly well hidden inside a 'mental bubble' with which he'd protected himself from childhood. When Joe was away, Frank fretted that she would find someone else and leave him, yet he trusted Joe to tell him the truth and rightly so.

Joe respected Frank's feelings for her. At one stage, they didn't see one another for two months but reunited as friends because they both missed each other very much. They argued occasionally, Frank would invariably back down and go back inside his 'bubble'.

---

[110] Case study used as part of the story in the novel: *2012, a twist in the tail*, by Paul C Burr, available in: paperback and kindle format from Amazon, epub format from Lulu.com and online at http://2012atwistinthetail.com/.

Frank was highly intelligent and a deep thinker. Joe was intellectually very bright, had a very fast mind and tongue, and was prepared to fight assertively and vehemently for her corner.

For those of you who know Astrology, Joe's rising sign (personality) was Aries, the most aggressive and short tempered of the zodiac signs. Furthermore, Joe was born with Mars in Aries - Mars, the god of war and weapons of destruction.

As a young child, Joe loved to box and was given her boy's nickname by her dad, after the world heavyweight champion boxer, Joe Louis. She maintained her penchant for boxing throughout her childhood into adulthood. Woe-betide anyone who tried to cross swords with Joe, physically or verbally.

Frank on the other hand was a gentle soul (Mars in watery Cancer), a Leo, a benevolent king of the jungle. The 'white hot blow torch' and the 'glowing fire in the hearth of the home', Joe and Frank both had strong fiery powers. That was part of their attraction to one another; they were more than close friends, much more. Joe and Frank were *soul mates*; they had a part genealogical, part past life connection.

Frank's Revelation #1

Frank's great grandfather, Jim, was an officer in the First Anglo-Boer War, who was killed in action in 1881. On returning to England, Jim's close pal and fellow officer, Michael, visited and comforted Jim's widow who was pregnant with Jim's child, they married before the child, Frank's grandfather, Alexander, was born.

Michael took on his parental role willingly; he didn't tell Alexander that he was his stepfather. Michael allowed Alexander to think that he was raised by his real father and mother.

Michael was very strict and a religious man, his disciplined approach to life influenced Alexander greatly. The two didn't always see eye to eye on everything, especially religious instruction. Nonetheless, and perhaps strangely, stepfather and son were inseparable as Alexander grew up; the two developed a very close bond.

Alexander was a highly intelligent man. In his early 20's, he joined a regional police force and within three years transferred to Scotland Yard in London. He soon met a girl and was married within a year.

Alexander's rise through the police ranks was meteoric in comparison to the standard in those days, so by the end of the First World War, in 1918, he was one of the most senior police officers in the country.

It was on a police business trip to Yorkshire that he met and fell in love with Frank's grandmother, Freddie. She became pregnant and bore a son, Frank's father, Bill, out of wedlock in a remote country hospital. The scandal would have damaged Alexander's career beyond repair. Alexander loved Freddie very much; they separated but remained in touch. He sent her money regularly until she married another man.

Alexander told his ageing stepfather that he had a grandson born out of wedlock. Michael was furious over Alexander's infidelity; he wanted nothing to do with his so-called grandson and they argued bitterly over the welfare of the child. In a fit of rage, Michael told Alexander that there was no blood relation between himself and the new born child. Alexander, aghast, left his stepfather's home never to return. The two would never speak together again – until the soul incarnated in Michael would return to earth and meet Alexander's grandson, Frank, in 2011.

In a previous life, Joe was Alexander's stepfather, Michael. Joe and Frank had unfinished business, it seemed. And so they had come together in 2011 as *soul mates*.

Frank's revelation added metaphysical reasoning, an ontology, for his and Joe's attraction to one another - if indeed his revelation was true. Frank's research on the internet revealed that some *soul-mate* relationships can be very intense and challenging because of 'unfinished business' in a previous life. This made sense to Frank. As much as he loved Joe, their relationship troubled his mind greatly, almost to the point of obsession. But what was he obsessed about? What was the purpose of him and Joe being together? What purpose did she reflect for him? What purpose did he reflect for her? Frank would find out more fairly soon.

Frank was used to having the occasional metaphysical revelation or dream every few months or so. The quasi-genealogical connection between him and Joe was his first in a while. He was surprised to have a further revelation less than three days later.

Frank's second revelation told him how, as a child, he developed the 'mental bubble' that he stayed inside to protect himself when facing a potential confrontation. It also explained Frank's occasional lack of willingness to communicate openly with Joe.

Joe had asked Frank on several occasions why it was always she that called him and he would hardly ever call her. Frank would return Joe's calls but very rarely called her just to see how she was. Specifically, Joe tackled Frank on why he hadn't called her at all for several days whilst she was away, staying with friends. She had called him twice during this period. Frank's second revelation explained to him why.

Frank's Revelation #2

Frank's mother, Mavis, left the marital home when he was 8 years old. Frank lived with Bill, his father, his invalid grandmother (Bill's mother) and a family friend who came to housekeep for them all. Bill, not wanting to hurt Frank, worried about his emotional welfare; he told young Frank a white lie. Bill said that Mavis had gone to the country look after her invalid sister, who was very ill.

As the weeks passed, Frank missed his mother. The weeks turned into months. Frank would ask his father, "When's mummy coming back?" No satisfactory or truthful reply was ever forthcoming.

Almost a year later, whilst on his way home from school, a woman whom Frank knew called him into their home and handed Frank some presents and money.

"They're from your mum", the neighbour said, assuming that Frank knew of his parents' recent divorce.

Young Frank, realising the consequences of the news the neighbour had unwittingly given him, reacted quickly. Holding back tears, Frank nodded in silent agreement, took the presents and money, gave a swift "thank you" and left. He ran down to the sea promenade near where he lived and grabbed the top railing of the sea balustrade with both hands to steady himself. Frank stared out to sea motionless, trying his very best to cope with the traumatic news that he had lost his mother and would probably never see her again.

Frank realised that the people he loved most in the world, his father and grandmother, had been lying to him. Frank's unconscious mind took over and protected him from his trauma. His unconscious mind wrapped all of Frank's fears, anger, sadness and shame inside a mental shield and locked them away. Frank developed compensatory behaviours instantly to deal with the crisis. He chose to remain complicit in the lie so he did not reveal that he knew of his parents' divorce and played the game of pretending his mother was coming back one day.

Frank, in effect, created a 'mental bubble' around him, outside of which he would not venture. He construed an 'illusory truth' created by his unconscious mind that his mother could not have loved him - and she left him because he was not worthy of her love. Frank rationalised that her departure was his own fault; that in fact he was the guilty party, not her. So if he tackled his father and grandmother about the truth - if he told them that he knew they were lying to him - they might well respond in the same way as his mother and leave him as well. Frank's childhood conscious mind couldn't handle that outcome. It allowed his rationale to become reality and so allowed his unconscious mind to lock his trauma away. Frank coped as best he could.

Frank realised that this 'mental bubble' he created as a child had stayed with him throughout his life. He found it very difficult, if not impossible, to face or ask for the truth from people whom he loved. He dreaded that any form of confrontation would lead to rejection. When Joe asked Frank why he didn't call her when she was away, he would answer something along the lines of, "I don't like to impose on your freedom". Frank now realised that, by calling her on the phone, he didn't want Joe to think he was checking up on her or incur her annoyance by chasing after her. Such behaviour might drive Joe away from him; he might lose her. This was a typical example of the effect the 'mental bubble' had on Frank's behaviour in most of the relationships he'd had throughout his life.

Frank was now aware why he was unwilling to tackle issues head on. Why a girlfriend many years ago had nicknamed him "runaway Frank". Frank's new found awareness gave him strength to release the fear of confrontation.

Frank sensed that the obstacles that he had allowed to bar a lot of openness between himself and Joe, at least on his part, had gone. Truth

could now flow much more freely between them. Not completely though because Joe still had a childhood bubble of her own to burst - but that's another story.
Ω

Like all couples, *soul mates* can have great fun, and/or settle down and have families, and/or share the same passions, hobbies and intellectual interests, and/or engage in fantastic sex, and/or enjoy a healthy level of independence - like 'two strings of a lute', in tune:

As the strings of a lute are apart though they quiver the same music.

Kahlil Gibran, *The Prophet*

They can learn to live together in harmony – physically, intellectually, emotionally and spiritually. Each secure in the wisdom of the purpose of their relationship; in tune with one another. Neither *soul mate* needing to trust because both share complete truth; a beautiful relationship, fuelled by love.

And you need to possess the feeling of love in order to share it with someone else.

Making Love - Spiritual Sex

Sexual desire stems from the indwelling desire to procreate; the *"species imperative"*, as anthropologists call it. As well as its procreative purpose, sex can be wonderfully recreational too. Making love (or *spiritual sex*) is both sensual to the body and fulfilling in our heart at the same time.

There may be no greater pleasure than making love which recreates the spark of all creation, unfettered. However the pleasure and gratification of sex for many of us, including me, has for the most part of our lives been hijacked by the *false ego*. I do not moralise here but speak of the *Laws of Attraction and Consequence*.

The *false ego* seeks to control. It seeks to dominate your psyche, sometimes blatantly and sometimes, when it finds the going gets tough, ever so subtly. The *false ego* controls you by getting you to not feel good about yourself, e.g. through shame.

Some people enact this relationship with their *false ego* allegorically. They play either the submissive or dominant role in their sexual fantasies. In elaborate circumstances they enact extreme sex, for example, flagellation or breath deprivation. Consenting participants seek either to dominate, or be dominated by, someone or something else. In very extreme cases they give up their power to the point where the consequences could be life threatening. They, in effect, play the role of their *false ego* OR themselves submitting to the desires of their *false ego*. The sensual joy, no matter how climactic and thrilling, has a short half life in comparison to higher vibrations of spiritual, sexual joy - I suggest.

Such sensual desires reside in the lower levels of the *desire body*. They don't make your soul feel good before or after the sexual act. Such desires can embed themselves as cravings to which you become addicted. Like a virus, they have no respect for the *Dense* or *Etheric Bodies.* They can grow into dangerous parasites that drain your life force from feeling fulfilled.

> *We make a good choice by how it feels when we think about it.*
> *Go with good feeling.*
> Jeanne Ayling, Spiritual Mechanic and Tai Chi Master, Hove, UK

In the context of making love, *"go with a good feeling"* is about both consenting partners feeling good in their *Sacral Centre*[111], as opposed to (false) egotistical fantasy (the mind). Their coming together is borne

---

[111]"Gut feel": *The Sacral Centre* is located a little above the tip of the coccyx, or in the sacrum above the coccyx. It functions to pump spinal fluid up to the brain, thus keeping the brain nourished and young. In eastern wisdom it is related to the quantity of sexual energy a person has.

of absolute trust, i.e. truth. The sexual union is tender and slow. Hours can pass like minutes. You are conscious of every subtle movement you both make. Your bodies are guided ethereally to give and receive complete joy and share love.

Before you climax, a coil generates spine tingling electricity through the generative area of the second chakra, across the base of your back, above your coccyx and below your stomach. The energy travels upwards, all your chakras connect. Your spinal column illumines. As you climax, the energy generates a profound connection with your partner. Together, through truth, you both enter the *Jade Gate*[112] *into the Garden of Unity*.

I have felt no greater earthly pleasure or sense of completeness in the physical world. You sense spirit in the ethers around you both. Your collective vibration resonates to an inaudible sweet tone. You both merge with the unseen; the memory of which stays with you forever. These are the best words I can come up with to describe the pure joy of *spiritual sex*.

Making love truly is thus devoid of invoking any form of mind control (e.g. shame) between two people. It begins, evokes and ends with beautiful and good feelings. Both feel good because they share the truth of and feel in harmony with the oneness of its recreational purpose - without necessarily seeking anything further, such as a long term relationship. Yet there are elements in society who attempt to teach us that recreational sex is wrong.

Some clerics still advocate today that human nature is innately depraved. They prey on fear to control their followers' minds. Mind control starts by getting a victim (in this instance, a follower) to not feel good about themself. When a follower's self esteem lowers enough, the follower ceases to trust their own judgement and so allows a 'better judge' to make decisions for them. Having waved the stick, those who judge use the carrot of salvation as a counterweight.

I remember my religious upbringing in which I was taught that lust and sex were forms of corporeal sin - and in particular, one specific

---

[112] The *Jade Gate* (sometimes called the *8th Chakra*) is located in the back of the head, on the pointy bone on the back of the skull. As you pass through this gate, you connect with the *source* or spirit.

'Hellfire and Brimstone' speech from a highly evangelical minister at a church I visited. Fortunately, I didn't have to sit through his rebuke every week. He scared the living daylights out of me. I recall feeling shameful before God about my teenage sexual fantasies and behaviour. I felt that my life was already doomed; that God would never forgive me. It's taken me over forty years to figure a better way to deal with my conscience.

Conscience is that 'still small voice' that speaks between your thoughts. It warns you as to when you may be about to do something that you do not feel innately good about. There lies the secret; go with choices that 'the small voice within' concurs with or ideally exudes joy over. The 'still small voice' speaks of your soul's desires as opposed to those of your *false ego*.

Your *false ego* fetters the vibration that your spirit signals to your DNA. I can think of occasions where my *false ego* 'won the day'. On each occasion I was not sharing my truth, in this context, about the purpose of the sexual relationship I was engaging in. I invoked a mismatch between my own and my partner's hopes or expectations about the nature of our relationship. I would induce negative *karmic* responses and hey-ho, the situation would repeat itself until I chose willpower.

Willpower = adopting spirit's vibration, in your mind and behaviour, to manifest that which your soul seeks.

Sex is not innately a sin. If there is one thing you sin against, it's yourself when you veer from truth. You have the onus of finding, becoming and expressing your true nature. You achieve that by doing those things which make you feel good in your heart. Allow *feeling good* to steer your thoughts and behaviour.

Should you continue in activities that make you feel not good, you deny your soul AND your soul can become bored.

And I shall give to each his rightful share
Of knowledge, weighing all his works with care.
But this I say to you, to all the rest,
Who in the Green Lodge lag in learning's quest.
Who have not sounded, as the saying goes,
The depths of mind — on you I shall impose
No other load; yet if you have one crumb
Of learning, hold it fast until I come.
From *The Message to the Hierarchy of Helios*, the awakening of the Sun God within us, 4th Chakra, the <u>green</u> sphere that glows with rays of gold, the heart.[113]

Think of the soul as wanting you to go through a door. You may choose to distract yourself from the task in hand. You may repeatedly fulfil a habit that makes you feel not good and avoid the door. You go around the room. Eventually, you find yourself back at the door again. You have learned nothing other than that your repetitive habit brings you back to where you were. You may feel remorse - which is the *false ego*'s 'gotcha!' Because remorse is one step away from low self esteem - which is one step away from low self trust which imbues indecision through fear. I repeat, "gotcha!"
Keep up the denial and your soul may eventually scream, "Enough!"

---

[113] Ref: *The Restored New Testament, The Hellenic Fragments,* by James Morgan Pryse, published by The Theosophical Press.

Tend (Y)our Garden

My Dark Cloud thickens.
Neither can I see within nor without.
I rage, I weep.
I fear, I alone.

Behind my pride, clouded in emotion,
My soul, thrown and tumulted,
At last cries...
"ENOUGH! Be gone.
Blacken my view, no more.
Let the storm clouds break".

I pour water on upset, resentment and shame.
An angel rescues me from the abyss.
The dark cloud (my fear) fades,
I see what lies beyond,
A mirror of my own self,
My unkempt garden.

I tend my garden.
And help you with yours.
Tis the same garden.
Not ours to own - but to share.

In that garden grows the Love I, not I, we have for all
humankind.
Tis' called Eden.

Keep up the denying of your soul further still and you may reach that point in time when you have chosen <u>not</u> to fulfil your *life's purpose*. There are two events that prompt death.

1. Completion – you fulfil your *life's purpose* and *journey*. You transcend to the next spiral up.
2. Incompletion – you have left it too late to fulfil your life's purpose and are no longer going to make it.

The good news is... you are reading this right now which means that you can still achieve your *life's purpose* borne of love. Go for it! ☺

Love

Love attracts and repels. Love is both a magnetising force and radiation, both particle and wave, as is light. Love is the highest vibration of light; the spectrum of light we do not see that travels faster than the speed of visible light, outside of the space-time continuum. Love is instantaneous. Its unseen force interpolates the ethereal world around you. Love is all around. Everything is love made manifest.

If you look inside the densest atom in your body, it is almost empty. Or to be more accurate, it is almost ethereal. You can't see the ethereal content of the space between the atom's constituent particles within. It is deemed empty by the conventional scientist because they cannot see or register anything physical there. To the occultist it's packed with ethereal information.

For example, when in and around your *Dense Body*, your *Etheric Body* interpenetrates every cell, every atom of your *Dense Body*. It's there; you just can't 'see' it yet with today's technology.

You manifest form through love when spirit is unfettered by the mind. That form may descend ethereally or come to you in your day to day life, face to face. Love's gifts are heaven sent; the right people, things, wisdom or events appear - when the timing is right – deterministically. Until that point in time you send out your 'signature-vibration'. It possesses a complex collection of frequencies created from the sum total or aggregate data in your *Etheric Body*. This is your day to day signature, limited or fenced in by beliefs; not necessarily your highest vibration - that of your *true self*.

It can contain signals that make you feel good, i.e. love. It can contain signals that make you feel not good, i.e. not love. Not-love manifests itself in the form of shame, anger, sadness and fear – *the four seeds of negative karma.*

If, for example, you seek love, you will not find it until you learn how to transmit love properly. The journey to love starts with yourself. When you learn to love yourself wholly - whole love is what you transmit.

Unconditional love has neither attachment nor detachment. If you have either, you place conditions on your love. Unconditional love has a non-judgmental nature, passion and composure.
But it is none of these things. It is a higher vibration.

Spirit moves one step at a time. Be patient. If you are like me, you will find that some steps take a lot longer than you might hope for. When the timing is right – 'shazam!'

When is the timing right?

Answer: when you project what you seek truly and possess the will to go for it. At such a point in time, you have unearthed all your hidden motives[114] so that your unconscious wishes and will are completely in line.

Until this point you attempt to attract what you think you seek which <u>may be part but not the whole</u> of what you truly seek.

For example, you learn about love indirectly through your ability to discern all the elements of not-love in the relationships you have had in the past. When you attempt to attract what you think is love but is in fact not love - that is what you attract, not love. You need to discern love from not love to attract it. And that journey starts with yourself; first apply love to yourself and everything you do.

---

[114] Ref: *Unearth Hidden Motives* in *Part XIII: What does it Take to Make Spiritual Steps Toward a Fulfilled Life?*

Discernment precedes transcendence.

Discern Love's Purpose

Love's divine purpose is oneness, wisdom and truth, unconditionally and eternally. If your relationship has any of these qualities missing you share something that is, in part, not love.

People, myself included, talk and write about different kinds of love. For example, the love of:

- Self
- A partner
- A friend
- A child
- A family member
- All humanity
- All that exists.

Here's my kind-of-revelation. We have been mistaken. There is only one love.

One love, stay cool.[115]

Your *true self* discerns the purpose of a relationship. Love energises and magnetises the relationship to achieve that purpose. Your wishes and will are in accord. You filter out inappropriate behaviour.

For example, you:

- Share a loving relationship with your partner. You give and receive love: physically, caringly, compassionately, intellectually, spiritually and purposefully.
- Filter. You can share all the same, wonderful and purposeful behavioural aspects of a relationship you have with a life partner (apart from sexual intimacy, which you filter out) with children, family, friends, humanity and yourself!

---

[115] Ref: A phrase I first heard on a Jamaican radio station - many, many years ago.

You love and filter out thoughts and behaviour according to purpose. You discern the purpose of your loving relationship with someone and act in accord with the laws of nature.

You give and receive attention equally, to and from that person. You give and receive help when they or you suffer, physically or emotionally. You share truth, the joy of oneness and wisdom. You raise one another's consciousness. You love.

Love's Absolute

We are borne of Love.
Love's life's tune.
We lend an ear, we hear.
Love's here.

Love's faster than the light
That speeds through space,
To the edge of time -
Because Love's already there.

Love's consciousness, the highest vibration
Entangles every shake, rattle and roll of...
Every galaxy, down to the smallest quark;
Love's everywhere.

Love's here, there and everywhere.

Love's wisdom.
Know Love and you know the universe.
Its vast seas of vibrations oscillate in time;
A mult-Imax movie in which you cast, direct and play
your own part.

Have you ever loved truly:
Someone or something?
Have you ever loved yourself?
So that you live....
Your life wholly?
Your heart, wholly fulfilled?
Your mind, wholly wise?
Your body, wholly at peace?
Holy, within yourself?

Love's journey starts with and within you.
Love's the path upon
Which, when you walk,
You become the path.

Love's the destination.
Love's the path.
Love's the journey
Back to the source.
Through the darkness
Where glory lies,
Through the portal of wisdom's light,
Beyond this cosmos,

You become divine.

Paul C Burr

Part XI: Synchronicity – When Two or More Worlds Collide

A few years ago, I worked in corporate sales. I didn't have much spare time during weekdays. Domestic chores, paperwork and house repairs would often not get done until the very last minute.

One morning, a water pipe had sprung a leak so I called an emergency plumber. He wasn't in but he was picking up his messages and called me back within two minutes. He was available immediately and less than fifteen minutes drive away - a nice coincidence.

I took advantage of this window of opportunity to catch up on domestic chores. I wanted to look up a local motorbike repairer to fix my Harley Davidson. I also wanted to sell a Knoll sofa that I'd purchased from Harrods a few years earlier. One further chore: I had an old portable Dansette record player that needed fixing, to play my large collection of 45rpm records.

The plumber arrived shortly on a magnificent Harley Trike. We got talking about bikes and he told me of a pal of his who could fix the bike cheaply - result!

That afternoon, I was talking to a computer engineer who was also very keen on electro mechanical gadgets, he offered to fix the Dansette – result!

Two days later there was a knock on the door, I welcomed in two visitors side by side; an insurance adjuster, who came to check out the damage to my flat, and the Harley-man. As we drank cups of tea the insurance adjuster noticed the table football machine and the Harley-man took an interest in the Knoll sofa pushed up against the wall at the far end of the room.

The insurance adjuster told me of his passion for Table Football at university. He offered to buy it for the asking price – result!

The Harley-man had just bought an old country cottage and was looking for antique style furniture. Instead of paying him to fix my motorbike, he took the Knoll sofa instead – result!

"I can't help it, if I'm lucky"[116] I sang to myself in a 'nasal-blocked' voice after they'd gone. I felt blessed.

Ω

Synchronicity does not always imply a happy outcome however. Let me return to Henry and Vivienne from the case story in *Part III: Experiencing Within (i.e. Going outside Life's Jigsaw's Edge)* chapter *Love, Not-Fear and Karma*.

Henry and Vivienne shared many synchronicities. They both shared the same dreams on the same nights. Out walking, one day, they talked of what sort of dog they'd both like to have – a Miniature Schnauzer. Just then a wee Schnauzer came ambling around the corner in front of them. Henry had been to a clairvoyant who described Vivienne intimately. Subsequently, the same clairvoyant described Henry accurately to Vivienne without Vivienne revealing that she knew Henry.

All these coincidences encouraged Henry, perhaps more than Vivienne, that he'd met a girl he wanted to spend the rest of his life with. It wasn't to be.

In hindsight, Henry now admits that he was way off beam in his attempt to partner up with Vivienne. He allowed synchronicities to convince himself otherwise. Had his *false ego*, hiding his innermost fears, attracted these coincidences into his life? And/or was it his soul, informing spirit that Henry was way off course from his *life's path*?

Either way, synchronicities accelerated the pace of Henry's *karmic* collision with his metaphorical brick wall.

Synchronicities are divine interventions or tweaks. However, when they occur, they don't imply that you are operating divinely. Instead, they hint that change is on the way. Keep a watchful eye. Listen to the voice within.

---

[116] From the song, *The Idiot Wind*, from *Blood on the Tracks*, one of my favourite albums by Bob Dylan.

Part XII: Make Sense of Life's Unwanted Changes

Change is the only constant in life. Each and every moment contains birth and death. Every moment is born, dies, and is born again to a new moment. Some moments bring about joy (a goal scored by your favourite football team), some bring sadness (a goal scored against). Some moments are ho-hum. Some are life changing; you are compelled to make a transition by them, an emotional transition.

Some time ago I came across two books by William Bridges on the subject of making emotional transitions. If you want an authoritative source on the psychological process of dealing with change, look no further.[117] I should add, if you suffer from change or grieve deeply, seek professional and qualified advice.

Change starts when something comes to an end. You may lose, for example: someone or something precious to you, a relationship ends, the death or departure of a loved one, your health, your job, your home. When what ends ends, you start the process to pick up the pieces, hopefully sooner rather than later. Next, you start the transformation process of getting over that which has gone. In time, again hopefully sooner rather than later, you eventually release the hurt and ready yourself to start a new phase in your life.

On the far side of pain lies wisdom.

If you choose not to release the hurt, you stagnate; life stands still. You may learn to cope but you cease to attract or learn from new possibilities. If you allow this cessation to continue for too long, you rot – emotionally and spiritually.

At the time I picked up Bridges' books, I wasn't rotting but I was 'starting to go off', as it were, until... one theme in particular from Bridges' works caught my eye. It spoke to my emotional state.

---

[117] Refs: *Transitions, Making Sense of Life's Changes* and *Managing Transitions, Making the Most of Change*, both by William Bridges

Change doesn't hurt us but the emotional journey to accepting and making that change can be difficult, if not cathartic.

I was in the hurtful throes of getting over a relationship breakup and recognised a pattern that had repeated several times in my life. I wanted to accelerate the healing process.

They say "time heals" but it takes so darn long!

I wanted something more; I wanted the wisdom of what to do differently. The bust up pattern had repeated itself too many times. If I didn't learn what to do differently this time then I would learn nothing. In all likelihood, the pattern would repeat itself again. I started by assessing where I was. In which of the three phases did I place myself?

Three Phases of Change

Phase 1: Something Ends

Something most precious comes to an unwanted and/or unexpected end. You find yourself in the pit of despair. You cannot contemplate life without that which you have lost. At its worst you wonder how you are going to get through the next 30 seconds of your life without cracking up. You cannot think. Your body feels like caving in. Pressure, up through the back of your neck, makes your head feel as if it is about to burst. You cry (and cry) long and loudly. You pray through your tears and scream out for help. It does not come.

Do any of the preceding words sound familiar? Was the ending half expected? Or did it come out of the blue? During this period of shock you cannot come to terms with what has ended. You find it difficult to think of anything else. You dwell on the past and brood over whom or what you have lost. It's too soon to start contemplating 'what next?' You haven't yet been able to acknowledge the change that's happened or happening. Remember:

I self-acknowledge means 'I accept what has happened and ready myself to learn'.
Acknowledge = Accept + Congratulate + Reward + Consolidate Learning

You cannot even wish for the healing process to start. You do not have the willpower to start it. The pain is all too much.

Pain is resistance to psychological and spiritual growth.
Jeanne Ayling, Spiritual Mechanic and Tai Chi Master, Hove, UK.

You might even agree with yourself where you are philosophically but that doesn't stop the pain. If naught else, philosophical wisdom will teach you one thing. It is important to understand that your next step is to get yourself into the state of mind where you are prepared to acknowledge what has happened.

This isn't an on/off switch like a light bulb. You may think, believe, and even feel that you are ready to accept what has gone is gone. Then a few days later you find yourself looking for ways to recover that which you have lost. Time does heal. The healing does get stronger, one day at a time. If I were to give you one piece of advice should you find yourself in this phase, it's this.

Find as many <u>healthy</u> activities and distractions as you can. I find physical exercise and running alleviates stress. I used to have a devil of a time putting on those jogging shoes until I reframed the exercise of jogging as an expression of gratitude to my body - for being fit and well enough to run four miles every couple of days. I used to feel good about myself after a run. These days I feel good about the prospect of running and the exercise whilst running as well. I call this a 'triple good' feeling: good before, good during and good after.

What 'triple good' hobbies and interests do you have or could you nurture? Go for them. Go and socialise with friends and family. Go on holiday. A change of scenery doesn't make the underlying pain go away but it does remove the visual and auditory anchors that remind your conscious mind of that person or thing you cherished and no longer have. Whatever buttons you press, practise self compassion.

I caution you to avoid doing what I have done in the past. Do not take yourself off to the pub! Excess alcohol, or whatever drug of your choice, may well insulate you in the moment from your pain but that moment soon ends. When the inebriation wears off, you wake up feeling lousy and perhaps guilty about your drinking habit. What can become the easiest way to stop feeling lousy and guilty? Have another drink; the unhealthy habit repeats. You perpetuate a state of denial to and about your grieving and wellbeing. You can come up with a number of hard and fast rationalisations to justify your actions. You live falsely. You appease your *false ego*. Your soul withers.

No matter what you do, avoid excess, go for temperance and balance. Avoid doing too much and not giving yourself time to heal. When your intentions are healthy, avoid turning into a health freak, a workaholic or its equivalent in any other passion you engage in[118].

One further point, avoid doing something on the rebound borne out of shame, anger, sadness or fear. This is a common occurrence, especially in the context of relationships. I've had one or two 'relationships on the rebound'. I've witnessed many firsthand. I can only think of one (not one of mine) that has survived. The rest died on the vine sooner or later. Why?

Relationships on the rebound are an effort to replace that which you had immediately. It's like buying a false premier marque watch, when

---

[118] Refer to chapter, *Balance/Temperance*

you've owned a real one. It looks good. It feels good. It ticks good. But "it ain't the same!" It's false.

Nothing but that which is borne of love will evolve into love. Anything else takes you away from the path of love which always starts, from wherever you are, with yourself.

Well I know the arduous labours you undergo,
Your patient waiting that defies despair,
And that faint-hearted men you cannot bear.
And those who falsely claim to come from me,
You placed on trial and proved their falsity.
With patience you endured for my name's sake,
And wearied not....

From *Message to the Hierarchy of Chronos,* the opening of the Base (1st) Chakra, ruled by Saturn, Regent of The Yellow Lodge[119]

Once again...

Spirit moves one step at a time.

Above all, allow yourself time to heal. Be kind, caring and compassionate to the inner child within you that seeks love and to learn. Be patient. Babies take baby steps. Children do not run as fast as adults. Help the inner child within you to heal at as fast a pace as it wants to go, no faster. Don't push it. When the time is right you will heal sufficiently to ready yourself to move on.

You will know when you are ready to engage in the next phase (2) of healing when you answer the following questions in the affirmative.

---

[119] Ref: *The Restored New Testament, The Hellenic Fragments,* by James Morgan Pryse, published by The Theosophical Press.

Ask yourself:

1. "Do I accept what has come or is coming to an end?"
2. "Do I want to move on?"
3. "Do I want to learn, what I have to learn to avoid this pattern repeating itself?"
4. "Do I have the will to start moving on?"

When the answer to all four questions is "yes," you have already started Phase 2.

Phase 2: Transformation

You may have been the instigator of change that got you here. You skipped Phase 1 or so you thought.

Whether you are here by choice or not, the beginning of this phase can still be a very uncomfortable place emotionally. You will not want to linger here. There may well be the urge to get it over with as soon as possible, for two reasons...

1. When you turn around, metaphorically speaking, that person or thing that you have left behind is no longer there. By definition you have already accepted that there can be no going back.
2. You are still very much attached to that which you have said farewell to. You still grieve.

Once again, avoid the temptation to do things on the rebound borne out of shame, anger, sadness or fear. For you now have a tremendous learning opportunity.

Some readers may well not agree with what I have to say next, especially those of you who grieve or hurt deeply.

You attract everything that happens to you, every change, happy and sad. There is no such thing as random.
Life is more than the pursuit of happiness. It's about learning wholeness. We seek to find, open, become and express our true selves - and thus find true happiness in a bubbling well within, not without.
The more we know about ourselves, warts and all, the greater the wisdom we have, to achieve what we set out to achieve. When we <u>choose </u>courage and willpower to act on that wisdom, the closer to true happiness we become.
So life is about a continuum of choices.
And life is about becoming.
It's a very tough climb at times.
Seek wisdom!

As you seek and act upon the wisdom you glean, you heal. You move in an upwards spiral day by day towards Phase 3. You have the opportunity to look objectively and calmly upon the actions you took in that period of the spiral below you, actions before and during Phase 1. You understand more of how the outcomes of those actions came about. With the right help,[120] you can look upwards at the image of the person you can become in Phase 3 and the actions you will take differently to bring about the outcomes you would rather have happen, in the future.

As you spiral upwards there are some vital reflections to remember:
- If you <u>think</u> you have gotten over someone or something whose memory is precious to you – <u>you have not</u>.

---

[120] Ref: http://paulcburr.com/making-transitions/ and
http://paulcburr.com/emotional-clearing/

- If you <u>believe</u> you have gotten over someone or something whose memory is precious to you – <u>you have not</u>.
- If you <u>feel</u> you have gotten over someone or something whose memory is precious to you – <u>you have not</u>.
- If you <u>know</u> you have gotten over someone or something whose memory is no longer precious to you – <u>you have</u>.

Illustration 23: Fear, Sadness, Anger and Shame Fade

You know you have gotten over someone or something precious when they crop up in your memory and you give their memory little or zero negative energy. By this I mean you give their memory only a nominal amount of your energy in the form of anger, sadness, fear or shame.

Once again, this diminution of negative energy is not a binary on/off switch. It's like a decreasing exponential curve. It doesn't get all the way to zero but as time goes on it gets closer.

I still have happy and fond memories of everyone whom I have loved or who has loved me. I have some memories that are sad too, not a huge amount though. I no longer feel anger or fear consciously. Recently I still had a little bit of shame about one or two people until I learnt what the term, 'self-forgiveness', really meant. Since then I've moved on.

True self-forgiveness happens when you feel like the event (that you forgave yourself for) never happened.

It was upon hearing the above phrase from Jeanne Ayling that I suddenly twigged that self-forgiveness is not about a good part of me forgiving a bad part - thereby creating and sustaining a divided self. Instead, it was more about evolving a state of mind as if whatever I did that I used to feel shameful about never happened.

How did I do that honestly and earnestly? By unearthing and learning everything I could about my hidden motives[121] behind what I did so that I knew how to avoid repeating such things in the future.

Phase 3: Begin Something New
During Phases 1 and 2, your mind dampens your spirit's will and expression. You are not yourself, especially early on. But as you edge closer to Phase 3 you begin to:
1. Rekindle your passion for life.
2. Raise your curiosity about new possibilities.
3. Remain composed. You no longer allow things that used to upset you (e.g. photographs of whom or that which you have lost), to drain your life force. Feelings of shame, anger, sadness and fear have diminished to an 'ok' level. You feel empowered.
4. Trust your intuition about what to do for the best.
5. Raise and articulate your awareness of where you are, and where you have been, openly.
6. Create new circles of friends and acquaintances.
7. Feel reconnected to Spirit.

As the metaphorical phoenix unfurls it wings, you ready yourself to fly again. The mind no longer sullies your spirit anywhere near the level it did in time gone by. You raise your vibration. You choose courage. You choose willpower. You ready yourself and shine.

---

[121] Ref: See chapter, *Hidden Motives* in *Part XIII: What does it Take to Make Spiritual Steps Toward a Fulfilled Life?*

Healing the Hurt

Looking back to the time I went through Phase 1 and the start of Phase 2, I studied Bridges' works and used my NLP training and experience to create a self-help process, to deal with the emotional changes I was going through. I became aware that it would best work if it addressed issues at a material, emotional, intellectual and spiritual level.

I could devise the self help questions readily that looked at hard facts and the logic of things. I felt okay about that but to address emotions I needed to work at the feelings level in my psyche. I needed to sift and sort all the feelings that I attached to each fact. So far so good but how do I hear what advice spirit has for me – how does anyone?

The answer is that for most us we cannot. To be more accurate, I should say we have forgotten. According to Rosicrucian teachings[122], hu-man had the ability to talk with spirit way back in the Lemurian Age that predates Atlantis. Many modern day occultists have learned how to channel with spirit.

I add caution here. Occultists are prone to error - especially the apprentices amongst us. I have found that *channelling spirit* takes a lot of practice. *Channelling spirit* has boundaries that are fruitless to cross. My apprenticeship in such practises continues.

You can express spirit through art, music, dance and imagery. I have clients who have said such things as, "The only time I can really feel free to be myself is when I'm dancing", or "...painting" or "...playing guitar". In business coaching, I use imagery to get clients create a picture of how they are now and contrast that with how they would like to be. By taking their mind off the logic and analysis of facts they open up the channel for spirit to be heard.

Spirit, the voice within, speaks to us all the time but we hear best when we focus on the here and now - when, rather than thinking, we wait for inspiration.

Here's a real example of the imagery I used to get me through an emotional transition I was going through a few years ago.

---

[122] Refs: *The Rosicrucian Cosmo Conception Mystic Christianity,* by Max Heindel, two chapters: *Evolution on the Earth,* and *Occult Analysis of Genesis.* Also refer to *Atlantis and Lemuria,* by Rudolph Steiner (1911).

I combined all the facts, logic and feelings I came up with for Phases 1, 2 and 3 respectively. With each combination I constructed three images, of:

1. The recent past – Phase 1
2. The current situation – Phase 2
3. A future new beginning. – Phase 3

I came up with the following three images of myself...

1. Phase 1 - A *ship* lost at sea beyond the point of turning back.
2. Phase 2 - A *pioneer*, fearful of the future, regretful of his past but still optimistic that life can and hopefully will improve if he keeps going. The *pioneer* is travelling through a distant and uncharted land; looking to secure a new life.
3. Phase 3 - The *pioneer* becomes a *settler*, arriving securely at the place he sought.

With these three images in mind and all the facts, logic and feelings pertaining to each, I began to ask some basic questions, for example:

1. "Which phase am I in now?"
    Answer: "The *pioneer*: fearful, regretful but with sufficient optimism to keep going".
2. "What is it about the *pioneer* that evoked such an image?"
    Answer: "I feel scared. I am alone in a new land. I have no idea what lies around the next corner. There's no going back to the old life, which was financially secure and moderately happy - but not fulfilling. I'm not sure how to find happiness where I'm headed. I know what I think I want but is that what I really want in my heart of hearts? More than anything, I fear being unloved and isolated. I may find a new life soon. If it takes longer, I'll just have to keep going".
3. "How will I know that I am ready for a new beginning (Phase 3 – the *settler*)?"
    Answer: "The fear has subsided. I feel ok (if not good) in my own skin. It's ok to spend time alone. I'm cool with the uncertainties that remain and have faith in the direction I'm headed. I no longer dwell on the past or feel hurt about the people I loved who have gone out of my life. I no longer feel guilty about those that I hurt albeit unintentionally. I look forward to the rising sun".

I thus enabled myself to create two vital, **'act as if'**, questions for every decision to be made.

1. "As I consider the choices available to me, what would a (Phase 3 image) *settler*, who has arrived securely at the place he sought, choose?"
2. "Failing that, what will move me towards becoming a *settler*?"

For each major decision to be made in life, I attempted to answer the first, if not the second, question. If the answer was forthcoming, I would do my best to act upon it. If it didn't or I didn't have the courage to act, I would acknowledge my plight and let it go. I found that by asking the same question and getting in touch with the answer, it would accelerate the process of acting upon it in the affirmative one day.

This process involves choosing courage and summoning the willpower to move on in identifiable and pragmatic ways. By taking action, one step at a time, to:

- Install new behaviours into 'muscle memory' of the *Dense Body*, e.g. physical exercise and regular meditation.
- Acclimatise the mind to seeking new experiences and friendships without focusing necessarily on the outcome, like a true pioneer e.g. join a choir, attend astrology and tarot classes – much better than boozing at the pub.
- Seek spiritual guidance to learn how and where I am going wrong, and put things right. Align the energy passing up through the chakras and release the shackles that hold me back.

Self-help Tool: Change your Perception and Character, Change your Life.

If you perceive life negatively for a few hours, people will think you're in a mood. If your negativity lasts a few weeks, others may think that you're depressed. If your negativity sustains over a longer term, others will define you as someone with a negative personality – a negative character.

Your perception and character, more than anything else, forges the events and situations you attract in life. I have attracted a few cathartic personal experiences some of which I was not proud of. I reacted negatively and chastised myself for not being stronger in will and character in the first place. I now do my best to work diligently on the part of my character that lacked courage and self confidence. I am getting there slowly, step by step.

I illustrate an exercise to help you make an emotional transition by using a client's case story. The process normally takes between sixty and ninety minutes to complete. Schedule interruption-free time and switch off your mobile etc. to complete the exercise in one go.

Case Story: Clare's Life Changes

Clare was born in Eastern Europe behind the then Iron Curtain. She had a desperately lonely childhood without love, security or any form of stability. Clare's mother suffered from a number of psychological disabilities, refusing to show Clare any affection whatsoever throughout her infancy, childhood and early teenage years. Clare's alcoholic father spent most of his time away from home and was prone to increasing bouts of violence. Clare and her mother would both be subjected to severe beatings. Eventually Clare was taken away from home and raised by a series of community and family members, without any sense of a permanent respite from her childhood plight.

Clare was desperate for love and some form of day to day security. A temporary 'carer' molested Clare when she was only eight years of age. Fearful of more desolation, Clare acceded to the carer's requests in return for some form, any form, of kindness and stability.

Clare's innate shame was overpowered by her fear of homelessness and isolation. Clare's childhood mind wrapped this shame deep within her unconscious memory. She developed a series of compensatory behaviours, refusing to acknowledge or contemplate love for anyone including herself. Clare refused point blank to express love.

Clare emigrated to London in her early twenties. By this time she had developed a muscular response to sex for love; able to enjoy sex sensually but not as an expression of love. Despite this, Clare bore three children from a series of relationships - none of which lasted for long after each child was born. Clare's psychological problems mounted.

At a deep level, Clare felt she loved her children but developed a neurosis of becoming like her mother. This inner conflict created a huge turmoil within her psyche. So Clare decided to go for therapy which she felt helped. She still found it difficult to make the transition; to express the love she had for her children. Clare heard of my newly designed energy healing process from a friend and approached me for help.

When we met, I asked Clare in which of the three phases she felt herself to be. "Somewhere toward the end of Phase 1", she answered. I informed Clare that the healing would only work if she was prepared to move on and acknowledge the changes to her life, that she (not I) would come up with. She agreed. Here are extracts from Clare's case notes which she wrote.

Phase 1: Where are you now?
- **Three Facts and the feelings you attach to each:**
  1. *I am in flux, uncertain - fearful, vulnerable, confused and panicky*
  2. *I am starting to realise the joy of life – happy, excited, loving and active*
  3. *I am learning to love – open heart, accepting, interested and loving*

- **What is a metaphor for where you are right now?**
  Answer: *A tug of war*

Phase 2: The Transformation Process
- **What is coming to an end?**
  Answer: *The old me*

- **What do you want to let go of?**
  1. *Guilt – I hold back*
  2. *Fear – I need to control situations and relationships*
  3. *Anger – I have an unforgiving nature*

- **What will you miss of *the old me*?**
  Answer: *The safety net of familiarity*

- **What do you want to change?**
  1. *Open myself up*
  2. *To be vulnerable without fear*
  3. *To be more loving and giving*
  4. *To pursue my hearts desires*
  5. *To be a more enabling mother*
  6. *To be less controlling*

- **What do you want to keep or maintain?**
  1. *Generosity*
  2. *The love I have for my children*
  3. *The good inside of me*

- **What is a metaphor for this Transformation Phase?**
  Answer: *Wading through water*

Phase 3: The New Beginning
- **What is beginning as you come to the end of the Transformation Process (all answers to be solicited in the form of affirmations and actions)**
  1. *I am calm, loving and happy in my life*
  2. *I am giving peace, calm and healing to others*
  3. *My children are thriving and happy*
- **What feelings do <u>you</u> attach to each of the preceding affirmations, and what do I see you doing more of to demonstrate those feelings?**
  1a. Joy – showing genuine happiness
  1b. Enthusiasm – open to new experiences
  1c. Energised – doing things that I want to do
  1d. Fulfilment - expressing my content
  2a. Pleasure – using new techniques, hugging, laughing, socialising, being adventurous
  2b. Relief – doing what I know I need/want to do
  2c. Rightness – doing what I know I need/want to do
  2d. Love – showing and telling people I love them
  3a. Joy – Letting others see my happiness for their happiness

217

3b. Satisfaction – Not controlling others, making allowances
3c. Love – Showing/telling my children that I love them and am proud of them too.

- **What is a metaphor for your new beginning?**
  Answer: *Dancing for joy*

Clare left the healing session uplifted and supported by a collection of self-created affirmations and 'act-as-if' exercises to move on to her new beginning.
Ω
There follows a blank worksheet for you to work through and make sense of any unwanted or unexpected change in your lives. After completion, perform the daily exercises to accelerate the emotional journey through the unpleasant aspects of change you have gone or are still going through.

Blank Worksheet: Make Sense of Life's Changes

Phase 1: Where are you now?
- Three facts and the feelings you attach to each:

    1.

    2.

    3.

- What is a metaphor for where you are right now?

Phase 2: The Transformation Process
- What is coming to an end?

- What do you want to let go of?

- What will you miss of *the old you*?

- What do you want to change?

- What do you want to keep or maintain?

- What is a metaphor for this Transformation Phase?

Phase 3: The New Beginning
- What is beginning as you come to the end of the Transformation Process (all answers to be solicited in the form of affirmations and actions)

- What feelings do <u>you</u> attach to each of the preceding affirmations, and what are you doing more of to demonstrate those feelings?

- What is a metaphor for your new beginning?

Daily Exercises:
Repeat the affirmations you create, seventeen times each, twice a day, for seventeen consecutive days. If you miss a whole day, the seventeen days start again.

As and when you feel willing to move on, act as if your metaphor for the *new beginning* were true. Do more things differently that would reflect the metaphor or image of yourself at your *new beginning*. If that feels like 'a bridge too far' to begin with then start with the image you come up with for the *Transformation Phase*. Ω

When you change your perception and character for the better, you heal; you attract a new beginning. So...

Let's get it on!

Paul C Burr

Part XIII: What Does it Take to Make Spiritual Steps Toward a Fulfilled Life?

And the Answer Is.... A Stronger Commitment to Self

People I coach, by and large, fall into two categories:

1. Doers – who trust and commit themselves to do the work assigned. They achieve what they set out to achieve. Some overachieve.
2. Reviewers – they analyse the exercises intellectually. They often look to see the purpose of an exercise. They then fall into their *false ego's* trap and don't do the work. They acquire lots and lots of information but don't apply it. They achieve 70% at best of what they set out to achieve. And many reviewers still come back for more coaching!

What's your commitment to taking responsibility for your whole life, both your inner and outer worlds? Are you more of a doer or a reviewer? The exercises herein give the opportunity to not only knowing what 'to shine' means, they equip you 'to shine' more radiantly, and apply your shining to your everyday life. They've helped me and my clients 'to shine" more light on to our truth and share what we find. My intent is that they do the same for you.

It's not a question of whether spiritual practises work; they do. It's a question of whether you apply them.

Before I go any further, I preface the faculties with which you can equip yourself with some simple definitions:

- **Data**: the bits and bytes of information you find here and there. A detective in a novel goes around looking for clues. They attempt to piece the clues together to find an explanation, something intelligible – the truth.
- **Information**: a meaningful collection of data. Letters (data) make up words (information) that pieced together can be constructed into sentences (knowledge)
- **Knowledge**: awareness of how all the information pieces together. If you do not go beyond this stage you can amass a vast sum of

knowledge but you have no experience of sharing what happens when you apply it. You, in effect, become a walking encyclopaedia; useful for reference but not action.

- **Wisdom:** knowing how to apply and share knowledge. It answers three questions you bring its way:
  1. What do I need to know?
  2. How do I apply this knowledge?
  3. How do I help others to do the same?

What follows will help you equip yourself and create the context to succeed in your spiritual journey within. Remember...

Not only does spirit move one step at a time, you'll find you cannot outpace spirit.

Wisdom versus Ignorance

Types of Ignorance

.....we have (three) different types of ignorance.... One type of ignorance, learned ignorance, allows the pure researcher to come up with new questions and thus also, explore new answers.... This type in my 'book' is positive in nature. It is active and, ultimately, creative. Another type, wilful ignorance, blocks inquiry, trying to preserve an orthodoxy. It is negative. It is active, but rather than creating, it protects a rather limited vision of the status quo.... It is reactionary and if we are honest with ourselves, we will recognize that to some degree, it is in us all.
Last of all, ordinary ignorance is the ignorance of the individual not involved and unconcerned. This type is

neither positive nor negative in its nature because it is passive. If it becomes interested, it becomes interested in knowing 'that', rather than doing. Of course, there are all kinds of different degrees of involvement or openness inside these three types of ignorance, but you can figure out the different shade on your own if you desire.

Extracted and paraphrased from a blog by john6912, Cold Fusion Now[123]

Much of the wisdom you receive on your spiritual journey doesn't come from a book or intellectual discussion. It comes from within: a dream, a waking idea, a daydream whilst running or perhaps a visitation from a spirit guide. Einstein got all his breakthrough ideas, apparently, out of the void within but his so called void wasn't empty. Neither is yours.

You acquire wisdom to lead a more fulfilled life in two ways:

1. Sometimes you get a download of information, an intelligible, steady stream of consciousness of wisdom. You acquire it, for example, from a course of study, a teacher, a book, a spiritual guide or your best pal. Were you to listen carefully, you might even get it from an adversary.

2. At other times, you receive snippets. You get dots of information about your inner world. You are left to your own devices to join the dots through personal experience. This happens in my experience during the latter stages of a spiritual step. The book or the master takes you so far; after which you persevere alone to connect the dots of the unknown within you.

I've woken up a few times in the night with a revelation. Occasionally I've experienced what I call an "overnight epiphany". Here is one of my

---

[123] Ref: http://coldfusionnow.wordpress.com/2012/02/17/types-of-ignorance/

more memorable evenings, releasing some unknown and unwanted dots.

Case Story: My 3am Epiphany, Shapes of Things Before My Eyes.
June 2011, I was part way through self-coached Etheric Cleansing Programme. I'd been conducting affirmations and exercises to complete the final stage my next *spiritual step*. I felt very much on my own.

At the start of the programme, in May, I was given information, from my *Higher Self,* that I could take the next major *spiritual step*, the week prior to the Full Lunar Eclipse on 15th June.

On the evening of the 8th June I retired to bed as normal only to waken at 3am. I felt energy in the room, a presence of someone or something. I opened my eyes. Above the bed I saw dark objects swirling around my head. The ceiling fan above my head kept distorting as when you see something in the distance through a heat haze. The objects, all black, looked like bits of broken wings, pieces of chainmail and other obscure but quite solid looking shapes.

Initially, I freaked out. This was a very powerful hallucination, if indeed that's what it was. I calmed myself as best I could. I sought neither to deny nor over-embrace what I saw quite clearly through my open eyes.

I didn't feel that I was experiencing anything divine. I felt no malevolence either. I was puzzled. I let my vision flow. I felt that I almost knew what these dark objects were but I couldn't form the words in my mind. Time passed. The swirling and the vision continued. After about 20 minutes I spoke out fairly loudly and directly at the dark matter. "Look, if there's anything here that's not from a divine source, you may as well leave. I have no interest in anything except that which comes from the divine. And if that's the case you may as well leave. So go now!"

I thought to myself. "Bloody Hell, Burr, you are talking to dark objects flying around the room. You are sober and you're not on any drugs. Have you gone off the deep-end? There's no point in denying what you see. Give it another few minutes!"

Five minutes later, still staring at the swirling black objects, I spoke even more loudly, "Look, if there's anything going to happen, I ask for it to happen right now please!"

Nothing happened.

Five minutes later, at about 3.30am, I spoke my last piece, "I'm going to sleep now. I've got an early start in the morning and I'm tired. Good night!"

I turned over and fell asleep soundly straight away.

I awoke at 7am feeling remarkably fresh considering the interruption to my sleep. I got up and walked into the sitting room at the front of my apartment. I stared out across the English Channel, yon side of the green lawns and promenade of Hove seafront.

I felt at complete peace. More than that, I felt love. I felt love for everything in front of me. Even more, I felt love for the whole of creation. There was more.

I felt a simultaneous attachment to and detachment from the universe at the same time. This was neither a clutching attachment ('I have to have you') nor an averse detachment (where I looked down my nose from a place of superiority). It was more a kind of wise and compassionate combination of opposites - as if I was experiencing the universe for what it was, a vast ocean of vibrations. As I took in this wonderful combination of compassion and knowing, a third feeling filled my body - the feeling of 'fearlessness' [described in *Part III: Experiencing Within (i.e. Going outside Life's Jigsaw's Edge) chapter Love, Not-Fear and Karma*].

I didn't feel fearless like a warrior; I didn't feel brave; instead, I felt that there was nothing to fear. That everything before me or that came my way served a purpose. That was about as intellectual as it got. I didn't feel the need to think through this feeling of fearlessness any deeper. It simply was what it was. I couldn't remember feeling this way ever before.

I stood before the morning sun feeling love along with a sense of wise non-attachment and a wondrous fearlessness. The feeling stayed with me.

The next day, I called my Spiritual Mechanic, Jeanne Ayling, who practises in Hove. I told Jeanne of my experience. Jeanne is very wise in matters like this.

She asked, "Have they (the black objects) come back?"

"No" I replied.

"You've just rid yourself of many dark habits that have been lurking around your subconscious for some time, possibly from lifetimes ago!" Jeanne exclaimed.

"You're right!" I replied.

I knew Jeanne was right before she got the end of the sentence out. I knew what these dark things were. I just hadn't been able to bring the words into my conscious memory to describe them. It had been not so much a 'tip-of-your-tongue' experience, more a 'tip-of-your-consciousness' feeling.

The fearlessness by and large stayed with me for a few weeks. It served two purposes.

1. It told me that I'd mastered one level of development, or completed a significant *spiritual step*.
2. It also informed me that I was naively fearless of what will be my next *spiritual step*. I am both 'The Magician' and 'The Fool' at the same time. Such is the Tarot.[124]

The story has a twist of strange synchronicity in its tail (or tale for that matter). A few days later I related my night-time experience to a friend, Emma Andrews, a hugely talented author and children's storyteller.[125] Emma was in the process of putting together illustrations for her book, *Dilly's Dog's Disguises*. Emma sent me the jpeg of an image she had reviewed a few days earlier. It staggered me beyond belief.

---

[124] *The Magician* card in Tarot denotes spiritual mastery, at some level, over the 4 elements, earth, air, fire and water, through hidden wisdom. *The Fool* depicts a childlike energy, stepping merrily, enthusiastically and naively on a new adventure in life.

[125] Emma Andrews' first book, *The Adventures of Baby Bat*, is published by Pegasus Elliot Mackenzie.

Illustration 24: The Magic Happened[126], by Sean Savage, from
***Dilly's Dog's Disguises*, written by Emma Andrews, published by**
Pegasus Elliot Mackenzie, March 2012

Ω

The last stages in a *spiritual step* are the most difficult to engage. You have gleaned wisdom. You set yourself a course of action. You stick with it.

But all the while, you keep a guard against your *false ego* diverting you from your path. As you journey through the darkness, it attempts to ensnare you. It can send events and situations which in the past would have invoked shame, anger, sadness or fear. Should you become clouded in emotion again, you realise that there are remnants of

---

[126] Ref: www.dillysdog.co.uk (Please note, the illustrations in *Dilly's Dog's Disguises* are in colour.)

subconscious counter intentions still to be cleaned out. You may not yet be ready to advance to your next spiritual step until you have a released these negative holding patterns.

Creativity/Variety

Let us return to the rhyme...

> *All works creative and all works that find*
> *Treasures of knowledge in the Cosmic Mind.*
> From *The Message to the Hierarchy of Helios*, the
> awakening of the Sun God within us, 4th Chakra, the
> heart.[127]

Take away creativity/variety and you restrict yourself to
that which you know already or develop in a linear step
by step approach at best. You limit your learning. You go
through the same loop in your lives several times. The
boredom or lack of learning starts to eat away at your
soul. You need to do something different (variety) and
ideally something creative.
Paul C Burr

Insanity: doing the same thing over and over again
and expecting different results.
Albert Einstein

---

[127] Ref: *The Restored New Testament, The Hellenic Fragments*, by James Morgan Pryse, published by The Theosophical Press.

Choose...

> *Creativity → new associations between things, people and ideas → wisdom → satisfied soul (especially when you share that wisdom with others) → connect with other people → shine and share*

Or...

> *Not creativity → stay where you are → your soul gets bored → lethargy → depression → your light dims.*

The Right Heart-set and Mindset

Passion and Composure

Take away variety and you limit the breadth of your learning. You avoid, or miss out, on all you could learn and experience. You need to change your tack and do something differently.

When you do something differently, you cannot predict the outcome. So it will help immensely for you to nurture specific qualities of the heart and mind respectively:

1. **Passion:** develop a passion for the spiritual journey as well as the outcome. The journey is what takes the time. It is how you spend your life so adopt a mindset to live life to the full. Give everything 100%. If you are at work ~ 100%; at play ~ 100%; at rest ~ 100%. A half hearted effort produces half hearted results and wastes precious time.

    Can you think about someone who is really passionate and bubbly about something - for example: football, work, family, reading, motor biking? They generate, promulgate and attract the trust of others because of their commitment and attitude. Furthermore, if they come across as both wise and bright (like a star) you trust their integrity and capability. They become your beacon or seer.

    Wise and passionate people shine even if they do it quietly. (I'm thinking of Gandhi whilst I write.) They attract seekers of the same light. They shine light into where those that follow them have darkness. Furthermore, passion attracts passion.

Passionate people attract others who are equally passionate, who seek to form a peer group. Together, they collectively form a *Group Spirit*. See later section, in this *Part XIII*, entitled *Group Working with Spirit.*

2. **Composure:** applies especially when you are close to a big breakthrough. Take some typical events - for example: a wedding, an exam or a big sales contract. When you attach your desire to a successful outcome too much; the closer you get to it, the more excited or nervous you can become.

Say you forget your lines in a ceremony; panic and lose your concentration in an exam; or express nervousness in a presentation at work; you underperform; you don't deliver to your best capability because of fear. Despite best effort and intentions, you miss out on what you wanted for yourself and others at the very last hurdle.

The same goes for when you get close to completing a *spiritual step*. Should you start to allow nervousness (fear) to creep into your thoughts then the *false ego* readies itself to pounce. You may find yourself tested towards the end of the step, to see if you are ready to move on to the next. Let's say something occurs that would have normally upset you in the past.

If you allow that event to upset your pride, you find yourself taking a back step. Upset means that some pertaining darkness still lurks within your psyche. Release light into that darkness by parking any animalistic/reactive response to one side and thinking things through. Raise any shame, anger, sadness or fear up to spirit[128]. At the same time, contemplate what you seek beyond the event. And then raise that which you desire up to spirit as well. Avoid over analysing. Go forth with love and support in your heart and manner. Become unassuming. Trust in spirit, to provide what will be best for you.

---

[128] I cover a technique to raise things up to spirit in *Part IX, chapter, The Law of Attraction: Heaven on Earth*

Exaltation and Humility

As you take each *spiritual step* your soul rejoices. You feel joy and fearlessness as you reflect on that which you have learned and absorbed. You can account for dark energies that hindered you in the past and you have now put aside. You see through their illusory powers that used to manifest themselves in the form of shame, anger, sadness or fear. You have learned how to harness this negative energy and transmute it into the positive. You exalt yourself.

Don't overdo it. Should exaltation transmute into pride, you set yourself up for an upset which in turn becomes a humbling experience. Instead, enjoy your successes and act with humility of mind.

How do you avoid such setbacks?

Answer: "Remain curious and unassuming".

Unassuming Curiosity

Imagine you are a very curious person. You want to get to the bottom of things. You seek to understand what goes on below the surface. For example, think of an iceberg floating in the sea as a metaphor for human relationships. You see less than 20% of its size and shape above the waterline. The rest remains deep beneath the waves.

And so it is with your spiritual journey. The visible 20% is the same stuff you see everyone else do: meditation, prayer, yoga, Tai Chi, martial arts, occultism, study groups, contemplation, diet and the like. The remaining 80% lies in the darkness below the surface. The real journey lies in how you internalise what you practise in the visible world; make meaning of what you find and apply it to your whole life.

Become curious in your feelings. Allow your 'gut feel' to influence your actions. Listen to the voice inside that speaks between your thoughts; it's your intuition speaking to you. Allow your curiosity to travel beyond intellectualising about what goes on within you.

Avoid the pitfall some people fall into when given what appears to be a simplistic exercise. They look at the exercise, figure out its purpose and then say to themselves: "Oh, I understand the purpose of what's going on. Therefore I don't need to do it". They do themselves a disservice on two counts...

1. Experience comes only from doing, not thinking or intellectualising. You don't get fit from studying physical exercise. By all means, you need information to work out the appropriate physical exercises that will get you to the level of fitness you want. In the end, you still have to work up a sweat by doing the exercises.

2. When you intellectualise about the purpose of an exercise, you can put limits on your learning unknowingly. Once you learn what you think you have set out to learn, you can make the mistake of switching off. You thereby miss the rest of what there is to learn. Stuff that you neither foresee nor leave yourself open to finding. You close down the opportunity to find out what you do not know. The wisdom you missed remains outside the edge of your conscious *Jigsaw of Life*.

Case Story, Kissing is Fun:

I asked a client to do something differently, as a coaching exercise, every day for a two week period. Normally clients come up with slightly different things like wearing a brightly coloured tie or holding a meeting standing up. This client surprised me when I later asked him about his most memorable do-differently.

"I kissed my wife in front of the children", he said.

"That was a do differently?" said I, somewhat tongue in cheek.

"My father never did it. He was a conservative Jamaican Pastor", came the reply somewhat stiffly.

"What did you learn from that?" I enquired humbly.

"It was amazing", my client exclaimed. "The kids ran over to us both, grabbed our legs and demanded kisses too. The whole family now has 'kissy time' every time I come home. It's truly wonderful."

And so my client found out something wonderful that he did not know, he did not know. And what seemed pretty a normal day to day activity to 'assuming' me, took courage and a leap of faith on my client's part - faith in himself. Ω

I have assumed an understanding of the nature of some darkness in my psyche at times, only to find far more than I expected. I ended up digging deeper into my unknown. I now make a conscious effort to never assume I have got to the bottom of it all. I do my best to remember that I cannot know. Instead, I do my best to remain curious, unassuming and place my trust in spirit.

Develop your Sensibility: Discern Truth

Choose truth, as best you can, given the wisdom you have acquired already. Dance to the rhythm of your own drum.

What you feel to be your truth is an approximation to - until you find, open, become and express - your complete truth. It's the closest you feel to your reality.

I recall a relationship several years ago with a woman I'd known a short time only. We had occasion to spend a few days together. We'd gotten close, very close, without there being any contact of an intimate nature. We would kiss when we met, perhaps a half second more than the norm, and we would kiss the same way when we parted company. One day whilst out walking, the woman took my hand. 'Bashful-me' obliged. We laughed, smiled and hugged occasionally as we walked for hours. We met several times in the same fashion. The relationship did not become intimate until....

Out of the blue, one morning, she 'texted' to me a mobile photograph of some fridge-magnet letters, she'd arranged. Her message read "I LOVE YOU". My immediate reaction was "Oh sh*t, I love you too. We're going to spend the rest of our lives together". That was my truth – or so I thought. I was mistaken. Within a few weeks she was gone, out of my physical life. A boatload of anger, shame but mainly sadness and fear ensued.

Ω

When you feel the negative emotions that make up such pain, you have the opportunity to work through and hopefully release them. When you do, you take a step closer to your truth, your beautiful truth. I used the aftermath of the breakup of the relationship to seek my truth further, by seeking out the root causes of my negative emotions. They were by and large unconscious memories from the first seven years of my life - and some were handed down to me genealogically.

I noticed the impact these 'negative subroutines' had on my whole life; the repeating patterns they attracted. As I found out more and more, I used a number of techniques to release the negative subroutines up to spirit slowly. I felt I was getting closer to my truth albeit ever so gradually. I say "gradually" because certain negative patterns in my life have stopped - but not all. I work on. I continue to seek out the best therapy, be it self-administered or not, for the little twists, turns, upsets and blocks I encounter on the way.

Sometimes blocks occur in the form of physical ailments, for example, knee or elbow ligament problems (mobility and flexibility), chesty coughs (stress) and back pain (self esteem). I look for the mind-body connections and determine the behaviours, thoughts or intentions that attract the disease - or on other occasions, a repeating habit or pattern. For example, a negative relationship pattern might repeat itself and the pattern has both deep and subtle nuances to it. Gauging where I am emotionally and clarifying my intentions, I go back to before things went wrong. I study the actions and responses which invoked the negative pattern. I seek out my hidden motives[129] - especially those that I am shameful of. I work through how I might act/respond differently in the future. I use relationships as an example because that is the area with which I find most people have the most issues. Like attracts like.

Sometimes the *false ego* blanks me out spiritually. I forget what my aim is and lose track. My *false ego* attempts to trap me in shame, anger, sadness or fear. The *false ego* sends you little tricks to see if it can invoke shame, anger, sadness or fear; all the things that make you feel ultimately not good about yourself. I keep mindful of my thoughts and intentions as best I can. I don't deny myself when I have negative feelings. Instead, if I catch one, I raise it up to spirit immediately. Sometimes I miss them and invariably attract the consequences.

When you vent these negative emotions into the world, even by thought alone, you attract a karmic response. Furthermore, when you

---

[129] See section, later in this Part, *Unearthing Hidden Motives.*

get emotional, especially when you attach anger and blame to someone, something or yourself – you learn little if not nothing at all. And so you attract the experience to repeat itself.

When you vent anger and blame outwardly, you project disowned facets of yourself, that anger you, on to others.

Some of us go to therapists to help resolve these deep rooted, dark memories that hold us back. Some use group work. Some practice self development. Needless to say, when I do nothing differently, the negative patterns keep repeating and repeating. Denial doesn't work. Hopefully, I stick my head in the sand less than I used to.

If there is one common aim or output of all therapy, group work or self development, it is to bring you closer to your *true self*. If it does not, it is effectively a distraction; not much different to sticking your head in the sand.

Willpower + Commitment + Self Trust = Faith in Yourself

Hu-man did not invent the wheel, the steam engine, the aeroplane or the nuclear bomb without the capacity to imagine each invention in the first place - along with willpower, commitment and trust in its own ability to create such inventions. The same holds true for the future you seek for yourself.

To invoke such 'magic' you need to perceive your 'image-in-ions' as highly desirable and have faith in yourself. You may find you need that faith in yourself for many other reasons too.

The road can be long and hard.

I found thousands of ways how not to make a light bulb.
I only needed one way to make it work.
(Paraphrased from) Thomas Edison

You can meet many setbacks and stumbling blocks. Being a Leo, I've found affairs of the heart to be the biggest area of learning. The area, more than anywhere else, where in the past I have disowned facets about myself. Such setbacks and heartaches required a vast amount of patience with myself as well.

You may be ridiculed, ignored and isolated.

All truth passes through three stages. First, it is ridiculed. Second, it is violently opposed. Third, it is accepted as being self-evident.
Arthur Schopenhauer

Revolutionaries: Albert Einstein, Mahatma Gandhi, Oscar Wilde and Pink Floyd were all ridiculed either by their peers or the media before the world accepted the beauty and wisdom of their works.
When truth attempts to usurp not-truth, those protectors of not-truth in power often do all they can to suppress it; without bringing it or the truth tellers to the public's attention.

Although I am a typical loner in my daily life, my awareness of belonging to the invisible community of those who strive for truth, beauty and justice has prevented me from feelings of isolation.
Albert Einstein

In my early years when I first got into spirituality, I was prone to be outwardly enthusiastic about my journey within. Most of the people around me were not into 'it' at all.
When, for instance at a wine party, I started spouting off about "shining light into my inner darkness", I would get different types of response. The minority would show interest but the silent majority would remain quiet and walk away to join another group who talked about 'normal' things. Some who objected strongly to what I was

saying would let me know of their views in no uncertain terms. Others would ridicule me face to face or behind my back. It is often easier to ridicule something than to face it; especially when that something invokes fear in you.

There's a paradox too. If I'm attracting ridicule, is it because I fear it? Probably yes. In the meantime, I do my best to avoid responding to ridicule with ridicule or any other animalistic response. Sometimes I fail.

You may choose to isolate or distance yourself.

I go to the occasional reunion where others see a superficial change in me. These days my hair is long as is my wispy goatee, unlike the corporate clean cut image I used to portray years ago. My appearance often places me 'outside the flock'. My appearance is a choice I took to change along with a few other things about four years ago. Conversations have on occasion become slightly stilted.

I no longer take much interest in 'normal' day-to-day small talk, like who is going to win 'the current Saturday night TV contest' or get thrown out of some 'reality' show. Many of my interests have changed and perhaps more significantly, my perspective has changed.

For example, I feel distanced when people complain about being the victims of an economic recession that we have collectively created. At the same time, I ask myself, "Why have I attracted this conversation? I wonder where I am not being accountable for what I receive in life; whom or what am I blaming?"

I do not consider myself superior in any way and do my best not to come across as an evangelist. It's that I've moved on. If people ask my opinion about the latest TV game show, I probably don't have one. If we're discussing global events, I speak my views.

I prefer to distance myself from day-to-day chatter or 'complaining about the system' - both of which I might have engaged in once upon a time.

I still 'rabbit on' a lot about two of my passions though: football and music (probably more than I do about oneness ☺) and, undoubtedly, I distance a few people from myself in the process as well.

You may be opposed violently.

When all other attempts at their suppression fail, truth tellers face their sternest test; to stand firm and risk physical harm from those who stand to fall by truth. I could cite religious, political and civil-rights leaders, pacifists and innocent people - all whom have been attacked, beaten and some murdered ignominiously to prevent truth from being revealed to, or sustained in, the world.

What others do not do to you, you may do to yourself.

Without willpower, you limit the depth of your learning; you only go so far and you only get so much in return. When you commit yourself 100% to a project, that's what you can receive in return, 100%. On the other hand, if you commit less than 100%, you get at best what you put into it and sometimes you get nothing. Ask any seasoned salesperson.

Act as if you make a difference. Act as if you count. Act as if and you will... Notice the focus is on your journey, more than the outcome.

Spirit takes one step at a time. It operates solely in the present tense and permeates like the wind into all moments.

Jeanne Ayling

When I say "commitment", I refer to the trust you put in yourself and your willpower at the times you need it most. An image I often refer to is of a serpent in the sky.

Ancient Egyptians used the image of a serpent to represent duality. In the book of Genesis, it symbolises temptation. Imagine trying to wrestle with a serpent. It's slippery and almost impossible to grasp. It can appear very friendly and give the animal in you what it wants, for example, sensationalism, fame, sex, drugs and rock n' roll. As fun as they are, I've found these things do not give me what my *true self* seeks.

Illustration 25: Serpent, *The False Ego*

The python, Kaa, in Rudyard Kipling's, *The Jungle Book[130]*, uses his serpentine hypnosis to rescue the "mancub", Mowgli, from the Bandar-log monkeys. He befriends Mowgli then later, Kaa hypnotises his animal friends, Baloo the bear and Bagheera the leopard. Mowgli is immune to Kaa's serpentine hypnosis because he is human. Kipling illustrates how the *false-ego* appeals to the animal within hu-man but it cannot mesmerise the hu-man itself, your true ego or *true self*. And the duality of your true ego is your not-true ego, your *false ego*.

Your *false ego* can be its most slippery self when you seek to illuminate deep unconscious patterns in the shadows within.

Here's the transcript of a chat I had with my very good friend and relationship wizard, Romilla Ready[131], recently.

"Just before you get close to your truth about a certain situation - that is when you need to have the most faith in yourself; the period when your false ego feels the most exposed. Your false ego recognises that its end is nigh, at least for this part of your spiritual journey. So it tries to get you

---

[130] Ref: *The Jungle Book* by Rudyard Kipling available in multiple formats. Kaa (the mesmeric voice of Sterling Hayward) sings Mowgli to sleep only to be undone by Shere Khan, the tiger (voice of George Sanders). If you haven't seen it, it's a must-watch. Check out clips on YouTube.

[131] Romilla Ready is Co-Author of the 100,000+ copies seller, *Neuro-lingusitic Programme for Dummies®* and *Neuro-lingusitic Programme for Dummies® Workbook*

to be angry or sad, for example. It attempts to bring out the animal in you - as it has with me of late.

I'm using affirmations right now about being sparkly, bubbly and bright. I'm using affirmations about my weight and fitness. I've used affirmations about a relationship I have with someone close to me right now.

My affirmations are all about my side of the relationship and me evolving to the good. And having the willpower <u>for me</u> *to contribute to the relationship to achieve what the other person and I are meant to achieve together.*

It's about evolving the relationship to the 'good' without being specific. The 'good' might be a loose friendship. It might be a close friendship. It might be more. I am not pre-judging.

If I pre-judge then I start attaching myself to the outcome. I become too fixed. I start attaching pride to the result. And if I start attaching pride then that's one step away from shame, anger, sadness and fear.

So it is like being in the boxing ring with your false ego and keeping on the balls of your feet; ducking and weaving; waiting for the false ego to get tired - and then eventually 'bang, slam-dunk'.

Float like a butterfly. Sting like a bee![132]"

Ω

Watch your Language, Especially When You Have a Setback

Words are an extremely powerful energetic force. A *Word* created the universe, we are told. Words create and destroy so speak them carefully.

I find that when I ask business clients about their successes, they will speak gladly and in detail about their experiences. If I use the term "failure", they speak comparatively little. That's because we often equate the word 'failure' with 'shame'.

---

[132] Quotation: not only the greatest boxer but one of the greatest sportsmen I've ever seen. I recall my dad waking me up in the night so that we could listen to, and sometimes watch on TV, the then Cassius Clay and later Muhammad Ali fights.

Avoid equating 'failure' to 'shame'.

Instead of "failure", I use the word, "setback". It has a less emotive effect and encourages the client to learn more from the things they didn't want to happen. This is a simple example of how a single word can have the power to influence your willingness to learn or not.

Use every opportunity for learning. Every success and setback brings you wisdom about what to repeat and what to do differently; wisdom that informs you how to be, to bring yourself success and how not to be and avoid a future setback.

Failure is when you choose to ignore the learning opportunity a setback brings, do nothing differently and hope to be successful next time.
Success comes from learning and applying that learning. Tis' otherwise called wisdom!

Exercise: When You Have a Setback in your Personal or Business Life.

Get yourself into an objective frame of mind. If you feel emotional about the setback be wary of allowing your feelings to cloud the learning. You can help yourself by repeating the following affirmation seventeen times before you start the exercise.

Preparatory affirmation: "I am calm, focused and composed as I study the learning opportunity from this setback".

Study the facts and chronology of your behaviours, no-one else's, that led up to the setback. Answer the following questions.

1. What was it you did or didn't do, knowingly or unknowingly, that caused (or somehow contributed to) the setback to take place? List three to five actions down to you. Be honest with yourself.

2. Look back and within. For each of these actions: if you were to go below the surface, what were your feelings about what was happening at the time that prompted those actions?

243

3. Where did you get those feelings from – especially the negative ones?

4. What childhood memories, if any, did they rekindle? What specific memory invoked them?

5. What unresolved issues surfaced from your childhood specifically with your parents?

By answering all the above questions, you can create a profound sense of accountability, without blaming yourself, for your part in the setback. You learn the ontology of all the things in your life that somehow contributed to the setback. You become consciously aware of red flags, i.e. generic behaviours and feelings that warn you of future pending setbacks. You give yourself the opportunity to transform future setbacks in successes.

You can work out what to do differently so that you do not repeat setbacks or avoid them in future. New set-backs bring new learning opportunities but it is preferable to avoid or minimise the setbacks in the first place - is it not? ☺

Case Story: Neville and Kate's Marriage Breakup

Neville and Kate had been married for three of the twelve years they'd lived together. Both had successful careers in large corporations. Money wasn't a problem but their relationship was going nowhere and they'd become bored with one another's company.

Kate had an affair and eventually told Neville. She couldn't decide whether to stay with Neville or not. Even after her admission, Kate continued the affair. Having tried for a year to win Kate back, Neville gave up and felt a failure. He had made vows before God at their church wedding which he now could not keep. Neville felt guilty, destitute and became clinically depressed.

The coaching session with Neville focused on learning from this huge setback which he felt to be the "biggest in my whole life". Here's a summary of the session notes, arising from asking the Questions 1-5, listed on the previous page.

Summary of questions: "What 3-5 things did you do or not do, knowingly or unknowingly, that caused, or somehow contributed to, the separation to take place? What were the feelings you had that prompted these actions? What were the sources of those feelings? What childhood memories do they/you rekindle?"

Answer:

1. **Behaviour:** "I asked Kate to marry me because the relationship was going downhill and this was hopefully a way of saving it. I'd allowed our relationship to become a convenient habit. We were both busy people so staying together was easier than breaking up – or so I felt. I started the marriage off on the wrong foot".

   Feelings: fearful of being on my own, of not being needed and low self worth.

   Source of feelings/childhood memories: "I had a very strict upbringing. I was raised as an only child. I spent many an hour on my own. I made do as best I could but I did not like it. I did anything I could to get my parent's attention. I felt I was an interruption to their lives. I felt I wasn't good enough for them".

2. **Behaviour:** "I spent many, many nights away from home, wining and dining with clients. I drank in excess and paid very little attention to our marriage, especially during the working week".

   Feelings: bored, relationship going nowhere.

   Source of feelings/childhood memories: "I would do things in extreme or naughty things as a child to attract attention to myself. I would overindulge in food to compensate for my childhood boredom and low self worth".

3. **Behaviour:** "I didn't tackle the real issue. I thought that by buying Kate whatever she wanted, that was enough. But I didn't give 'me'".

   Feelings: "I felt that I was doing enough. I felt that by being generous materially that would suffice Kate's needs. Giving myself emotionally and spiritually didn't occur to me. I cared for Kate in the best way I knew how – up to a point".

   Source of feelings/childhood memories: "I would steal money to buy treats to share with other kids so that they would keep me company. My parents never played with me. We didn't have anything in common. They would spoil me with presents and money".

4. **Behaviour:** "I never sat down with Kate and created something in common for us both to work towards together. I allowed us to drift

from day to day. We'd be like passing ships in the night, most evenings".

Feelings: bored.

Source of feelings/childhood memories: "I can't recall ever planning anything with my parents. I never recall them taking an interest in my career - other than promising my father I would do my best to go to university. And once there I would work hard".

5. **Behaviour:** "When our sex life started to fade, I didn't do anything about it. I allowed the spice and variety to go out of our sex life. I allowed the frequency of our love making to trail off".

   Feelings: Distracted – I found the company of other women more exciting.

   Source of feelings/childhood memories: "My father was the same with my mother after my birth. Subconsciously I blamed myself for the lack of love between my parents. I copied my father's behaviour".

Neville's answers gave him a number of 'red flags' to be wary of.

Neville's 'Red Flags':

Generic behaviours: avoiding tackling the root cause of relationship problems, drinking to excess, allowing self to be easily distracted from what's important, drifting from day to day without focusing on common ground or planning the future.

Feelings: boredom, distracted, "what I'm doing is enough", fear of loneliness, low self worth.

Neville's first lesson was to make himself aware that if he found himself indulging in any of the above behaviours or feelings, he was probably heading for a setback – especially in the context of a relationship.

The remainder of the therapy session with Neville focused on clearing out the negative emotions he attached to his childhood memories. Neville wiped the slate clean. I then supported Neville to construct self help exercises to avoid those old 'red flags' and create 'green flags to wave' instead.

Ω

Over time, by collating the answers to Questions 3, 4 and 5 (listed immediately prior to the case story) for setbacks encountered, you will start to notice the key events that have shaped your life. Childhood setbacks or emotional abuse tend to be the most powerful influence on behaviours that carry on throughout adult life.

The journey within requires you to get in touch with your feelings or emotions as much as your thoughts. Emotions act as a navigator to find your *true self*. If you find yourself taking actions borne out of shame, anger, sadness or fear, watch out! You are deviating from the fastest path to your journey's destination, your *true self*. And attracting *karma* to boot!

When you feel shame, anger or sadness you live in the past. You relive, sometimes unconsciously, a past memory. You live in the past tense. When you feel fear, you are living an undesirable outcome in the future. You live in the future tense borne out of a past setback. Fear zigzags between the future, the past and the future again. You are at no time in the present tense, the domain of spirit, your highest vibration. At sixty years of age, I have only recently cleared out a lot of shame and anger from childhood. I still have some sadness to clear out, along with some fears that linger. I work with spirit every day and am determined to free myself of the remaining negative holding patterns and cellular memories.

Spirit lives in the present tense, it dwells in the heart. It does not judge and neither does it fear. It radiates love, one love. That is the direction I seek in life, love, unconditional love.

Feel Good in the Moment - and if You Can't Feel Good, Feel Better

Like attracts like. If you feel good, guess what? Good attracts good; you attract good things into your life. Feeling good is your emotional cue too. If you feel good about doing something, do it. If you don't, that's spirit's little message to say, "Do something differently that you will feel good or at least better about!"

Later on I write more about when the going gets tough but let's think about some of those moments when you're down in the pit of despair. Short of a miracle (and you can attract them at anytime) you might not think of something that will transform your unhappiness into high joy instantaneously but.....

You can always do something to make you feel better. Here are a few things I do when I'm down and on my own....

- Go for a walk or run. Get some fresh air, ideally in the sunshine where you can stare at the horizon or faraway places.
- Exercise
- Listen to your favourite music or an uplifting audio recording. I recommend anything by Joe Dispenza, Eckhart Tolle, Joe Vitale, Esther Hicks, Andrew Watts, Marianne Williamson, Ali Campbell, and Rupert Sheldrake.
- Use an EFT[133] tapping technique. They only take a few minutes and some are available free to follow on YouTube. I had a very wobbly few days last week and came across *Fear and Panic Right Now - EFT Tapping with Brad Yates.*[134]
- Do something creative that you enjoy - for example: cooking, dancing, art, writing, singing and so on.

Avoid the pitfall of lying around and moping as I have done on a few occasions. Wallowing in the muck never got me clean.

Also think about the sustainability of taking your mind off your sorrow through alcohol or some other form of sense nullifying stimulus or activity. I'm not saying "don't", I'm saying "take it easy!" Here's why.

Balance/Temperance

Remove balance in life and you limit your perspective. The workaholic might not give themselves the time to enjoy a healthy personal life. The addict can't see outside the control of their habit. The drunkard inebriates themselves from sobriety. In all three cases, the protagonist lives their life in denial.

---

[133] EFT: Emotional Freedom Technique
[134] Ref: http://www.youtube.com/watch?v=ajW1b-6jgJY

Should you avoid temperance, not only do you limit your learning, you can do yourself harm – physically, mentally, emotionally and spiritually. As such, you harm the environment you live in and those nearest and dearest to you. Lack of temperance, by definition, means an excess of, or gluttony for, one thing over another. Be it work, alcohol, drugs, mindless TV or computer games – the excess means that you deny yourself health, which has consequences.

Have you ever watched downhill tobogganing on TV? The more often a sleigh hits the wall, the more it slows down through friction. And when it bounces off sideways the team are using their energy laterally to get back on track. Whilst it's traversing it has to travel farther than a direct descent down the middle of the run. The middle way is the fastest and smoothest.

Illustration 26: Temperance
Major Arcana card from the Tarot of Jean Dodal, 1712.

Study the *Temperance* card, from the 18th Century, *Ancient Tarot Deck of Marseilles*, by Jean Dodal.

(This book is in greyscale, so please use your imagination.☺) You observe a grounded female angel clad evenly in red (fire, hot, male) and blue (water, cool, female). Her arms are dressed in red, to signify strength and power of Mars. Her blue covered torso signifies the love and beauty of Venus.

Water from the higher cup flows into and cleanses that of the lower. Not a drop is spilt or wasted; the flow is steady and harmonious.

Her wings reveal she is an angel who may advise, guide and protect us. Her work embraces the harmony of opposites.

The *Angel of Temperance* teaches us that life's direction leads eventually to the middle path. We do not need to swing extremely and continually between feast and famine, peace and war, love and hate, mercy and severity, prosperity and poverty, abundance and scarcity, riches and debt, victory and defeat, mine and yours, property and theft. When we embrace both aspects of duality as one, we create oneness. Something is only good for one, when it is good for all. There is no us and them, there is no me without not me. There is only us, together we become oneness.

When we bring temperance into our lives, we exemplify oneness.

Exercise: Promote Temperance

For 17 days, curb all excesses in your life - for example,[135]

- If you drink alcohol, abstain or curb your intake by 50% or more. If you smoke, curb your intake by 50% or more.
- Eat, healthy, fresh food, free from artificial additives. Eat balanced meals in moderation and avoid regular snacking.
- Avoid overwork or overstressing yourself. Cherish the inner child within. Take it easy.
- Cut out caffeine towards the end of the day. Drink decaffeinated drinks, ideally natural herbal teas, fresh juice or fluoride-free water.

---

[135] Seek professional advice before you change your lifestyle significantly.

- Take a warm (not hot) bath before retiring to bed every night. Pat yourself dry with a towel rather than rubbing vigorously.
- Curb your temper; avoid animalistic responses to things that annoyed you in the past. Stay calm.[136]
- For those who do little exercise. Do some moderate exercise, meditate, yoga, tai chi or similar - daily, just for a few minutes. Go for gentle walk, get some fresh air.

Keep a daily log of what you do temperately. In it write:
1. What you did temperately.
2. What you did temperately which differs from your normal habits in the past
3. How you stopped yourself from repeating the old habit.
4. What did you say to yourself or picture in your mind?
5. How did that differ from what you said to yourself in the past (rationalisation)?
6. What happened as a consequence?
7. What did you learn from the activity?

'Sweat the learning'
As you finish a sentence keep asking yourself, "So what do I learn from that?" - until your learning 'runs dry'.
Note - it is vital that you keep a log and write the answers to the questions posed, rather than just think them through. By taking time to write, you open yourself up to receive much richer intuitive insights that will surface as you pause your thinking to reflect.
And when I say "write", I mean with a pen or pencil. You open up far more neural pathways writing by hand than typing.

---

[136] *3 Ways to Stay Cool,* page 124, *Learn to Love and Be Loved in Return* by Dr Paul Burr, published by Bookshaker.

Do-Temperately Log

What did you do temperately?	How does what you did temperately differ from your normal habits in the past? How did you stop yourself from repeating the old habit? What did you say to yourself or picture in your mind? How did that differ from what you said to yourself in the past (rationalisation)?	What happened as a consequence?	What did you learn from this?
Date:27 Nov 2011 Stayed cool when someone close blew their top at me when I was genuinely trying to reassure them about something important to her.	Instead of venting an angry response, I paused. I felt the hurt from someone I care a lot about but I trapped my response there. I asked myself "what's going on here?" I realised my friend was venting, at me, her frustration with a situation that she couldn't deal with. I looked at her in the eyes and said nothing. In the past I might have allowed my hurt to transmute into anger and give back as good as I got.	Within a few seconds my friend saw my hurt and apologised. She thanked me for my kindness, love and support.	When two people go to war, one has to back down before the other, to start the peace process. The glory is found peacefully through negotiation and equitable handling, not victory. Transmuting upset to uplift takes courage.

Date: Ongoing I restricted myself to eating half a biscuit after lunch instead of the normal two or three.	In the past I would have said *"oh it's only a couple that won't hurt."* I have used this rationalisation often, over the years, when having one or two drinks too many. Instead, I pause again. I picture the level of fitness and health I have committed myself to attain. I say to myself, *"I achieve the fitness and weight through little bites, one at a time."*	This little visualisation technique and mantra combined has helped me to rid myself of my unhelpful snacking habit and over indulging in fast food.	Like spirit, wellbeing evolves one step at a time. Chocolates and biscuit treats taste twice as good when I feel I have earned them.
Date: Ongoing – Curbing Laziness Instead of grabbing a glass of wine and gawping at mindless TV for hours on end - I read, meditate or cook and schedule or record the specific programmes that interest me. If I feel tired, I take a cat nap. (and so on...)	In the past, at the end of the working day, I would say to myself, *"I need to relax and have a drink."* Now I schedule my evening time as well as my work time. I plan my rest and play. I say to myself, *"work, rest and play are equally important. I plan all three wisely."*	I no longer watch TV programmes to rest my mind. I rest and spend my time doing something more creative or learning. I spend more time singing and conversing with people.	I find I enjoy reading and writing far more than watching mindless TV. When I watch TV purposefully, it relaxes me far more. I no longer feel guilty about wasting time. I am more productive. I feel more fulfilled.

Group Working with Spirit

By group I refer to many levels of working.

1. Your *Dense Body* is a group of human cells. Each of the cells within a specific organ combines to make a group. The organs collectively with the connecting and protective matter form the *Dense Body*. The *Dense Body* and *Etheric Body* are formed by a group spirit, your spirit, in the physical world.

2. You may join a homogeneous group of like minded people, who have similar interests and spiritual yearnings as yourself. You may hope to accelerate the pace of your spiritual journey and that of your fellow group members.

3. You may choose to ally yourself to a nation, a continent, the earth, a species, a gender and so on.

Every group has its own spirit. The principles of working with spirit apply to all archetypes within each category.

These are the basic precepts.

• Spirit represents will - the will of your heart, the will of the nation, the will of a species. The spirit's will is to raise the vibration of <u>all</u> the group members, willing to stay the journey, to that of itself, the spirit's level. (There is a dreadful pun here but maybe it's not so dreadful after all. Because a line is not level when part of it lies below the level of the remainder. When the group members elevate their vibration and wisdom to that of the group spirit, its task is done; their spirit is level with the group spirit.)

• The group spirit, when called upon in the right fashion, will manifest collectively the experiences which each group member needs to undertake according to their own path in order to join the spirit at its level.

• When we form a homogeneous group, we create a group spirit.

• Agree the purpose of the group consciously. Otherwise it can be like setting off on a long journey in a group where everyone regards their personal map and compass as sacrosanct above all others. You place yourself at the mercy or severity of *karma* should you go off course.

- Put aside petty desires and connect with the greater good. Create a group purpose that is congruent with but over and above all constituent members' individual yearnings.
- Recognise that what is truly good for you is good for all. The 'good for one and all' is precisely what the group spirit helps you engender. Act as if you are that group spirit acting humbly and respectfully with yourself and others.
- The dynamics within the group change. The first one now will later come last, as the song goes. Whatever or wherever you are, in the group programme of development, there will come a time when you encounter someone who is not doing as well as you. Help them. Conversely when others, who are doing better than you, offer their help, accept it.

Courage and Oneness

Courage is a choice you take, not a trait. We can all choose courage to overcome that which holds us back.

It takes courage to allow your fear into your consciousness and neither embrace, fight or deny it. Fear feels very real until you let it be okay, accept that you are not perfect and practise self compassion and self love. When you love your whole self, your consciousness including your fear, that fear has no purpose anymore. Then you realise it was an illusion all along. An illusion created by your *false ego* to hold you back, for a purpose: to retain its sense of separateness.

> *Separateness, created by your false ego, is at the root cause of everything that holds you back in life.*

Separateness is an untruth and untruth breeds untruth. Thus the source of all untruths, in and about yourself, is your sense of separateness. Untruth, separateness is as such, an illusion. When you let go of this illusion, you learn the wisdom you have hitherto denied yourself. We are all ultimately of one spirit and when you let go of separateness, you let go of the fear it breeds.

Why do you fear being unloved, unwanted or isolated?
Why do you feel the need to be loved and connected to
someone else?
Answer: "Because you have separated yourself from your
true self. You neither connect with nor love your true
self"

When you learn to love yourself wholly, truly and
unfettered, you connect to oneness. You learn the
meaning of love for all, unconditionally and immediately.
And by 'love yourself' I mean – enkindle your soul with
love.

"*Enkindling your soul with love*", releases the not-love (sense of separateness) from the shadows of your psyche. You shine light into the shadows. You do not find fear there though. Fear is not hidden in the shadows; it is only the encasement or packaging. It takes courage to pass through the encasement and venture into the shadows but once through the encasement, you find wisdom eventually. You step nearer to your ultimate *true self* and with hindsight you realise there was nothing to fear about this wisdom in the first place. Your being fearless transforms into fearlessness; not so much a state of being brave, more a state of wising up; you had nothing to fear.
The brave warrior thus transforms into the now wiser alchemist.

Choose courage.
Find wisdom and fearlessness.
Let go of separateness.
Choose oneness.
Become One-Love.

Unearth Hidden Motives

That which you possess in a prideful way possesses you.
David Loxley, Chief Druid, the Druid Order, London

Can you remember when you wanted something or someone's love badly, perhaps even obsessed over having it? Who or what had control over the situation? Who or what commanded the power?
Can you recall your motives for trying to possess or have control over that thing or person? Did you make ALL your motives clear and put ALL your cards on the table - or did you keep some of your motives hidden, even from yourself?

Everyone has a special way of trying to get people to be who they want them to be, some expectations, some rules, some opinions etc.
There is a level of hidden motives about which most people do not speak, even to their best friends. Can you put them on the table, out in the open, on the greensward, in full view of all?
If you can, then truly there will be no shadows. Hidden motives can cripple relationships at the beginning. Later on they can surface and destroy them. [137]
David Loxley, Chief Druid, the Druid Order, London

Whether conscious or not, hidden motives are what separate you from those around you and more importantly, your personality from your *true self.*
Mercury/Hermes (as your immature personality borne of the past tense) began life as a thief. He steals light from the sun (spirit) and

---

[137] Ref: *Learning Not to Know (Mercury, Gemini, Pituitary)* - a druid meditation booklet from the Druid Order, London, (Yew Tree Printing).

withholds it from the moon (the potential to be your *true self*). *Mercury's* message links your personality with your *true self*. When you let pride (in the form of shame, anger, sadness or fear) control your personality, the link breaks.

You repair the link by speaking and being your truth - which involves speaking your hidden motives. When you speak your truth, as best you know it, spirit will manifest what's best for you at that moment.

If you hide your motives, you'll still get what's best for you - that's *karma*. It might not be what you think you want up front - or you end up getting what you think you want which leads to an ethereal brick wall to turn your head around to face what your soul really seeks. It wants you to unearth and immediately allow your hidden shame to be.

Exercise: For Two Weeks, Unearth Hidden Motives

Write down some of your hidden motives, the ones that come easily are not that deep. When you cannot think of one or the well dries up so to speak - that is when you need to be more persistent. That is when you have reached the ones that you find shameful.

As you unearth your hidden motives, you reveal your deepest sources of shame. Don't dwell here. Allow your soul to rejoice because your conscious mind now has a much richer picture of the whole you with which to work on. Remember, your heart never judges. You now have far less of the unknown (subconscious counter intentions, or negative emotions caused by impressions of memories that no longer serve a useful purpose for you) to sully spirit's power to fulfil your soul's quest. In short, put all your shame on the table, send it compassion and allow yourself to love yourself.

Avoid the Pits I Have Dug and Fallen Into

Some of these pitfalls can be a devil to get out of. Things have to sometimes go really badly before you even recognise you have dug yourself a pit. Here are three such pits I have dug, some on more than one occasion. I check continually that I have not dug one again - hopefully.

1. **Pitfall: Denial of Self Worth**

   a. Some of us choose to become ascetic and turn our backs on material belongings at least on the outside. But if we still long inwardly for the pleasures and luxuries that money can buy, we deny our worthiness to receive wealth. To avoid this pitfall: take on the notion that you receive what you feel you are worth and then build the self esteem to receive what you wish for.[138]

      Or... choose asceticism because it really feels really right for you on the inside.

   b. "Look after yourself so that you can look after others", is a phrase I share with most clients at some stage. In your quest to better serve your friends, families and fellows, you go to great - lengths to assure their wellbeing as best you can. They return your kindness hopefully with words such as "Thank you, you are... wonderful, very kind, a star and so on".

      Kindness, generosity and compassion are the salt of humanity. However you can fall into a trap. Should others' thanks become your sole source of esteem, you run the risk of giving away your power.

Case Story, Self-worth: Patricia's Tale

Patricia came to me in mid-2011. She doted on her 18 year old daughter and husband. She worked part time in an office. She had many friends who came to her for advice on many topics because she was both wise and very capable in helping others with all sorts of problems. She also committed time to a children's charity.

Patricia had been trialling new techniques that she had developed personally to help children with learning disabilities, to raise their

---

[138] Raising your self esteem: may I refer you to the exercises in the final chapter of my book, *Learn to Love and Be Loved in Return*. You create self esteem by keeping agreements, decluttering your life, completing any task you have started, setting and keeping to the daily goals you set yourself and acknowledging your vulnerabilities and achievements.

own self-esteem and self-reliance. Patricia epitomised a marvellous mother, wife and contributor to society. She worked for and helped others, all the hours she could. You know what comes next?

Patricia served and looked after everyone but herself. She was taught this behaviour in her childhood. Patricia had received a very strict upbringing by her domineering father. As the eldest child, in a large family, she was brought up to help her mother and look after her younger brothers and sisters. This 'looking after others first' had been programmed into her from a very early age – and she was chastised should she neglect her duties. Nonetheless she gave her all to her family and gave gladly.

In early 2011, Patricia's daughter left home to start a career overseas. The relationship with her husband had been dysfunctional for several years. Patricia's husband decided to move away from the marital home soon after their daughter had left home.

Patricia grieved deeply and her self-worth plummeted. Patricia's life had transformed significantly but now found she had much more time on her hands. Time, for instance, to document the new learning techniques for children she had developed and follow the due process to have them approved by government. The results of the development trials were most promising but Patricia still baulked.

She did not have the self esteem to visualise herself with the recognition and success that her learning techniques would bring. She feared failure. Instead of acknowledging and pushing through her fear, Patricia turned her attention to doing extra compensatory work for others; she filled her time serving others. In this way Patricia put off doing something for herself first and this impacted her ability to help others in due course.

It was at this time that Patricia approached me to take her through an *Etheric Cleansing* programme. She focused on releasing her 'look after others at your own expense' programme. Patricia erased the programme (erstwhile manipulated by her fear) and created a void. I was then able to assist Patricia to create a self help programme with which to fill the void. Patricia put together a balanced programme taking into account her own needs and wants before others, in order to better serve them.

The programme encouraged Patricia to *act as if* she already had the self worth and success she so richly deserved. She started by committing to get fit and, for the first time in years, she purchased a new wardrobe of clothes. Furthermore, she had her hair styled and cut by an up market hairdresser.

With a new look and new fitness regime, Patricia acted as if she had a new outlook too. She created time to complete the trials of her development work for children and submit them for approval.

Within one month Patricia had turned her life around. The healing programme and self help exercises had saved her "months of frustration and grieving" (her words). Perhaps more importantly, the 'new' Patricia was much, much more powerful than the old. With a new-found and healthy level of self worth, Patricia applied herself far more strongly to helping others. She no longer required the thanks of others to feel good about herself.

Ω

When you focus on others completely at your own expense, you end up giving only half of what you could be giving because you have not found nor use your true power.

That power starts by giving your soul the experiences it seeks to fulfil its quest.

Look after yourself first so that you can look after others - far more powerfully than ever before.

2. **Pitfall: Evangelism** – When you start your journey within, at some stage, you adopt a framework of being totally accountable for everything that happens to you. Nothing is random anymore. You start to see the world in a way that many others do not think about or perhaps even want to think about. You get enthusiastic or about your evolved outlook. In a rush of enthusiasm and good intention,

you may wish to spread the word vociferously about your new chosen path – only to be knocked back.

It takes skill, patience and simplicity to articulate the nature of spirituality to the uninitiated. Indeed, ancient wisdom informs us that the highest frequencies match with lowest to create the harmony of opposites. That is,

> ## *It takes the highest master to teach the lowest in wisdom.*[139]

Your intentions are good. But beware, if your evangelism is borne out of separateness – a sort of 'me and you' or 'us and them' outlook. You will attract suitable *karma* from such an untruth.

To avoid this pitfall: curb your enthusiasm and speak quietly from the heart. Cleverness and wily conversation are no substitute for genuine love and support. If someone is genuinely curious, their teacher will arrive. That teacher might be you or you might be the channel or conduit to that teacher. Listen to your intuition and pace your measured responses to their questions and comments.

3. **Pitfall: Spiritual Snobbery** - You start your journey within. You discover insights about yourself and life in general. You intellectualise about the illusion of all that is 'not-spiritual'. You patronise and place yourself above those that remain focused on the material and sensual.

   Eventually you see in the mirror that at which you scoff. You look around at the material possessions that you have gathered. You realise that you were really pointing the finger at yourself.

---

[139] I mentioned this phrase to Charlotte Blant, CEO of *Youthforce*, based in Hove, UK – see www.youthforce.co.uk. Charlotte has vast experience in teaching and facilitating workshops with corporate leaders, university students and young delinquents respectively. She is a master at her craft. Charlotte replied, "You're right. It's far more difficult to work with young people, with no little or no prospects, than it is with university students or executives. It's ironic that youth-workers are the lowest paid when they have the toughest job".

*Projecting disdain outwardly, avoids you facing
the disdain you have for part of yourself.*

Avoid this pitfall: remain unassuming and allow each to choose their own path in their own time – as you have yours.

4. **Pitfall: *Spiritual Power* v Fantasy**

Spiritual Power enables you to think and express yourself with great subtlety, allowing you to express ideas and feelings that you usually cannot; therefore it is very favourable for all forms of influence and artistic expression.

Be careful that you don't let your new power go to your head; let it sit with grace in your heart. What you think is power becomes (false-) egotistical fantasy. You can end up with fanciful ideas about your own station; your power to command influence over others. When you act from the head alone, without attending to what your intuition advises, you're about the hit a proverbial *spiritual banana skin*. You've attempted to race ahead of spirit. You've left it behind – except you haven't. *Karma* has subtle and sometimes not-so-subtle ways of giving you feedback and bringing you down to earth.

When your imagination transforms into unclear thinking and confusion, that's *karma's* way of saying that what you are trying to achieve does not have lasting value – for you or others. You are chasing an illusion.

You are not in a race with spirit. Serve spirit, it knows best. Spirit knows how to manifest the path your soul seeks. Pace yourself accordingly and follow its direction, *spiritual step* by *spiritual step*.

To avoid this pitfall: Hand anything you want or want to avoid up to spirit. Let spirit guide you. Tune in to your intuition, *intunition*. Trust spirit completely and you trust the divine in you.

5. **Pitfall: Forgiveness Is not about Absolution; It's about Being Like whatever Happened Never Happened.**

The sun shines on us all regardless. The Heart Chakra, your 4th chakra, is the domain of Helios, the Sun King. The heart doesn't judge; it thus has nothing to forgive.

Forgiveness is not about the good or saintly absolving of the sinner. It's about evolving a state of mind such that you release any anger, shame, hurt or fear you attach to an incident in the past - as if that incident had never happened.

On the surface, what I write next might seem to go against the grain of what some leading spiritual authors teach us. Then again, maybe it doesn't. It took me a while to tune into its subtleties. After writing it, I had to read it several times to make sure I was explaining myself as best I could. (Maybe it stands somewhere between the 'bleedin'...' and the 'obvious' but it was hard for me.)

The best book I've ever read on helping yourself through hurtful relationships is called The *12 Steps of Forgiveness* by Paul Ferrini. I recommend it heartily. I'll try and sum up the whole of Ferrini's book in one sentence.

When you forgive yourself wholly, you realise that you neither have nor ever had anything to forgive - of others.

And here's what I've learned and put into practice as best I can since reading *12 Steps....*

Instead of forgiving others, thank them for the gift of learning they brought you about yourself. When you forgive yourself completely, forgiveness disappears.
Jeanne Ayling, Spiritual Mechanic, Hove, UK

At the time of reading '*12 Steps...,*' I was coincidently going through a period of feeling very hurt by someone. That hurt often turned to anger - which I didn't like about myself for many reasons. When anger subsides I always feel guilty. Ferrini, in a caring and simplistic style, helped me to realise that I was responding to the other person by projecting my own shame, anger, sadness and fear on to our relationship. I'd attracted, once more, a series of repeating patterns that limited me from learning, namely:

1. I feared that the other person didn't love me the way I loved them.
2. I feared that they would subsequently leave me.
3. Because of 1 and 2, I was ashamed that I could not love anyone wholly. I feared that I was not worthy of receiving love. Therefore I was not capable of giving it.

By forgiving myself, I allowed my fears and shame into my consciousness. I let them be and contemplated my fears and shame for a few days without feeding or fighting them with fantasies. Instead, when they cropped up, I placed my shame and fear in an imaginary bubble and shone light and compassion on to them. When I felt ready, I used the exercise in *Defrost your 'Energy Freezer', Defrag your Soul – Case Story* to find the purpose of these negative emotions – to become and express what the not-these-negative emotions are, namely: **I love wholly, regardless**.

Once I enable myself, using the exercises referenced earlier, to bring about an innate ability to love wholly then I have no need to absolve anyone.

Humankind is not empowered to forgive one another in the 'good versus bad' sense. That form of *false forgiveness*, as such, is a trick of the mind which results from a sense of separateness. Separateness causes the negative emotions that two people project on to one another.

When someone else *'trespasses against us'*, we are encouraged to *'forgive them'*. When we trespass against others or even ourselves, we are encouraged to repent and ask for forgiveness – but whom from: those that you wronged, God, or yourself? Consider the phrase, *God empowers each hu-man to judge themself.* When you forgive yourself, who or what is forgiving whom and for what? Forgiveness, in this context, presupposes that part of you has the right to pass judgement on a second part of you about what that second part has done and holds that second part accountable. Self-forgiveness, in this context, thus requires separateness, an 'I and not I'. The same principle applies when you forgive someone else in the same way. You create an 'us and them'.

Us and Them = Separateness (ask *Pink Floyd!*[140])

Back to self-forgiveness: some part within you looks down upon and judges the other. YET, there's no higher authority within you than your heart. Your heart doesn't judge. Your soul seeks wisdom, borne of oneness; not judgement borne of separateness. The soul judges yes or no on the efficacy of what you have done toward fulfilling its quest. It judges whether what you've done has worked well or not well. It doesn't judge your thoughts, words or behaviours from a moral perspective. Spirit will manifest *karma* to guide you back to your *life's path* should you have veered from it. Spirit will bring to your attention to the need to learn and act accordingly.

The process of self-forgiveness is thus acceptance that what you chose to think, say or do didn't move you forward down your *life's journey*. It's acceptance of any ensuing or continuing anger, sadness, fear and shame you may have. Your soul is saying "It's ok! I love you and it's ok for you to love me".

Avoid this pitfall: when you forgive yourself, avoid self admonishment. Accept any negative feelings into your

---

[140] *Us and Them*, one of my favourite *Pink Floyd* songs, written by Roger Waters and Rick Wright.

"'Us and Them' is the philosophy of life that enables one to hate. This philosophy is one of exclusivity that can never create anything but strife. It is this principal of comparison that allows us to sit on our teeter totter where we find ourselves Up looking down at those below us or Down looking up at those above us. Either way we lose because with comparison we never find a state of equanimity. "Us and them" living is the way of life that ultimately leads to an end known as war. There is no us and them; only we. I think this is what PF was getting at."

Nat Scott, Brunswick, GA, ref: http://www.songfacts.com/detail.php?id=1690

consciousness. Avoid dwelling on them, denying them or fighting them. Instead, accept them so that in time you can release them. Send the negative emotions your heart's love. That's the heart's job, to shine light and love on everything, including the space between you and other people – so that you become one. Act as if your heart shines brightly. Be uplifting and raise your vibration from separateness to oneness.

> *"I believe if there's any kind of God it wouldn't be in any of us, not you or me but just this little space in between."*
> Quote by *Celine*, from the film *Before Sunrise*[141].

I don't concur entirely with *Celine's* belief but I've added it in because it got me thinking about the pervasiveness of spirit in everyone and every interaction between people.
When you focus on oneness, your vibration will spread. You journey to love wholly.

> *Unconditional love leads to magic, divine magic – because you become the change the world awaits.*

When the Going Gets Tough and You're at your Lowest

I do not know of any fellow *Apprentice in the Light* who is not having a hard time over one thing or another right now. Perhaps we're having the passage into our own dark shadows accelerated. Perhaps there is a quickening and we will find ourselves needed, sooner rather than later. If that is the case and I do not know for sure, my attitude now is...

> *Let's get on with the awakening to spirit.*

---

141 Ref: http://www.imdb.com/title/tt0112471/quotes

Nonetheless, I have found that spirit does indeed move one step at a time and the going can get slow and very tough. For me it has proven cathartic at times when I've felt the (my) journey appears to take a backwards turn.

In his venerable poem, *The Dark Night of the Soul*[142], St John of the Cross, the catholic mystic, describes some of the trials and tribulations you face in your journey within. Such tests challenge your disposition for the journey ahead and validate the completeness of the *spiritual steps* taken thus far.

St John of the Cross, cites two phases in which you face your stiffest challenges.

1. **The Passive Night of the Senses:**

   You may find yourself going back to old sensual habits that no longer serve you on your journey, e.g. overeating, laziness, excess drink, drugs and gratuitous sex, to name but a few. This apparent backward step proves not to be backward at all.

   It is more of a validation process, to revisit old habits to ensure you are willing to 'kick them into touch' once more and hopefully for always. You, in effect, spiral to the same place you were some time prior only higher (in wisdom), and ready yourself to move on.

   You re-present yourself to old sensual habits - so that you see through them and no longer feel the need to revisit them ever again.

2. **The Passive Night of the Spirit:**

   You start to find the spiritual practices you engage in, such as meditation or yoga, lose their potency. As you shine more light into your dark shadows, you venture deeper and deeper into your psyche. The shadows get darker and more elusive to find. The light you shine does not seem bright enough to light up these deep caverns within.

In both phases cited, help is always at hand and you can help yourself. Here are some tips...

1. **Patience:** acknowledge that the darkness which lies in the deepest shadows of your psyche is unconscious. It may be from a previous

---

[142] *Dark Night of the Soul, St John of the Cross,* translated by E. Allison Peters, published by Dover Publications Inc.

life, in which case it is very deep and very dark. You do not know what you do not know. But you sense its existence because you feel its effects in recurring situations that invoke shame, anger, sadness and fear.

Part of the transition through this phase requires you to have patience with the process you are undertaking and, more importantly, have patience with yourself.

2. **Invoke help as if you have already received it:** this is a simple task to help with that which you feel holds you back.

- Negative holding patterns... e.g. emotional blocks to promoting self.

- Destructive cellular memories... – e.g. unhelpful habits picked up from parents or handed down by ancestors and specific relationship issues.

- Physical issues.... e.g. sexual problems, illness, and physical hindrances.

Exercise: Construct and Recite your own Invocation

You can ask spirit for help at any time but this technique is especially helpful when dealing with the unknown.

There may come a time in a major *spiritual step* when you find remnants of unknown darkness within. Unsure of its precise nature, you may not be able to intuit the source of this darkness. It's dark. It's deep. That may be all you know about it. You know it exists because it attracts situations or people that manifest shame, anger, sadness and fear in you.

Other techniques, such as using affirmations, to integrate this darkness into the light may help. But if you don't know what lurks in the darkness of your psyche, how can you affirm precisely what the not-darkness is.

I will show you how to construct your own invocation, by way of three generic examples that I crafted. Invocations to spirit empower rather than make a request.

"I invoke all destructive cellular memories, physical issues and negative holding patterns – related to love, sex and relationships –
be found, opened and released to the light. It is done. It is done. It is done. Thank you."

The second invocation example relates to upbringing and legacies of ancestors.

"I invoke all destructive cellular memories, physical issues and negative holding patterns – that remain from parental upbringing and ancestors -   be found, opened and released to the light. It is done. It is done. It is done. Thank you."

The third invocation example relates to blockages...

"I invoke all destructive cellular memories, physical issues and negative patterns – that hold me back from finding the contract I made for this lifetime – be found, opened and released to the light.
It is done. It is done. It is done. Thank you. I now invoke the healed self."

The three invocations have an identical beginning and ending, *"I invoke all destructive cellular memories, physical issues and negative patterns - .... – be found, opened and released to the light. It is done. It is done. It is done. Thank you"*. Complete the invocation by inserting a phrase that describes what you want to focus on. Make sure it looks right when you've written it, sounds right when you speak it out loud and feels right. Allow your intuition to judge. You may even sense its energy as you recite it. Rehearse your invocation in your mind.

If you're not comfortable with invoking, here are some alternative statements, in the form of affirmations:

I free myself from all the destructive cellular memories, physical issues and negative patterns...

- *Related to....*
- *That remain...*
- *That hold me back...   ....and so on*

Recite your invocation or affirmation, like a mantra, for ten minutes daily, for seventeen days[143] consecutively.

Before you start:

- Sit up straight in a comfortable chair, arms on lap or by your side, feet flat on the floor.
- Close your eyes and relax.
- Regulate your breathing to the count of "4" in and "4" out.
- Focus on your *Brow Centre* – just above and between your eye brows.
- Imagine a circle of light, like a neon tube circling around you in an anti-clockwise direction, i.e. it passes behind down your left hand side and emerges from the right.
- As you breathe in, illuminate your spine from its base (coccyx), up through your chest and neck, around the back of your head, and down through your brow centre (like a shepherd's crook), emitting an orange flame out from your forehead.
- As you breathe out, illuminate your whole body, so that you shine, literally.
- If you break the sequence, start it again at any time and keep going.
- Now start your daily 10 minute invocation or affirmation.

---

[143] Some texts recommend forty days to change your consciousness completely.

- Focus on the energy of the words by allowing them to fill your body without allowing your mind to wander.

After a few days, memories of childhood events, or even further back, may develop or spring into your consciousness. Notice any shifts in your feelings and experiences. You may even have an epiphany!

If you have such an experience, write it down as soon as you can.

---

3. **Imagination:** If you were to release the biggest issue or drawback you face in life,
    - How would your life differ?
    - What would you do differently?
    - How would the major relationships in your life change?
    - What would you achieve?
    - For what purpose?

    In order for you to create something, you must imagine it first. This is not as easy as it sounds. Because in order to imagine something you may have to park some form of fear that holds you back. For example, several clients have baulked at entering into a serious relationship for fear of being hurt, dominated or repeating some unhelpful childhood memory of their parents' relationship. Some business clients feared making sales presentations or starting projects that involved risk, for fear of failure or perceived incompetence. Fear really does lock the door to fulfilment in your life.

    The answer lies not in ridding yourself of the fear. All you have to do is park it and let your imagination run free, not wild. No one can hurt you when you imagine. (See exercise in *Part XIV: The Matrix for the Life You Would Like to Have, Imagine*)

    When you engage fully, patiently and wholly in invocation and imagination, you open up the channel to receiving feedback about that which you seek. That feedback may not always be what you want, hope for or expect. Nonetheless when the unknown becomes known, you put yourself in a much stronger position to deal with it. Contemplate.

Patience + Invocation + Imagination = Contemplation

4. **Gratitude:** Count your blessings every day. Count every little or big thing you can be grateful for and give thanks to spirit. If you have love in your heart and the willingness to keep going – be grateful for that. Show gratitude to others who help you. And when life is at its very lowest, be grateful for making it through the night.

5. **Blessing:** Bless everyone and everything. Make blessing a daily practise. To bless is to wish the best of everything in great waves of abundance.

6. **Persevere:** Know that you can make your way back to the path. You wouldn't be breathing otherwise. So be grateful for that too. Pace yourself gently, one step at a time.

7. **When in Conflict, *Let Go, Let God*[144]:** Relinquish emotional control and no matter how bad things seem, trust the present situation to help and teach you. Trust your ability to push through any shame, anger, sadness or fear that you feel. Go to a quiet place within and acknowledge how you're feeling. Articulate it.

   Recite the following words to yourself - your mind, body, soul and spirit:

> *"I made a mistake* (in what I created)
> *I am sorry.*
> *Please forgive me.*
> *I love you.*
> *I hand it up to spirit"*[145].

The above phrase, on the surface, appears to contradict what I wrote earlier about forgiveness being a trick of the mind. In this instance you are asking of spirit or, if you prefer, the inner child within you - not that spirit/the inner child needs to hear it. It's an acknowledgement that you take full accountability for what you've

---

[144] I got the phrase, *Let go, Let God,* from *The Healing Runes,* by Ralph H Blum and Susan Loughan, published by *Connections Book Publishing.*
[145] Derived from a Ho'oponopono cleaning technique to clean the part of you that you share with another. Ref: http://www.hooponoponoway.com/

attracted and seek to clean the 'separateness programme' that runs within you that attracted it.

Speak your truth to whoever else needs to hear how you really feel deep down inside. When you speak truth to someone else, you engage in transmitting love. If you get not-love in return, you are now wiser because you now know that the other person does not have that love/wisdom to return. If things get emotional, avoid responding with anger. Let the other person blow and wait until they've exhausted their anger. They are probably angry because they cannot cope. They may need to retire to think things through for themselves. Allow them that space. It may get really wobbly, but you have spoken your truth from within. Speaking your truth involves no loss, only learning. When you speak truth everything you say or do serves love and acquires wisdom.

Afterwards, regardless of the outcome, set up a boundary so that you never go back to that space of shame, anger, sadness or fear. Be truthful to yourself and trust in spirit. When you live in truth, you set spirit free to create unlimited possibilities.

Setting spirit free can be tough. If you do not, your shame, anger, sadness or fear, pesters and festers. It only gets worse. Instead, push through. Open the door to where you think your biggest fear lies. You'll not find it though. Instead, yon side of the door stands an angel. She knocked on the door earlier. Did you not hear her?

Behold, I stand before the door and knock:
If any man shall hear me, and unlock
The door with welcome, I his guest will be.
And I will dine with him, and he with me.
From *The Message to the Hierarchy of Selene*, the
Moon Goddess, the 7th Chakra[146]

---

[146] Ref: *The Restored New Testament, The Hellenic Fragments,* by James Morgan Pryse, published by The Theosophical Press.

When you welcome her in, you see that your fear was all an illusion and you might also get the surprise of your life.

All Together Now...

There's a lot to focus on simultaneously. Like spirit, focus on one area at a time, one step at a time. Let it embed in your daily thinking and routine.

Seek wisdom.
Apply creativity.
Explore variety.
Adopt the right heart-set and mindset:
Be passionate and remain composed, accept
exaltation with humility and adopt unassuming
curiosity.
Develop sensibility.
Discern truth.
Exercise willpower + show commitment +trust self
= have faith in self.
Practise feeling good or at least better
Balance your lifestyle.
Embrace temperance.
Work with companions.
Seek seers.
Choose courage.
Unearth hidden motives
Avoid: self denial, evangelism, spiritual snobbery
and fantasy (instead of spiritual power).

*Practise forgiveness: as if whatever happened
never happened.
Be patient.
Invoke (i.e. ask for) spirit's power.
Imagine.
Show gratitude
Persevere.
When in conflict, let go
Above all, choose oneness.*

And when you apply all the aforementioned, you find yourself just over the border of the known with the unknown; beyond the edge of the *Life's Jigsaw* you have pieced together so far.

Principles for Researching the Epistemology[147] of the Scientific and Mystical World(s) You Live In

Your journey within is an encounter with the unknown, truth and fantasy. As you make your journey, you gather evidence of what works and what doesn't work, what's truth and what's not truth. You learn to discern between truth and egotistical fantasy.

Working with spirit is not an intellectual exercise. It's a process of finding your true feelings, listening to your inner voice, having faith in yourself and choosing the courage to heed the advice spirit provides.

Something, an outcome, a supposition, a philosophy to life or causal effect is only a theory when there is no evidence to support it. **As soon as you have evidence that supports the theory, it transmutes into likelihood,** however small or unlikely that likelihood may be.

---

[147] Epistemology: the study or theory of the nature, sources, and limits of knowledge. It defines the boundary between that which we believe and that which we know to be truth.

Four Research Axioms: Quality, Validity, Impartiality and Consequences

1. **You can <u>qualify</u> evidence under 3 headings** to support/dispel a hitherto theory[148], now a likelihood:

   I. What evidence exists?

   II. What kind or quality of evidence exists (e.g. is it scientifically verifiable)? Do you have: a credible eye witness account, expert opinion and personal experience - or is it hearsay? The less scientific the evidence, the more of it is required.

   III. How much of the evidence exists?

   As the amount and quality of evidence grows, what was a likelihood now becomes a probability.

   As and when more evidence emerges you get to a point, e.g. in a court of law, where you reach a verdict based on evidence which points to the "probability of an event beyond reasonable doubt". You judge something to be true. If you don't have sufficient evidence you judge it as not true.

2. Your discernment about **the <u>validity</u> of a theory can be correct in two ways and incorrect in two ways as well.**

Two Ways to Discern Correctly and Two Ways not To:

	In fullness of time it proves to be: →	True	An Illusion
Discern something as: →	True	√	X
→	An Illusion	X	√

---

[148] Ref: *Philosophy of Religion,* by Professor James Hall, PhD. A marvellous 36 x 30 minute lecture series, available from http://www.thegreatcourses.com/tgc/courses/Course_Detail.aspx?cid=4680

I.   You are correct when you discern something to be true (or illusory) and it actually is true (or illusory) as the case may be. Otherwise you are incorrect.

II.   You can discern incorrectly when the evidence points to something being....

    a) True when it is, in fact, illusory (e.g. a long term relationship).

        I recall a long time ago when I fell in love with someone. They declared their love for me. I felt a strong emotional connection. Our love making was great. We had the same values and beliefs about what's important in life. We both wanted the same things. Synchronicity and fate somehow seemed to have pulled us together. Everything seemed right. I loved this girl deeply. Within the space of a few weeks, it was all over. The large amount of evidence that promoted the theory in my head about a long-lasting if not lifelong love - was incorrect.

    b) Illusory when it is, in fact, true

        There was a girl, I knew at school, called Charlotte Robins. I was in Upper 6th year and she, a year below me. Charlotte was stunning; tall, long blonde hair, fabulous looking and she knew it, in a very cool fashion. She only went out with the pick of the young men. I discerned that I wasn't amongst those who would get picked. At school, Charlotte hardly gave me a first look, never mind a second glance.

        "No way, José!" I thought to myself.

        I had just been given permission to drive my dad's car. One Saturday night, I agreed to give Charlotte a lift from a dull party to hopefully a better one nearby. We got about half way and she told me to pull over.

        I obeyed. Before I'd even turned the ignition off Charlotte leaned over and gave me a long, deep and passionate kiss. I was gobsmacked – literally. I'd hardly caught my breath when she said – "I've wanted to do that for some time, Paul. Let's not bother with the party. Take me somewhere else". Wow!!!!

I certainly got my supposition, from the evidence presented (i.e. not giving me first or second looks) about me <u>not</u> being a "pick of the young men", incorrect there!

Ω

The two examples cite day to day events that happen. When journeying within, the evidence is ethereal and experiential. Take one step at a time (when forming a judgement about the validity of inner experiences), spirit does.

3. **Impartiality, <u>objectivity</u> and vulnerability:** you can see from the two examples in the previous item how difficult I found it in my younger days to remain detached when I'm engaged in something close to my heart. When it comes to falling in love, I remain vulnerable. Most of us are - are we not? Love conquers all – especially impartiality, objectivity and in my case, coolness. Me, a-heart-on-sleeve Leo, with Leo rising (personality) with Moon in Cancer (very caring and vulnerable emotionally) - I don't stand an emotional cat-in-hell's chance of remaining cool in love, with regard to my vulnerabilities ☺.

It took me years to recognise the importance of allowing my vulnerabilities to be okay in life. The more uncomfortable they are the less objective I am and the more prone to error in judgement I become.

Many of us deny our vulnerabilities, our fears. As discussed earlier, when you attempt to deny your feelings, you cannot be selective. When you deny your fear, you deny yourself access to your *true self*.

When you deny yourself truth,
you deny yourself happiness and fulfilment.

4. **Acknowledge the fear of <u>consequences</u> of expressing the truth.** When you see truth, you no longer need to believe or feel something to be true. You know it regardless of what anyone else thinks, says or believes about you. When you act on or speak of truth, others make seek to deny it. They may seek to ridicule you and in extreme cases those in power may seek to defile you.

Working with a Pendulum

I have been working with a pendulum, also known as dowsing, since 2005. Dowsing takes practice and care. In a client session, I dowse with a pendulum to communicate between the client's and my higher self. My higher self receives and channels answers to questions from the client's higher self to my conscious mind.

Dowsing

A basic dowsing pendulum consists typically of a crystal or weight suspended by a light chain. There's nothing precious inherently about the crystal pendulum itself but in a short time it attunes to you. Before you hand it to anyone else, ask if it will remain effective for the other person too. Remember to cleanse it in fresh or salt water when they hand it back to you.

If the other person's vibration is close to you, the pendulum will probably answer "yes" because they are attuned to you. A total stranger though may well not be able to get results.

Use the thumb, the index finger and, if you prefer, the middle finger of your dominant hand to hold the chain of a pendulum. In addition, I point my index finger of the other hand forwards whilst pressing the thumb and middle finger together to form a circle.

Bend your wrist and fingers as illustrated with the string or chain hanging unimpeded freely. Find your programme for the "yes" and "no" movement for your pendulum. Simply ask your higher self to give the signal for "yes" then ask for the signal for "no".

Illustration 27: Hold Crystal in Dominant Hand and Use other Hand as a Tuning Device

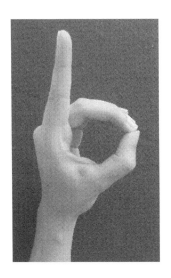 

Different people receive differing signals. For me, the pendulum swinging back and forth means "yes" whereas a swinging from side to side means "no." A diagonal movement means "maybe" or "something is incomplete", or the question needs rephrasing. Sometimes the pendulum swirls anticlockwise for releasing unwanted emotions. Occasionally it swirls clockwise which means that new powers or wisdom are being handed down. If the pendulum remains stationary, this often means, "no answer" or "wait a few moments". If the pendulum shakes or wobbles without any discernible movement, it often means I am not in the right frame of mind to ask the question objectively. When so, take a few deep breaths and relax your muscles.

By and large, I use a pendulum to answer 'yes-no' questions. After you have had a chance to 'play' with it for a while, you can ask the pendulum to shape signals for phrases such as "it's still undecided" or "ask me later". Pendulum dowsing is much more than asking 'yes-no' questions.

For example:

- In certain client sessions, I scan pre-written lists of feelings (for example: low self worth, feeling drained, angry and so on.) to discover which negative emotions are holding a client back. When my finger passes over the right word or phrase the pendulum switches from a "no" signal to "yes".

- I can pick a card out of a tarot or oracle deck, directed by the client's higher self, during a remote session by simply shuffling the pack, splitting it into two piles and asking if the client's designated card is in the first, or the second pile. Discard the unneeded pile. Split the cards that remain into two piles and repeat the process, until there are five or six cards left. Then lay the cards side by side and ask if each card, working from one to the next, is the chosen card. You end up with the card the client's higher self has chosen.

  You can select a series of cards by arranging the deck face down in piles of five, each arranged like a fan. Move the hand not holding the pendulum quickly over the piles asking the pendulum to indicate the location of the pile the client's card is in. Then by pointing to each card in the pile selected, the pendulum will indicate which of the cards has been chosen by the client's higher self. Repeat the process until you have the complete sequence of cards required.

- Clients and I can have a three way conversation with the client's higher self. For example, I may ask a client where a specific emotion came from. The pendulum often starts swinging positively (to confirm what the client is about to say) or negatively (to disaffirm what is about to be said) before the client speaks because their higher self is already aware of what they are about to say. Sometimes I get an answer directly from the client's higher self, without the client thinking or saying a word. I then use the pendulum to confirm I have understood their higher self's message correctly in my conscious mind before vocalising the answer.

Dowsing proves a very effective tool to probe the subtleties of what goes on within the clients (or my own) subconscious. There are many sites that will help you get going with dowsing.

Http://pendulumdowsing.org/ will give you a quick introduction and point you to other reference sites. Here are some tips to help and pitfalls to be wary of.

Choice of Crystal

I use two pendulums, a clear crystal and an amethyst. The clear crystal can be used as a 'recorder' it is very powerful for delving into a client's history and pinpointing the source of an issue. I use the amethyst for relatively quick yes/no answers or to confirm that messages are correct.

If no crystal is available, all you require is a weight, a ring for example, at the end of a thread.

Cleaning and Maintenance

Crystals become de-energised after use so need to be cleansed before re-use. You can soak or wash a crystal pendulum in cold salted water or ring a pair of Buddhist temple bells over it to rejuvenate its power. Tibetan bowls may also be used to create a 'sound bath.' I am lucky to live by the sea and wash crystals in fresh sea water which is a very powerful method of rejuvenating their healing and listening qualities. The seawater needs to be in a bucket or receptacle before you revive your crystals in it. Never place your crystals in the sea as they can lose their power completely. Crystals also enjoy a good bask in sunlight or moonlight especially placed in the earth in a garden or window box.

I once dropped a pendulum onto a hard floor and a small chip broke off its pointed end. I asked the pendulum if it needed to be replaced. My higher self signalled "yes". I asked should it be returned to the land or sea. "No", came the answer. The crystal now rests very happily among other crystals in its retirement home. (Stop press, I met someone whom the crystal is now meant for. It's had its rest and is now at work again in the service of humankind.)

Develop Calmness and Objectivity

Practice, practice, practice: in the early days of dowsing I became a little anxious when using a pendulum to get to a coherent answer for a client. I was working with the unknown for the first time and hadn't yet convinced myself that dowsing would bring valid results. It took a few tries to feel comfortable and confident to go beyond asking simple 'yes-no' questions.

With practice I developed the patience to clear the mind, ask a question, avoid pre-judging the outcome - and wait for the answer to channel into my mind. The trick is to sit and wait with a 'blank canvas' mind. It seems like ages but spirit-mind is relatively fast. Within one or two seconds you can fill the blank canvas with insightful answers and develop the logic verbally to explain complex situations.[149] Sit, listen and wait; don't force the answer.

Ask the Right Question, in Context

I reiterate, remain calm and objective when you choose to work with your higher self. You will ask about things important to you, otherwise why ask? When something is very important, we tend to be attached to the answer. For example, I used to my pendulum for advice about a very important relationship that was going wrong for me.

I would ask a question like, "Does she love me?" "Will we get back together?" I found that these are inappropriate questions and would usually get an unreceptive response. Why? Because the questions refer to an event or outcome that goes outside of the sphere of my personal power. I do not have the authority to ask what another person will or will not do without their permission. It took me a while to figure this out.

Instead, I found that only questions which pertained to me and no one else delivered direct answers. For example, instead of asking if someone else loves me or if we will get back together, I could ask: "Am I doing all the right things to evolve this relationship for the good? Is there anything more I can do? "What does spirit advise me to do next to bring happiness to us both?" Even then, I could have served myself better by taking care with emotionally charged questions. I did not until I learned from some further pitfalls.

If I asked an emotionally charged question and got the answer I wanted – a swinging "yes", literally and metaphorically, I would fire another two or three relevant questions, to confirm the "yes". I would get excited and dig deeper and deeper. The pendulum would

---

[149] For example, in *Part XIV*, chapter, *Defrost your 'Energy Freezer', Defrag your Soul – Case Story*, I summarise a fairly detailed dialogue with a client's higher self.

eventually signal that I had gone past the stage of sensibility. I found it difficult to accept the simplicity and directness that my higher self wishes to use.

When the answer signalled "no", alarm bells of panic would ring. I found myself conjuring up a plethora of different questions that, in effect, all asked the same or a similar question. All would typically still result in the answer, "no". So I would then ask questions to try to arrive at a compromise and I would get half answers. Eventually, I would get a stationary pendulum that refused to budge. This meant my interrogation attempts had become futile. Crestfallen, I would put the pendulum away, thank my higher self for the advice given and retire.

In one or two very hurtful periods, my holding hand would shake; usually in the direction I wanted the pendulum to swing. It became obvious that I could not trust the answer.

My advice is plain and simple. If you cannot remain calm and objective whilst dowsing with a pendulum, do not even pick it up.

Paul C Burr

Part XIV: The Matrix for the Life You Would Like to Have, Imagine

If you've seen the movie, *the Matrix*[150], you see a world in which perceived reality is created by a huge computer programme. Well that's just about how your physical world works AND you get to run the computer programme yourself. You specify the outcomes you want. All it requires is your imagination (= image in ions/atoms). You put the image of the life you would like spirit to manifest for you into a matrix. There are a few guidelines:

1. The image is good for all concerned – the good for you that is good for everyone.
2. If you want to place specific people in your matrix, get their agreement to be in it beforehand. Contemplate how you want the image to appear collectively. Otherwise be non-specific about the others you engage with.
3. You feel passionate about it. It represents fulfilment to you or at least a step towards what fulfilment means to you.
4. Your intuition tells you it has the *right feel* about it. The matrix contains what your soul seeks to experience and learn from.
5. It takes you closer to your *true self* and doesn't involve too many potential distractions.
6. If you attempt to abuse the above guidelines, you may invoke a karmic response according to the *Law of Consequence.*

The main body of the computer programme contains the oneness of the 'spirit code' of your *Higher Self*. It works perfectly. But the logic of the programme passes through subroutines (sub-conscious programmes) in your mind where lurks the separateness of the *false ego*. Until they are cleaned up, these subroutines sully spirit's code. Spirit attempts to manifest your *Higher Self's* will (the higher levels of your *desire body*). Whereas the *false-ego* can fetter spirit's will with

---

[150] Ref: Check out *The Matrix* at The Internet Movie Data Base website, www.imdb.com/title/tt0133093/.

petty desires and wishes (the lower levels of your *desire body*), borne out of shame, anger, sadness and fear.

What you project forms the matrix, your matrix - a mirror of all the light and darkness within you. Your projection creates the relationships you form, your job, health, everything. Randomness doesn't come into it.

With the tool below you can create an image of the matrix of the life you wish to have – consciously and proactively. It will help you focus firstly on what's most important in your life: a relationship, money, a job or good health. Keep the guidelines listed on the previous page to hand as you build your matrix.

Self-help Tool: Build your Matrix

The top row of the matrix contains *category* headings for everything that's important to you – see diagram that follows. For example, here are the category headings I use.

- Spiritual/personal development
- Life Contract – the most important thing you seek to achieve in this life
- Partner
- Family
- Work
- Home
- Wellbeing
- Finance
- Friends
- Leisure and Hobbies
- Passions (e.g. causes, charity work, serving the community, group working and so on)
- Other.....

Down the side of the matrix, place 7 *Levels of Operation:*

1. Purpose.... What purpose do you seek to achieve under this *category*?
2. Identity... Who are you or what phrase would you use to describe the identity of what you want under this *category*?

3. Values and Beliefs... What's important to you about this *category*? What do you need to believe in to make it happen, about: yourself, the others involved and the task in hand?

4. Traits and Characteristics... How would you characterise your feelings and emotions about this *category*?

5. Skills and Competencies... What skills and competencies do you want to demonstrate or develop for this *category* to be a success?

6. Behaviours... What is it that you will be doing, especially doing differently, to make this *category* turn out the way you want it to be?

7. Environment... Describe the environment you intend to create to make this *category* a success.

I have demonstrated how to complete the matrix by filling in two *categories* from my *Life Matrix: Spiritual/Personal Development* and *Work*. The examples are to help you understand sufficiently how to populate your own matrix over time. Don't attempt to complete the whole matrix in one sitting, focus on the most important two or three categories only. Fill the column under their headings of other categories as they crop up in importance.

The contents of each box within the matrix are 'cast in sand, not cement'. You can change them at any point in time – especially when your intuition tells you to. Check for consistency and resolve any conflicts up and down each column - and along each row of the matrix as you complete them. As you continue to build column after column, your matrix becomes a conscious picture of the life you seek.

I'll cover how to energise the matrix when complete, or column by column, after the example that follows.

Example of Two Completed Columns from *The Life's Matrix I Seek*

Questions to ask of spirit		Spiritual/Personal Development	Work
What purpose do I seek to achieve through my • Spiritual / personal development? • Work?	Purpose	To shine as bright as any human can. To share wisdom, to help the world move from separateness to oneness?	To help clients/readers release the shame, anger, sadness and fear that holds them back from finding, opening, becoming and expressing their true selves.
Who am I in this category?	Identity	Someone, with an abstract mind existing independently and apart from desire, who radiates light and wisdom in accord with spirit. Or higher!	A seer that helps others to become seers in their own right.
What's important to me about this category? What do I need to believe in to make it a success? (e.g. in self / others / the task in hand / the world)	Values and Beliefs	I live in truth. • My own self worth • Wisdom comes from my core • Everything evolves to the good. • Spirit knows best • Oneness	I operate from my heart and sacral centre. • I am competent and caring at my work. • Giving and receiving are of the same coin. • You are capable of things far more than you can dream. • What you attract is a mirror of something within you.
What traits and characteristics describe this category?	Traits and Characteristics (continued)	• Truth • Courage • Willpower • Compassion • Oneness • Curiosity	• Passion • Curiosity • Sensibility • Articulacy • Self trust • Collaborative

		Passion / Perseverance	Composure
What skills and competencies do I seek to develop?	Skills and Competencies	• To give and receive love wholly • Intuition • To trust and abide by spirit's governance • To express my core/true self unfettered by false ego	• Writing • Coaching • Healing • Public Speaking • Leadership • Business
What shall I see happening?	Behaviours	• Diligent study and research • Meditation and reflection • Individual and Group working • Experimentation • Acknowledgement – of self and to others	• Writing • Coaching • Healing • Business Meetings • Global travel
Describe the environment to enable this category to happen.	Environment	• Teachers who arrive at the right time • Peaceful and welcoming surroundings • Home comforts • Tidiness • Decluttered • Space and light • Companionship of fellow apprentices in the light	• Professional • Quality travel and accommodation • Competent support network • Companionship of savvy business professionals

The Life's Matrix I Seek

Questions to ask of spirit		Spiritual / Personal Develop-ment	Life Contract	Partner	Home	Work	Finance	Friends & Family	Leisure and Hobbies	Other
What purpose do I seek to achieve?	Purpose									
Who am I in this category?	Identity									
What's important to me about this category? What do I need to believe in to make it a success? (e.g. in self / others / the task in hand / the world)	Values and Beliefs									
What traits and characteristics describe this category?	Traits and Characteristics									
What skills and competencies do I seek to develop?	Skills and Competencies									
What shall I see happening?	Behaviours									
Describe the environment to enable this category to happen.	Environment									

Energise your Matrix, column by column.

When you have completed a column, find somewhere quiet to sit and contemplate it. Study the column from top to bottom and back again. Build up the picture. Integrate each line into the picture and see yourself in the picture. Close your eyes, go into the picture and see the people and things around you - as if you are looking through your own eyes. Hear what you are saying and listen to the responses of others. Check for any sounds, smells or tastes. Remember, do not include specific people unless they agree to be in your picture beforehand.

Ask yourself "How does it feel to achieve exactly what I want in this important area of my life?" Immerse yourself in the feeling. Immerse completely in the feeling for 17 seconds as you gaze through your own eyes, imagining the scene around you.

When you have completed the 17 seconds, raise your arm straight up above your head, palms facing upward. Say the following: "I raise this feeling of having received that which I seek of .... up to spirit, knowing that spirit knows what's best for me. I raise it up and let go of it". As you say the words, imagine the feeling in the picture rising up to spirit. Detach the feeling in the picture from your person and mind as it goes. Let go of it completely.

Spirit needs your mind's complete cooperation. When you let the feeling go of that which you desire completely, spirit is free to work on your behalf as it sees fit. Repeat this 17-second exercise for 17 days straight. If you change the picture, start the process again.

At first, I found this letting go process to be difficult. I wanted the feeling so badly, I felt I couldn't let it go. I later realised that my unwillingness to release the feeling was because I might start focusing on not being able to have what I want instead, i.e. scarcity. I later realised the likelihood of focusing on scarcity proved equally true if I kept myself attached to the feeling. The issue wasn't about letting go of the feeling; the issue was about allowing myself to focus on scarcity.

When you focus on scarcity, you invoke the negative emotions associated with that scarcity. You, in effect, create your own 'scarcity subroutine' and scarcity is what you might get if control of the computer programme flows into this 'scarcity subroutine'. You have the power to avoid scarcity and the final say in the vibration that your

DNA sends out into the universe. What you don't control are the consequences of that vibration - that is down to *karma*.

If, for example, you seek wealth and fame and spirit concurs that's what will help you on your *Life Journey*, what you seek will come your way. On the other hand, if you try and succeed in manipulating spirit, your 'success' will bring *karmic* consequences that you may not want.

This leads to a second reason as to why you might not find it easy to raise the feeling (of having what you want) up to spirit and let it go.

Just at the point of letting go, stop and listen. Is there a little voice inside of you saying, "Are you sure you really want what's in this picture? Are you sure that you are not asking for it out of fear?"

This is where your innermost feelings are your compass. Listen and act accordingly.

Finally there's a third reason, closely aligned to the second reason, why you can't let the feeling go. Is the voice saying, "You know, I really want this but I can't see any way that it is going to happen and so I'm not going to ask for it wholly"? If you don't ask (i.e. you don't raise up the feeling to spirit) wholly, you don't invoke wholly spirit's full power.

The answer to all these scenarios is the same....

1. Picture what you want wholly and only wholly.
2. Sit in the feeling of having achieved what you want already.
3. Raise it up to spirit and let it go.

One last word...

Many people, like me, worldwide have practised amateur occultism with the *Law of Attraction* to get what they want in life. Material things such as money, a job, a lovely home and whatever else was chosen brought me comfort if not a sense of fulfilment. In my case, the half life of any material fulfilment was fairly short lived. (That doesn't mean I was or am ungrateful. Quite the opposite, I feel truly blessed by all the abundances I enjoy in life.) True joy for me is found within by receiving what I ask for and being able to share it as well. So when it comes to sharing, I suggest that there's nothing more abundant than love, truth, compassion, wisdom and healing – to help others on their journey. Giving and receiving abundantly is nature's way.

Defrost your 'Energy Freezer', Defrag your Soul – Case Story

This section contains a case story of a 'negative-emotion clearing' process I first learned in 2009 and since then integrated into the majority of material I now use.

I pay homage to Lucille White[151] who taught me how to dowse effectively with a pendulum and use scan sheets to channel answers. There's nothing unique about using these materials in energy healing. What is different is the application I evolved from Lucille's initial teaching. Put simply, it's quick and effective. It's far quicker than any other technique of its type that I've come across.

You can find testimony to my work on the Internet: http://paulcburr.com/private-client-testimonials/.

Case Story: The Tale of Connie and the Anger She Locked Within

Connie called me, she was desperate; she didn't give me the time to say, "How can I help you?"

"My friend Edie recommended you. I binge drink every 2-3 weeks. When I do, I behave deplorably. I vent anger. I don't drink in-between but after my last bout, this weekend just gone, my husband has threatened to leave me. He wants me to go to Alcoholics Anonymous but I'm not an alcoholic. I want to make an appointment with you please."

"I can probably help you. Would you like to know what I do first or do you want make an appoint...?" I replied curiously.

"When are you next free?" Connie interrupted

"3pm, today."

"Good, where's your office..." Less than two hours later, Connie buzzed the door entrance.

---

151 Lucille White creator of the diagnostic process, The Truth Model™, now resides in South Africa. Ref: http://lucillewhiteblogs.wordpress.com/

The Healing Starts

Connie confided immediately how bad things had become between her disabled husband, Peter, and her.

Peter had been injured, some ten years prior, in a car accident whilst driving at high speed. His body was severely disabled and he had suffered brain damage. He was prone to fits of temper because of the frustrations of living in a disabled body.

Connie and Peter were separated at the time of his accident but Connie chose to return to the marital home because she felt guilty; "Peter might not have been speeding if we'd been together".

During Connie's last drinking binge, things got really out hand. Peter and Connie started to argue in front of one of Peter's carers about the quality of healthcare Peter received. Connie raged at the carer in a drunken temper. Taken aback, the carer gave her notice and left immediately. Then Peter lost his temper. He let fly a volley of abuse at Connie about her drinking and behaviour. Connie couldn't find the words to justify herself. She felt trapped in a clouded mist of shame and rage. Lacking self control through inebriation, Connie's animalistic instincts kicked in and she struck Peter. Three days later, Connie felt "destitute" and, in her words, "deservedly so".

I started the investigation of Connie's problems by reframing the purpose of her negative emotions in the context of duality. [In order to appreciate an enabling emotion fully (e.g. patience, confidence, self worth and love) we must first know its opposite, disabling emotion; what not-that-emotion is (i.e. not – patience, confidence, self-worth or love).] Connie accepted this explanation of duality's purpose.

She began to consider that all the negative emotions she had suffered for many years, somehow served a purpose in the bigger scheme of her life. We got down eliciting all the current negative feelings and emotions (in the form of shame, anger, sadness and fear) Connie felt about herself, not Peter, that she allowed to hold her back in life?

(Note: This is a most challenging part of any healing process for a client to go through. Finding and opening the source of your emotional issues is a major step in itself to help you self-heal.)

Connie allowed three, key negative feelings to hold her back. Each feeling consisted of a combination of two or more of the four fundamental negative emotions: shame, anger, sadness and fear.

1. Anger, sadness and fear: "I am lost and without direction".
2. Shame and sadness: "I am living a lie because of my past".

   Connie carried huge shame about things she'd done in her teenage years that she had refused to tell anyone about since. I didn't need to know them. She confirmed that, at one level, she had returned to look after her husband out of shame. In effect, she used this giving of energy to her husband as a distraction from facing the shame she carried about herself.

   I wanted Connie to focus on her early childhood because when clients recall emotional events in their adolescent or adult years, such events are usually an 'emotional harmonic' of things that happened to them in their early childhood.
3. Shame and sadness: "I'm exploiting my soul".

   I paraphrased to Connie that her soul was declaring "I've had enough. I'm bored with these same old repetitions. Time to move on!" She concurred.

Connie answered and reflected deeply about more detailed questions into her personal history.

- Where did these negative emotions come from?
- Who gave them to her?
- When?
- What impact have these negative emotions (developed in childhood) had throughout her life?
- How did these negativities evolve or change as she developed from childhood, through adolescence, to adulthood?
- Specifically, what are all the big decisions Connie made in life out of fear?
- Which decisions is she still making now out of fear, as opposed to those which will take her down the path to her real purpose in life? Those which give her a sense of fulfilment and afterwards 'feel right'.

Connie brought up a host of associated childhood memories. She was raised as a single child by her mother who suffered from acute alcoholism. Connie recalled the abuse she received throughout her childhood. One specific event stood out.

One evening the apartment, where Connie and her mother lived, caught fire. Alone, the five year old Connie used the fire escape to get herself to safety. Her mother, later rescued, was too inebriated to help herself or Connie or vice versa. Later, Connie's grandfather beat her mother mercilessly when he found out what had happened. Connie called this "my moment of separation" from all her family.

Connie recalled how helpless she felt throughout her childhood. So like most if not all of us, she blamed herself and felt at fault for what happened to her as a child. She carried anger for sure but that anger was cocooned in shame.

Connie allowed shame and the behaviours shame manifests to rule her everyday life. She had developed a number of compensatory behaviours to disguise this shame to others but not to herself - and so on occasion, she would drink excessively. Alcohol insulated her from the shame but at the same time exposed Connie to her anger. When she sobered up, the shame would return.

Connie and I identified the anger (cocooned in shame) that her unconscious mind had locked inside an 'energy freezer' within her *Living Matrix/Etheric Body*. In effect, Connie kept the anger and shame 'frozen solid' during her normal and sober conscious day, most of the time. She could control her anger but the shame was still prone to 'leak out'. With her permission, I tapped into Connie's *Higher Self*.[152]

Connie's Higher Self Revealed:

- How excess alcohol opened the 'freezer door'. How the contents would defrost and be exposed to external stimuli. When something happened that reminded Connie of her childhood helplessness, in a mirror-like fashion, she would either:
  1. Let fly and vent her anger on all around her or...

---

[152] The Higher Self – that part inside of us that knows the blueprint for perfect physical, emotional and psychic health.

2. Sometimes, be able to show profound depths of empathy and wisdom. Connie had learned all about helplessness, fear and anger. If only she could tap into it to help others.[153]

Alcohol predisposed Connie to bouts of anger but it didn't predetermine that she would get angry. Connie's issue was her increased susceptibility to bouts of anger under the influence of alcohol - should something trigger her childhood memories consciously or unconsciously.

- Connie couldn't change her childhood experiences but she did have the power to change the feelings attached to those experiences that no longer served a useful purpose. **In doing so, she would 'defrost the freezer contents', hopefully forever - and throw away those items (shame, anger, sadness and fear) that were way past their 'use-by date'.** What remained was wisdom, gained through a profound empathy for adults who suffered in the same way during their childhood - and children suffering right now. Connie extracted the wisdom, now 'useable at room temperature', and brought it into the light.

This reminds me of a sentence that I heard some while ago.

"The best therapists for drug addiction were once addicts themselves; now making good."

- The lack of care her husband had been receiving had exposed his helplessness further. When sober, Connie connected her husband's helplessness to her own helplessness within. However, as well as empathy for her husband's helplessness, his condition triggered shame, a profound sense of shame within Connie. When Connie

---

153 I remind the reader of Brene Brown's amazing video presentation, http://www.ted.com/talks/lang/eng/brene_brown_on_vulnerability.html, also available on YouTube. How, when we filter emotions we cannot be selective. When we filter sadness, for example, we filter joy at the same time. I have found. When we lock away shame, anger, sadness and fear, we also lock away the deeper wisdom we learned from the experiences, from the events that triggered those emotions. When we filter hurt, for example, we filter empathy.

could not take the shame anymore, she would insulate herself from it by drinking alcohol; she would unlock the freezer door and defrost the contents (anger) within until she sobered up; by which time she would feel ashamed, yet again.

- Bottom line: Connie connected the helplessness she saw in her husband with her childhood memories. In the past that connection had not been conscious to her. Connie now saw the vicious spiral that which without intervention would continue to take her downwards.

Connie now Realised with Conviction that the Time Had Come to Turn her Life Around.

I helped Connie to find out what useful purpose, her life-limiting emotions served, namely: "...lost without direction", "living a lie..." and "...exploiting my soul". I did this by asking a simple question, for each of the negative emotions consecutively - *"How would you like to be or feel instead?"*

Through careful dialogue, Connie identified what "<u>not</u> lost without direction", "<u>not</u> living a lie" and "<u>not</u> exploiting my soul" meant to her. Here's what she came up with:

1. "I feel laid back and happy with myself".
2. "I do things that I find challenging and make me feel whole".
3. "I am excited, optimistic and compassionate".
4. "I am brave and useful to myself".
5. "I like and love myself".
6. "I am patient and understanding with myself".

Connie crafted a series of affirmations to help her take her next *spiritual step* to emotional wellbeing; to get closer to her *true self.*

Where would that *spiritual step* take Connie? What was the vibration that she headed toward? I helped Connie give herself a seventh affirmation.

7. "I operate from the highest vibration" (Connie's next *spiritual step*).

Next, we found out which of the three negative feelings cut the deepest into her psyche - such that if that deepest negative feeling (*major conflict*) was released, the other two would release themselves at the same time.

Answer: "I'm exploiting my soul".

Using this simple statement I channelled Connie's *major conflict* in life: "I cannot operate from the highest vibration because I exploit my soul".

We tuned in and removed the effect of the major conflict and remnants of any remaining negative feelings from Connie's matrix, i.e. her *Etheric Body*.

Conceptually...

This Process Created a Void in Connie's Overall Vibrational Signal.

We set about mapping[154] out a pathway forward by which Connie could fill the void with positive vibrations or enabling energy patterns. The path would have two vibrational 'stepping stones' en route, for her to complete her next *spiritual step*, "I operate from the highest vibration". They were:

1. "I accept myself, for who I am, where I've been and all that's happened in the past. I accept that now is the time for me to move on".

2. "I am cool" (due to happen within 2 months of the healing session, assuming Connie kept to the exercises she was about to create for herself). "Cool" in this case meant composed, focused and taking everything in.

Filling the Void

With the map of the journey now in front of Connie, I asked the same question twice:

1. "As you think about 'accepting yourself...' what would you or I see yourself doing more of or differently – which would tell you that you were 'accepting yourself...'?"

2. "As you think about being 'cool' what would you or I see yourself doing more of or differently – which would tell you that you were being 'cool'?"

Here are the actions that Connie came up with:

---

154 Note, the 'map' is not the 'territory'.

- "Go for walks".
- "Go to the gym regularly"
- "Rejuvenate my interest in jive dancing for fitness and expressing myself".
- "Pause when something that used to upset me happens".
- "Be polite and respectful to my husband's carers".
- "Write my book".
- "Remain calm no matter what the circumstances".

Connie was now equipped with a combination of seven affirmations; namely: "1. I feel laid back and happy with myself 2. I do things that I find challenging..." and so on, and a series of seven actions to take, on a day to day basis. These were the exercises by which Connie would replace her hitherto negative feelings with new positive emotions and fill the darkness within herself with light.

She was to repeat out loud each affirmation seventeen times, twice a day, for 17 days - and focus on listening to and accepting each affirmation's vibration into her body. Furthermore, Connie would put the exercises into action until she integrated them into her muscle memory. Once integrated, Connie would exercise, write, be respectful, pause and remain calm naturally without having to think much about her actions.

Connie left the session uplifted and committed to turning her life around. She called me three months later. She enjoyed a drink occasionally. The binging and bouts of anger and shame had long since gone! Ω

I have not figured out a way to transfer a complete *Etheric Cleansing*[155] self development process into print concisely. It would take up a whole book of itself and take a significant amount of practice with the tools used, to gain an acceptable degree of confidence in the process.

At its core, *Etheric Cleansing* focuses on:

1. Clearing the negative emotions that hold you back, namely in the form of shame, anger, sadness and fear, but in your own words

---

[155] I offer a 1-1 *Etheric Cleansing* service to clients over the telephone or Internet. Contact Doctapaul@paulcburr.com.

2. *Spiritual step* -by-step, exercises to find, open, become and express your *true self.*

Self-help Tool: Transmute Negative Emotions and Characteristics into their Positive, Enabling Counterparts and Act as if You Had Released Them.

This exercise uses the duality principle that, for example, you learn and appreciate love completely only when you appreciate not love completely too. So when you feel a negative emotion and study its origins, consequences and think things through – you indirectly are learning about its positive counterpart. I illustrate the exercise by way of an anonymous client example. (Note, if you've practised some dowsing[156], you can use a pendulum to fine tune your answers.)

1. **List the top 4-5 negative emotions that you hold about yourself and only yourself (no one and nothing else)**

   Client example:

Negative Emotions and Feelings about Self	
i.	I am angry at myself over my own folly
ii.	My soul feels bored with how I spend my life
iii.	I feel bad about something I did.
iv.	I feel baffled. I do not know what to do to get out of this.

---

[156] See *Part XIII*, chapter, *Working with a Pendulum.*

2. **List, alongside each negative emotion, how you would like to feel or be, instead.**

Client example:

Negative Emotions and Feelings about Self	Positive Counterparts in the form of Affirmations (Repeat each of the seven affirmations below 17 times, twice a day, for 17 days)
i. *I am angry at myself over my own folly*	i. *I have freed myself up from rage and grief* ii. *I have released myself from my chains* iii. *I am at peace with myself*
ii. *My soul feels bored with how I spend my life*	iv. *I commit myself to fulfil new ambitions* v. *My soul is excited*
iii. *I feel bad about something I did.*	vi. *I feel fresh, clean, washed and clothed, emotionally and spiritually.*
iv. *I feel baffled. I do not know what to do to get out of this.*	vii. *I feel in tune with the right path. I know where I am.* viii. *I am healed. I am whole.*

3. **Repeat each of the affirmations, in the right hand column of Step 2, 17 times, twice a day, for 17 days.**
   In the client example, in Step 2, you find eight such affirmations.
   List up to ten affirmations. If you have more than ten affirmations, do the first ten for seventeen days. Do the next ten, or remaining, affirmations for the next seventeen days and so on.

4. ***Act as if.* List three or four things that you would do more of, or differently, to act out each of the affirmations.**
    Client example:
    1. *Focus on the new business expansion programme I have wanted to start up.*
    2. *Be proactive in connecting people and things together. Put myself out there.*
    3. *Commit myself to a coaching programme to develop myself and my business.*
    4. *Keep myself physically fit and eat healthily.*

    In addition to the affirmations, as and when you feel up for it, start to do more of the things in your '*act as if* list.'

    Act as if *you have made the transformation you seek.*

Paul C Burr

Part XV: The Contract You Made: Between your Last Life and This One

You chose this life for a purpose; to find, open up and become your *true self*. In exchange you contracted to serve humankind.

It's a two way deal. You receive help so that you can help others. Some of us only stick to one side of the deal. Some are very kind and caring, others are not so inclined. Either way we attract *karma*.

Some very kind and compassionate people devote their lives to others and struggle with or ignore their own material, emotional and spiritual needs. They get their esteem from others in the form of "thank yous" and recognition. But they do so at the expense of their own inner wellbeing. Not valuing yourself means you've missed the first half the journey. I reemphasise.

Put your own oxygen mask on before you help others to put on theirs

These well-meaning people ignore their own self-worth issues by busying themselves completely in serving others' needs and wants.

When you filter out, ignore or deny feelings of low self worth, you filter out self worth as well. Remember the 'wet and dry' of life. You can't know one without the other. So life is about knowing self worth and its shadow, low-self worth. When you understand both, and how to transmute the shadow into light, then you understand the alchemy of life.

You perceive the positive and negative for what they are. You acknowledge both sides. You take up a sort of superposition from where you can see the duality and so discern your truth - through and from which you learn to express your true self-worth.

Some people cut themselves off from even thinking about their self worth. They refuse to speak of their innermost feelings about themselves; instead they absorb themselves in work, caring for others, drugs, shopping, gambling, drinking, charity work; things that may be good or not good for their health. (See section, *Balance/Temperance*, in *Part XIII*). They encase the shame, anger, sadness and fear - that they allow to shield them from their *true self* - with another shield made of distraction.

They live outside two layers of shielding from their *true selves*:
1. Outer shield: distraction or escapism.
2. Inner shield: shame, anger, sadness and fear.

They pretend that all's well but often suffer from a series of frustrating situations and events in the material world around them. They attract constant hold-ups, things that go wrong (e.g. lost keys or mobile phones, minor sometimes major accidents and travel delays), all external signs of things ignored within. Such problems increase their busy-ness further, their frustrations escalate until one day they or their body screams "enough!" They may suffer a (near) breakdown in health: mentally, emotionally and/or physically.

This happened to me not so long ago. I got myself distracted in drink, computer games and relationships. I went through a few repeating habits that I was all too familiar with. Eventually, I had enough and got myself thankfully back on my *life's path*. I readied myself to find out my own *Life Contract*.

Like any contract, your *Life Contract* may contain events, dates, service level agreements, methods of working and all forms of detail that you could find in a normal business contract. At birth and throughout your life you are given the resources to complete your next milestone within the contract.

Once you consciously read your Life Contract, you will realise (real eyes) that there is no going back.

You made your *Life Contract* between your last incarnation and this one. Your *Life Contract* can be very precise. If the timing is right when you find and open your Life Contract, you will get far more detail than an overarching *Life Purpose* statement. You receive the right amount of detail appropriate for you at that point in time. As you progress towards achieving it, you can ask for more details.

You contract to achieve specific objectives or outcomes in each and every lifetime. The contract is locked away in *The Akashic Records* which are stored in a vault beneath the foundations of a very special cathedral or temple. When you arrive outside the vault's door, you can have access to your contract by simply asking permission to see it. Here's how you get there.

Case Story: The Cathedral

Only now do I realise where to find the Cathedral. It lies within and is accessed only by meditation at a very deep level. No-one can describe it as every person's inner space is different.

I sat straight in a comfortable chair – straight back, upper legs, lower legs and feet – all at 90°, perpendicular to one another – not rigid though, relax.

I closed my eyes, steadied my breath; count to 4 as I breathe in, count to 4 as I breathe out, slightly deeper than normal, yet gentle and focused. I forgot who I am and why I am here. I let go of my past and everything that led up to this present moment. I present myself to the present tense.

I surround myself in a circle of white light. It travels, like a neon tube, anticlockwise (right to left) about my person.

I illuminate my spine, from its base, up through my neck, arced around the back, top of my brain, down again and out through my Brow Centre, like a flame of gas. Light fills up my whole body on my in-breath. I shine on the out-breath.

(The illuminated spine, symbolised by the Shepherd's Crook. Often used by Church Officers who may not realise its true symbolic meaning.)

Illustration 28: Spinal Column of Light

SHEPHERD'S
CROOK

I contact my higher self, my 'inner CEO', if you like. I ask for the grace of the Holy Spirit to guide and protect me on my journey. A wave of energy shoots up my spine and fills my body. I tune into the feeling of 'my vibration'. I, at peace, can't help but smile uncontrollably – joy in the moment.

Eyes closed, I approach an unlocked, large wooden door. My energy swells as I push it open using my arm to mimic the gesture. I enter. Again I mimic the gesture to close the door behind me. Energy-swells in my body tell me the door is closed. I face forward.

Before me lies a yellowish dusty path with green pasture to either side. (I don't see it as such; more like I feel it. I can describe what I feel clearly. 'Insight' to me means a process by which I feel what I see.) I follow the path.

I begin to ascend what to begin with appears to be a hill. The climb is steady, straight and not overly strenuous. I can't see very far. Green grass to either side, the path remains clear. I have no way of getting lost. My energy swells again as I reach the top. Before me lies a vast, high plain and I can see clearly across the flatland. I walk on.

After a short time, I see the outline of a building with tall roof spires in the distance. I head towards it. As I progress, I notice that the spires seem to appear not that much nearer. The building remains distant. It must be very large for me to see it from where I am. I pick up the pace. As I get closer, I approach what appears to be a huge cathedral. I see two spires although I feel there will be more. Its vast structure now stretches from the horizon on my left to the horizon on my right. The path enters a semicircular clearing. I arrive before the Cathedral's large wooden double fronted door. My energy swells further. I realise for the first time that each energy-swell signals that I'm on the right track and I've come to a significant landmark in my journey.

It soothes my trepidation. I recall how I prepare for all the important moments in my life. I focus and build an inner calmness to prepare for what is to come.

No need to knock. Like before, I mimic the gestures to open and close the right hand side of the double door behind me. Inside, aisles, rows of pews and towering pillars stretch for miles into the dark distance before me. I turn left and make my way, keeping my left shoulder close to the rear wall of the giant hall. Another long walk ensues. I walk briskly.

Another energy-swell informs me that I've reached a corner of the great hall. I turn right and continue down along the left hand wall until an energy swell tells me I've reached another wooden door. I enter.

Inside, I begin to descend a long straight stairway. Down and down I go. At its base I proceed along an underground corridor. At the end of the corridor I come across an opening, off centre, to the right. I enter a small candlelit room inside, slightly to the right again, stands an elderly man. His long curly beard brushes slowly down the front of his robe and up again; his silent nod acknowledges my presence. I nod lower and slower – to express the humility, trepidation and joy I feel. I stand before the *Keeper of the Keys to the Locks* - to the *Akashic Records*.

These words are his, the chaste reality,
The keeper of the portal's golden key,
Who opens Wisdom's door, and none can close
To those on whom his welcome he bestows,
And closes it to minds unpurified.
And none can open who are thus denied.
From *The Message to the Hierarchy of Hermes*
(Mercury), the Regent of the Brow Chakra (6th)[157]

The Keeper stands before a huge vault, not unlike the bank vaults in the Harry Potter movies.

He speaks, "Welcome".

I nod again and reply timidly, "Hello".

"How can I help you?" The keeper asks.

"If I may, I'd like to know the contract I made for this lifetime please. The contract I signed up to before I was born, between my last life and this."

The Keeper enters the vault and returns with a parchment. As I open it, a voice speaks its content[158]..."You are here to become who you already are. The acorn already has the imprint and design of the Oak tree it becomes.

In the distant past you were very powerful. But you did not use your power from the highest integrity. Just the opposite, you committed heinous acts of violence and sex. You have spent much time learning the nature of your cruelty and not-cruelty. You have recently rid yourself of many of the dark unconscious remnants that have held you back. You are ready now to proceed.

---

[157] Ref: *The Restored New Testament, The Hellenic Fragments,* by James Morgan Pryse, published by The Theosophical Press.
[158] Some people are able to read their *Life Contract,* others get what feels like a download of information as if from the Internet. You receive as much information as is right for you at the time. You can revisit *The Cathedral* at any time to learn more.

You don't have far to go but first you must take it easy. You have travelled a long way during the last five years. You need not rush for now. Take it easy for a short while. You are to continue the book (*Defrag your Soul*) which you stopped writing a short while back. Start again when the time feels right. You'll know it when it arrives.

For now rest, have fun and wait for your time to move on.

Follow your path and ....." (The rest I will reveal when the time is right.)

I, overwhelmed, wept bitterly. I begged forgiveness for the dark deeds of my past.

"Forgiveness was and is not appropriate only learning. And you have learned what you needed to transmute darkness into light. Go in peace!"

I thanked *the Keeper* and 'felt' my way back the way I came - to the first, large wooden door at the start of my journey. Energy-swells signalled the landmarks again on my return journey. I walked back through the door and returned to my body.

I roused myself gently to make sure I was thoroughly grounded.

Later, the energy-swell, 'my vibration', kept returning. I continue to practise tuning into it as best I can.

Only now, I realise *The Cathedral* or should I say, *The Temple*, is built within me.

Paul C Burr

Part XVI: Where Next? The Return to Oneness

We have the power to put an end to the fiefdoms in politics, religions, nations and business in this 'winner takes all' world we've created; a world where one person's vulnerabilities and mistakes are seized by others for their own gain.

We can begin a new world where property, wealth and 'ownership' are based on equitable negotiation and usage, not forfeiture - where one person serves all as part of a social contract. Leaders do the leading, rulers do the ruling, Kings and Queens do the king-ing or queen-ing. They are jobs with responsibilities and accountabilities, not just titles or inheritances.

We create such a world firstly by imagining it of our own volition. When enough of us sit in the feeling, we shall transform this world of separateness into a world of oneness.

At that instant, we shall return to *The Desire World* we came from.

The Desire World

Love is divine. Anything that is not love is not divine.

Imagine if you will, a world in which all your desires are fulfilled. Everything you want, you are given. You only have to visualise its image in ions, i.e. use your imagination and have faith. Manifest the image as strongly and as often as you want. You and everyone else in such a world can choose to achieve fulfilment; you are empowered. Welcome to the *Desire World*, a stepping stone between heaven and earth.

Humankind does not have the language to describe heaven. We are restricted to the limits of the language and syntax of the mind and our imagination. The *Desire World* is thus a manifestation of heaven in terms that the human mind can understand. In it, matter manifests ethereally as if it were real just like in the world around us, if you can imagine such a paradox?

For instance, imagine you wanted to climb a tall mountain and the climb is difficult. Somehow you have just enough strength, endurance, technique and wisdom to make the climb – every time and anytime you want to. Eventually you exhaust all the possible climbs this mountain offers – the steep, the long, the quick and the gentle.

In another instance, you desire to climb a mountain that might or might not exceed your climbing capabilities. You seek a challenge that might take you beyond the limits you set yourself. Let us say that your attempt to climb the mountain fails. You halt and turn back to base camp or perhaps you take a tumble and fall. You spend a night in the *Desire World's* virtual hospital that you have already created – just in case of such a fall. The next morning you awake, fully repaired and ready for a new climb - for in this *Desire World*, you do not need insurance. You can protect yourself against all eventualities; you simply go there in your imagination and desire it.

All that exists, in the *Desire World*, is Divine. You live a life without shame, anger, sadness or fear – because everything untoward can be averted or put right with the snap of an imaginary finger. You live a life free from all that is not love. In your imagination, you live as close to heaven as you can. You can choose anything intellectual or recreational that you are passionate about, for example, mathematics, crosswords, music, football, sex, stamp collecting or organic farming (to name the first few things that came into my head). The *Desire World* was created for a 'part' of you to play in safely. That 'part' of you was and still is an Archangel archetype. It appreciates fully the notions of desire and abundance for all - through a sense of 'oneness'.

As wonderful as this heavenly image of a world is, it has its limitations. Because you preset the conditions and safeguards to the climb, you realise that a challenge - such as the mountain climb - is not a challenge after all. You enjoy the fulfilment of your passion unhindered. You climb successfully or select an unknown result to your climb by choice.

Should you fail in your climb there is no loss of personal pride through defeat because there is only 'oneness' in heaven. Everyone in the

Desire World is intrinsically linked to everyone and everything else through spirit. Everything desired is abundantly available to everyone through this inherent 'oneness', until you choose the desire to create an emotion or sense that had not existed before - 'separateness'.

The Archangel Michael sought to extend the challenges of the *Desire World* by desiring separateness with tangible and emotional trophies for victory - and penalties for failure, in the form of physical and emotional pain. Pain required separateness. Because oneness means when one suffers, all suffer.

What is (not) good for you, is (not) good for everyone.

Thus Michael created the double bind of separateness and pain. Personal differences in identity and power (but not honour) would evolve between entities. Separateness evolved during the latter phases of what is known as the *Lemurian Age*[159] and early phases of the subsequent *Atlantean Age*. By desire, separateness of consciousness created a boundary between the individual and the divine. So man was empowered to create in his own image, with his own imagination, with his own image-in-ions.

The divine empowers humankind to manifest and discern, each for themself.

Humankind was empowered to create its own boundaries. It built the 'wall' that surrounds the *Garden of Eden*, *Mother Nature*. Within the 'wall', humankind empowered itself with the will and imagination to create and destroy things by its own volition. But humankind could not empower itself to destroy *Mother Nature*, Herself. Humankind transgresses *Mother Nature* and if it continues - that's a battle that only *Mother Nature* can survive - but that's not what *She* wants.

Mother Nature wants humankind to be at one with *Her* and thereby be at one with one another. The divine never withdrew humankind's nous

---

[159] Ref: *Atlantis and Lemuria,* by Rudolph Steiner PhD, translated by the *Theosophical Publishing Society,* London (1911).

to tear down the garden 'wall' and return from separateness to oneness.

Separateness means me and not me, you and not you. Humankind experienced duality for the first time but it did not lose its capacity to experience the harmony of opposites. You create warm water by creating the right mix of hot and cold water that feels temperate to your skin. You enjoy the warmth of the sun by being shielding yourself from overexposure. Humankind may have developed separateness but it never lost its capacity for temperance. Thus temperance is a stepping stone between separateness and oneness.

Humankind evolved separateness of consciousness and the physical body to house it. Separateness of consciousness gave the individual the choice to experience personal victory at the expense of others - and block out the pain and suffering of others that their victory created.

Winning and losing, victory and defeat, joy and suffering became a personal experience; the notion of winning and losing fostered pride. From pride evolved upset: hurt, fear, anger and, later on, shame – the karmic seeds of not love.

As humankind evolved into separateness, it became more and more detached from love. Self proclaimed political and religious leaders labelled aspects of not-love as sins. They introduced the notion of good and bad. Humankind thus evolved the notion of shame. Individuals, representing the divine would judge others for their good deeds and their sins. Oligarchs would manipulate hu-man to feel bad about themselves - which is the first step we use to control one another's minds. When you control someone's mind, you disempower them. This is not (the way of right divine, of) love.

Your works and your devotion, faithfulness,
Your drudgery and patience under stress,
And that your final deeds shall far outshine
The first ones, when you rule by right divine.
From *The Message to the Hierarchy of Helios,* the Sun
King and Regent of the fourth chakra, the heart.[160]

In the beginning love resided at the heart of everything, at the core or coeur. The core of every human is love. The core of our solar system, the sun, is love. The sun shines its light on everything and everyone, regardless of race, colour, creed, species, belief system or behaviour. The light of your truth is there to be seen unless you choose to shield your eyes from it. We receive light or love everyday but we do not all accept it, i.e. those of us who choose not love.

Not love has no place in the heart; instead, humankind evolved the brain, the data processing centre for the mind which became the domicile of personal joy and suffering - and the willingness to allow others to suffer through one's petty personal desires.

Humankind's personal desires to achieve and be victorious over one another evolved in the head. But here lies the rub. Victory, be it a football game or a world war brings short lived self gratification and, by contrast, long term suffering. The victor's pride and sense of achievement dwindles.

Humankind creates trophies to preserve the pride of victory and stores them on a shelf in a cabinet in a trophy room. Visit Manchester United or Liverpool football clubs. They have many such trophies. But they are all history or past tense.

The meaning and power of a trophy, like any fresh food in a greengrocer shop, has a shelf life. We yearn to keep that sense of achievement and pride but we cannot. We want that feeling of victory and pride again so we return to theatre of football or war to regain it.

---

[160] Ref: *The Restored New Testament, The Hellenic Fragments,* by James Morgan Pryse, published by The Theosophical Press.

We attempt to make the past present by winning another trophy. If we do not, our pride suffers. We get upset, so much so, we may seek revenge to regain our lost pride.

We see such wars today based on the false ideals of right, wrong and of divine retribution where both sides claim, *"God is on our side".* The victors store their trophies in the form of land, people and large private bank accounts stored away in remote untraceable bank vaults. We want more so we fight more.

Through repeated violence, a minority of us have developed a lust for killing. Such is the nature of the physical world we have evolved. Such is the nature of separateness of consciousness without oneness.

By desire and design, separateness always has winners and losers until humankind says

Enough! I've had enough of winning and losing.
I can only exert a limited amount of power.
I can only spend a limited amount of money.
I've had enough of the power of politics.
I can only create so much suffering before I kill off
those over whom I am victorious.
I can only suffer so much when I lose.
I have exhausted all the possibilities of winning and
losing in the material world.
I now choose temperance.
I return to the harmony of opposites, the yin and yang,
the will and imagination, to return to The Desire World.

Humankind arrives at the end of the game. The time has come to gather all the pieces, the money, the cards and board of play - and put them all back in the box from whence they came. Humankind passes the game on to the next species who seek to play with it.

So this is where humankind finds itself today, at its endgame. It has two choices:

1. Destroy itself.
2. Collect and organise all the pieces of ourselves to go back to oneness, only wiser, much wiser. Because we fully appreciate oneness for what it is - not separateness.

We are either at the beginning of the end or the end of the beginning - the never or return to forever.

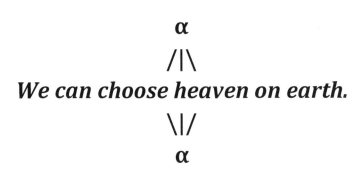

α
/I\
We can choose heaven on earth.
\I/
α

Paul C Burr

Post-Poems

Know then thyself, presume not God to scan,
The proper study of humankind is Man.
Placed on this isthmus of a middle state,
A being darkly wise and rudely great:
With too much knowledge for the Sceptic side,
With too much weakness for the Stoic's pride,
He hangs between, in doubt to act or rest;
In doubt to deem himself a God or Beast;
In doubt his mind or body to prefer;
Born but to die, and reas'ning but to err;
Alike in ignorance, his reason such,
Whether he thinks too little or too much;
Chaos of thought and passion, all confused;
Still by himself abused or disabused;
Created half to rise, and half to fall;
Great lord of all things, yet a prey to all;
Sole judge of truth, in endless error hurl'd;
The glory, jest, and riddle of the world!

Alexander Pope, extract from *Epistle II*

Never again will we stand
On the threshold of a new age.
We that are here now are touched
In some mysterious way
With the ability to change
And make the future.
Those who wake to the wonder
Of this magic moment,
Who wake to the possibilities
Of this charged conjunction,
Are the chosen ones who have chosen
To act, to free the future, to open it up,
To consign prejudices to the past,
To open up the magic casement
Of the human spirit
On to a more shining world.

Ben Okri, from *Mental Fight, An Anti-Spell for the 21st Century*

Appendix: About the Legend of Beowulf[161]

Written some 1500 years ago, by an anonymous bard, Beowulf tells the story of a gallant hero who travels north to Denmark to slay the swamp beast, Grendel.

Grendel would visit the local King Hrothgar's castle and set about killing all whom it encountered, carrying severed limbs and bodies back to its lair at the bottom of a deep dark lake.

Beowulf slays Grendel. That night there is much merriment and feasting, Beowulf and his men retire to a far part of the castle. A second creature enters the hall where many still celebrate. The creature, Grendel's mother, the source of the problem, wreaks her revenge. Like Grendel, she retires to her lair and Beowulf sets off after her.

The presenting problem is never the real problem. The real problem lies behind all the presenting problems.
When the real problem disappears,
so do all of its presenting problems.
A phrase oft used by Psychologists and NLP
Practitioners

Beowulf approaches the edge of the lake. Below him in the deep dark abyss lies the beast in her lair. Before he descends there is great temptation to withhold and draw back but with courage - afforded by the finest sword, shield and armour - Beowulf steps forward and descends into the darkness, <u>his darkness</u>. Below, he and the beast engage in battle. He finds the magnificent sword, shield and armour - that protect him so well on the surface - serve no use in the darkness. Beowulf casts them off. He reveals his unprotected self, his complete

---

[161] Adapted and extracted partly from my first book, **Learn to Love and Be Loved in Return**, Appendix 1.

vulnerability. Beowulf and the beast become one in combat and as they wrestle, Beowulf finds a luminous sword of light that hangs on the wall of the lair - a sword with which he slays the beast.

As Beowulf rises to the surface to reveal the beast's head, he finds that the luminous sword dissolves. The luminous sword that worked in the darkness has no power in the known world. It leaves Beowulf unable to demonstrate its power. For others to understand the sword's power, they must descend into darkness and find it for themselves. They must experience their own victory. They must choose courage.

We cannot stare at the sun in a noon-day cloudless sky.
Light cannot be seen in the Light.
At midnight, the cloudless sky reveals infinity.
By clouds, I mean 'clouds of emotion' - shame, anger,
sadness and fear.
Glory comes from our journey into the darkness.

This story illustrates the experience of my own inner darkness. Not to be feared, the darkness beckons my light. I often feel hesitancy, fear and vulnerability and am tempted to withdraw and go back to my old habits. But I shall not.

Ω

About me, Paul C Burr

Photo © Stephen Cotterell

The Skills and Passions in Me

I help clients to smoothen and accelerate the emotional journeys they need to take, to make changes in their lives.

Life doesn't get better by chance, it gets better by change.
From *Global Healing Exchange* on Facebook.

Corporate clients use me as a 'business coach', personal clients probably see me as more of an 'energy healer'. In both cases I help people to shed the internal stuff that holds them back - so that they can cultivate and apply their innate willpower, imagination, courage and creativity to achieve the outcomes they seek.

I've over thirty five years of 'b2b' corporate sales and management experience, fifteen years of which overlap with my business and personal coaching work. I've a PhD in Statistics and a First Class Honours Degree in Mathematics. I'm qualified as a *Master Practitioner* in: NLP, this/past life regression and hypnotherapy.

I study and practice ancient druid wisdom, astrology, casting runes, dowsing, the I Ching and the Tarot.

I love listening to music – rock, jazz, country… you name it. I sing a bit too.

I'm a passionate football fan of Newcastle United Football Club, in "Geordieland", in The North-East of England.

The Author in Me

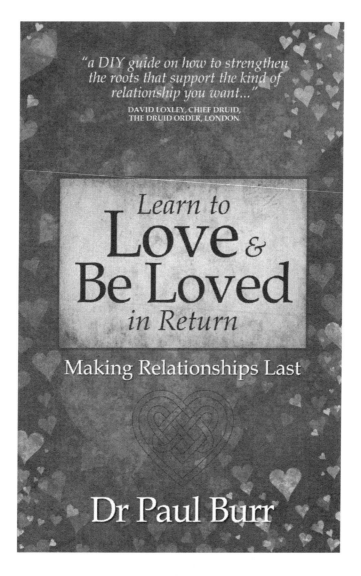

"a DIY guide on how to strengthen the roots that support the kind of relationship you want..."
DAVID LOXLEY, CHIEF DRUID, THE DRUID ORDER, LONDON

Learn to
Love &
Be Loved
in Return

Making Relationships Last

Dr Paul Burr

"Uplifting: this is one of those books that arrives in your life at just the right time, when you need it most. The author is able to convey a very deep and meaningful message in an easy to read and understand format with a step by step guide on how to achieve this. The best type of love is unconditional and what better place to start than with yourself."   Rhedd (Amazon reviewer)

"This is a compelling story for our troubled times. Paul C Burr writes with passion and compassion about moral uncertainties and the quest for salvation and spiritual fulfilment. Go with the flow, trust your inner-self and enjoy this humane and optimistic tale."
Professor John Ditch, York, UK.

My first book, *Learn to Love and Be Loved in Return*,[162] was published in 2010. Since publication, it's polled a '5 out of 5 stars' status on Amazon.

My second book (see next page), *2012: a twist in the tail*,[163] was first published in kindle format, on Amazon, in May 2012. This novel-with-spiritual-insights is now available in paperback in major outlets and in epub format from Lulu.com. It came as a twist in the tail-end of completing *Defrag your Soul*, at which time I assumed was to become my second book.

In late 2011, I was informed by a 'higher authority' that I was to write a novel that would be 'channelled'. I was to start on 3rd March 2012 and complete it by 18th April 2012.

Not really knowing what was going on; I hadn't channelled anything like this before; I hadn't written any fiction before (but I didn't want to pass up this new adventure); I chose courage and surrendered to spirit.

The Blogger in Me

I host a number of Facebook pages that have amassed an aggregate of over 20,000 followers. The most popular page, *Beowulf*,[164] links to extracts from my works as well as the words from people who inspire me.

My blogs[165] cover a broad number of topics to help you in your personal and business life. The 'wisdom' shared comes from what I pick up from day to day life, my research and my client work.

Client Work:

Most of us <u>don't</u> achieve what we set out to achieve. If the outcomes you sought were down to a purely intellectual exercise then you would have achieved them already - would you not?

---

[162] Ref: http://paulcburr.com/learn-to-love-and-be-loved-in-return/
[163] Ref: http://2012atwistinthetail.com
[164] Ref: http://www.facebook.com/PaulCBurr
[165] Ref: http://paulcburr.com/

Every 'journey' in life is two parts emotional to one part intellectual - i.e. **we are twice as likely to hold ourselves back because of self-imposed emotional blocks as opposed to intellectual problems.**
I help clients to release the emotional blocks by which they hold themselves back - so that they cultivate and apply their innate willpower, imagination, courage and creativity to achieve the business and personal outcomes they seek.

My Promise:
"The material I use is powerful, very powerful. I know of nothing quicker or more effective. It's non-mainstream - which means you get non-mainstream results".

Testimonials:
- **Private Client:** *"You have been so instrumental in the positive changes in my life, I set quite a few goals, and one by one my goals are being achieved, thanks to you, showing me how".*
Debbie (via Skype) Cape Town, South Africa.
- **Business Client:** *"I have worked with Paul periodically over the past 8 years to gain solutions to a number of people issues / opportunities. If you are looking for a Personal Coach to make a High Performer / High performing Team even better (particularly a senior player) – I would not hesitate to recommend him".*
Sandra Ventre, Management Development Director, Reckitt Benckiser (now with Qantas).

Further Details of Services I Offer over the Internet
You can find out about the quality of the products and services I offer to business and private clients alike, along with a synopsis of my business coaching experience at:
- http://paulcburr.com/testimonies/
- http://paulcburr.com/beowulf_coaching/

The business coaching and energy healing sessions work equally well either face to face or over the Internet/ telephone services.

For the *Etheric Cleansing* (formerly known as *Emotional Clearing*) service, refer to: http://paulcburr.com/emotional-clearing/.

For the *Change your Character, Change your Life* (formerly known as *Making Transitions*) service, refer to: http://paulcburr.com/making-transitions/.

For queries, please contact me via http://paulcburr.com/.

Thank you for your consideration.

/|\

Paul C Burr PhD

Stephen Cotterell, Photographer...

... A London based photographer, qualified with the Guild of Professional Photographers.

His background covers many, too many in his view, years working in management within the corporate sector and more latterly in the capacity as a consultant.

From a very early age he has had a love affair with photography and has owned many cameras. Over the past few years he has devoted more and more of his time to photography and has invested most of his energy and quite a lot of money in skills development, cameras, lenses, lighting and other equipment that helps him to produce the highest quality photography to the best of his developing capabilities.

He values love, light and laughter; each of these is reflected in his work as a photographer and he has permanently committed his life to people and photography. His particular passion is portraiture which enables both him and the client to create a special connection and capture an important photographic moment.

In addition to spending time creating photographs, especially of people, Stephen hosts and produces a podcast, Photography 121. It is about photographers rather than cameras or techniques and it can be downloaded for free from iTunes.

Samples of his work can be seen online by simply searching for Stephen Cotterell photography or by visiting his website at http://stephencotterell.com.

Made in the USA
Charleston, SC
20 February 2013